American Sucker

Also by David Denby

GREAT BOOKS

AMERICAN SUCKER

David Denby

LITTLE, BROWN AND COMPANY

Boston   New York   London

First Edition

Grateful acknowledgment is made to *The New Yorker,*
where parts of this book appeared in different form. Excerpts from "Provide, Provide" from
The Poetry of Robert Frost, edited by Edward Connery Latham, copyright 1936 by Robert
Frost, © 1964 by Lesley Frost Ballantine, © 1969 by Henry Holt and Company. Reprinted
by permission of Henry Holt and Company, LLC.

Library of Congress Cataloging-in-Publication Data
Denby, David.
American sucker / David Denby.
p. cm.
Includes bibliographical references.
ISBN 0-316-19294-5
1. Investments — United States. 2. Speculation — United States. I. Title.
HG4910.D456 2004
332.6'0973 — dc22   2003058853

10 9 8 7 6 5 4 3 2

Q-MART

Design by Bernard Klein

Printed in the United States of America

To Max and Thomas,
Who Have Heard from Their Father
of Things They Should Do
and Now Must Hear
of Things They Should Not Do

We're going to make lots of money together. Making lots of money—
it's not that hard, you know. It's overestimated.
Making money is a breeze. You watch.

—Martin Amis, *Money* (1984)

Contents

PART II

THE YEARS 2001 AND 2002 — LOSING MONEY

An Introductory Note

In January 2000, as my marriage was breaking up and my life wandered off the tracks, I began keeping a journal of what kept me sane and made me crazy — my adventures as an amateur investor. A new life created new needs and new passions, and every night, in my computer, I noted down the movements of the market and the alterations in my finances, and other things, too — musings about technology and change and such personal currents as desire and regret, and indeed anything that seemed joined to the obsession of the moment, which, as anyone could see, was money. I tried to take notice of money's related manias, like consumer envy and status. Busily, I raced around New York, horning in on investors' conferences, eager to meet a financial guru or an entrepreneur who could teach me something. I kept track as well of my periodic disaffection from investing and the stock market — the longueurs, the intervals of rebellion, the *loathing* of the market. For even if we become obsessed with money, most of us love the rest of life no less than before. At least we try to love it no less. What, I wondered, did money hunger do to a man's yearnings for love, for work, for entertainment and art? To his sense of himself, his place in the world? As the nineties boom gave way to the uncertainties and scandals of a new century, and a great many Americans fell into financial troubles of one sort or another, these questions seemed very much worth asking. For a writer, the questions are sharpened by habit. If a writer loses his dignity, he can still retain his wits; he can say when the baggy pants dropped, he can set down the ways in which greed overwhelmed the longing for consistency and self-esteem. I wanted, if possible, to restore to financial behavior the dimensions of psychology and morale as well as the crowding interests and conditions of daily life normally left out of writing about the market.

I have quoted a few passages from the journal and also a few excerpts from the movie reviews I wrote at the time for *The New Yorker*, treating the reviews as a kind of unintended public confession. Working over my materials, I tried to observe a simple ground rule: I did not ascribe to my thinking at any given period ideas that came to me later. I made note of doubts, questions, skeptical or outraged moments (I had many), but, at the risk of trying the reader's patience, I kept faith with my bubbling enthusiasms, too. What could be the point of burying New Economy naïveté in a deluge of hindsight? Such revision would do nothing but provide an easy victory over history. To capture, in context and over time, the motions of belief and disbelief, illusion and disillusion, fog and clarity — that was my goal. To paraphrase a remark of Mary McCarthy's: Anyone who acted so stupidly cannot cancel his debt to society by the mere process of getting older. I was not young when I blew myself up, but the debt remains the same.

I hope it will be clear that I knew — I always knew, right from the beginning — that I was in a privileged position. Not just in a money sense. To make a book out of one's difficulties is a luxury not easily available to a man or woman trying to put food on the table and stay out of the street. Hearing of this volume, anyone with serious troubles might say, "He has a good job and a Manhattan apartment to sell. What's his problem?" And a wealthy player might say, "This is a small-timer who got in over his head and should never have invested a penny without professional help." Both these statements are true, but they do little but point up the difficulty of writing openly about money. As any psychiatrist will tell you, most people are far more forthcoming about sex. They will boast of their perversions before admitting a bad investment. No one writing about money, therefore, can expect entirely to escape the envy or contempt of his readers. But I hope that some aspects of my behavior will inspire self-recognition as well.

What I have written is too fragmentary to stand as anything more than the most subjective account of the stock market in the period 2000–2002. Readers will immediately notice, for instance, that having thrown in my lot with technology companies, I closely followed the Nasdaq composite index, where the tech stocks mainly live, and became relatively indifferent to the Dow and the S&P 500-stock index. I did not follow the bond market or soybean futures or the price of gold. I couldn't have cared less about the price of gold. Readers will also notice that my attention to the market was much greater in 2000 than in 2001 and 2002, when the endless bear began to grind down my interest and I got caught up instead in technologies that seemed to promise an opening to the future. I have provided just enough market information to make the context of my own actions clear — information that will seem rudimentary to the financially knowing but perhaps necessary to the uninitiated. I offer the book not as market history but as a portrait of a single American living within money obsession during the first three years of the millennium — a wild, dangerous, and, finally, tragic era in which hope, folly, and disenchantment came together in amazed combinations, as if none had ever been aware of the others' existence before.

—June 2003

PART I

———

THE YEAR 2000— MAKING MONEY

1

Speeding

Quarterly Report, January 1, 2000
Cumulative Net Gain/Loss 0

SOMETIME in early January 2000, I became aware that I was jabbering. I was on the phone, in my little study at home on West End Avenue, in Manhattan, and speaking as breathlessly as a cattle auctioneer in full cry. Jumping over verbal fences, mashing participials, dropping qualifiers . . . I was talking to an old friend about movies, and I said something like this: *Movie people think platforming works only with quality-word-of-mouth and slow-building three-four-million-a-week pictures in which buzz rolls into multiple viewings like* The English Patient *or* Shakespeare in Love . . . I had trouble saying one thing at a time. I had to say two things, or three, tucking statistics into my words as I talked, and I seemed to be grouping ideas or pieces of information rhythmically, by association, rather than by cause and effect. As I hung up, I wondered, Who is this *nut,* gathering and expelling information in charged little clumps, like a Web site spilling bytes?

Babbling-brook behavior is common among journalists, and also, perhaps, among ambitious New Yorkers, who like to imagine that they are moving on a fast track leading somewhere — to the best table in heaven, perhaps. In part, the habit may be regional and occupational. Certainly the tempo of Al Gore's discourse, a procession of potted palms thudding across a wide desert, drove me crazy in that election year. But, then, it seemed to drive everyone crazy, even people from the South and the West, so region may have very little to do with it after all. And journalists, now that I think about it, talk at all speeds. At my magazine, *The New Yorker,* no one wastes words, but no one assails his listener like a jackhammer, either. It isn't dignified. Soon after the phone conversation with my friend, I thought back over the previous few months. I remembered ranting on and on at a party. No one interrupted, but no one commented, either. They were waiting for the storm to pass. Cowed, they sighed and rolled their eyes as if I were trying to impress them, when from my point of view, I was just trying to get it all *in.* What was causing the rush?

By the beginning of 2000, my life had changed in a number of extraordinarily important ways, but most of it was still in place. As I saw it, my job, as always, was to build a family, build a career, observe, observe, learn a few things, write them down, and get them into good enough shape to publish in a magazine or a book. I was a married, middle-class professional, a critic and journalist — an Upper West Sider, and therefore one of God's sober creatures, a householder and provider living among Manhattan's brown and gray buildings. The Upper West Side was the land of responsibility, a family neighborhood, hardworking, increasingly prosperous — and pleasureless, some would say. There were parks, there were dogs, there were many places to buy broccoli and diapers, to get suits pressed and prescriptions filled. But there were few elegant people (even the wealthy dressed like assistant professors), few art galleries or clubs, no wicked entertainments to speak of. You could walk for blocks without finding so much as a neighborhood bar.

My wife and I had added two boys to the swarm of children laughing and shoving on Broadway and shooting basketballs at the netless rims in Riverside Park. They were skinny boys, both of them. We fed them virtuously with fresh vegetables and fruit purchased at the long produce counters of the great Fairway Market, at Broadway and 74th. At breakfast, I plowed through the *New York Times* and the *Wall Street Journal*, and at night I watched the news (the stentorian Tom Brokaw, holding aloft the national virtue) and political chat shows (Chris Matthews interrupting God as He explained His policies on the third day of creation). I made my living writing for *The New Yorker* (and earlier for *New York* magazine). I went to Woody Allen movies and sometimes (as a type) appeared in them. I had been reviewing movies in one place or another since 1969. At the beginning of the nineties, when it became obvious to anyone with eyes to see that American movies, under conglomerate control, were not going anyplace wonderful, I wrote *Great Books,* in which a middle-aged man—me—slapped himself out of unhappiness by returning to his undergraduate college (Columbia) and rereading some of the Western literary and political-theory classics. Defending the books against the ideological manhandling they were being subjected to from left and right, I had made a few enemies to be proud of with that book, and a few friends, too, also to be proud of.

Thus the armature of routine, the thick-barked trunk of family love and work for a man of fifty-six. But in the months before I heard myself chattering, my daily habits had changed: I had become obsessed with piling up money, obsessed with the stock market, and I spent hours most weekdays watching CNBC. The men and women of financial reporting, my new friends, went on the air every trading day at five in the morning. They remained on the air all day, mopping up after the market closed at 4:00 P.M. with various recaps, surveys, predictions, and so on, continuing until eight, at which point the hard-blowing Matthews and the somber Brian Williams took over with the less important criminal, political, and constitutional entertainments of the day. Like several hundred thousand other Americans, I had become addicted to the reporters on CNBC, our joshing chroniclers of the national hopes. They were *with* us.

On New Year's Day of 2000, the market was closed, and I relinquished CNBC and went to a party. A terrific group had gathered together, teachers, lawyers, journalists, editors, novelists, smart people, and nice, too—*good* people—and I ate smoked salmon and drank mimosas and spoke too rapidly to a great many of them. I wanted to talk about the market, and they wanted to talk about politics, journalism, and children, and after a while, I thought, Pleasure! What a waste of time! Every other weekday morning, I would take my post in the kitchen, looking at the little TV perched on the granite counter. *A half hour,* I told myself. *Forty-five minutes, that's all!* The kitchen was not a comfortable place to watch TV. But then, ignoring the cat, Daphne, who rubbed against my shins and nipped at my ankles, I would sit there for two or three hours, fascinated by the stock tickers running at the bottom of the image, by the declining thirty-year-bond yield and the shocking new Producers Price Index Number. Everything that happens in the market is related to every other thing; it is a gigantic puzzle whose parts move as unceasingly as the tentacles of an underwater creature. It was all new to me—*the Consumer Confidence Index! Wow!*—and I was amazed. Even though I knew that some of what they said was hooey, I sat patiently through interviews with strategists from the big brokerage houses, with CEOs and money managers, with gurus and savants of various sorts who spread their blankets and displayed their urns and gourds and gave their opinions of shifting currents in the bazaar. It was a rattle of semi-worthless but spellbinding words. I loved it.

Speaking over the din of a brokerage trading floor, many of the CNBC reporters and their guests raced like corsairs. They had very little airtime in which to say complicated things. But more than that, they were driven by the tempo of the market it-self, the pulsing, darting flow of money around the globe, all of it intensified, as the CNBC anchors broke for commercials, by that rhythmic clickety-clack of electronic noise needled by a snare drum . . . *dig-a-dig-a-dig-a-dig-a-DIG-a-dig-a* . . . Were all the beats the same? Or were there, as I imagined, little emphases which turned the pulse into the music of money? Speed was in-side my head, and I couldn't get it out.

At that moment, in early 2000, you were sure that if you could just grab hold of the flying coattails of the New Economy investments, you could get rich very quickly. The newspapers and CNBC were filled with stories of twenty-four-year-old millionaires, start-up companies going through the roof, initial public offerings outlandishly doubling and tripling their price on their first day of trading. And the market! In the previous year, 1999, the Nasdaq composite index went up 85.6 percent; it went up by more than 39 percent the year before. And, as the market soared, you could feel it. You would have to be insensi-ble *not* to feel it. All around, in the suddenly resplendent corpo-rate pomp of once-dreary San Jose in Silicon Valley; in the crisp linen and sparkle of a downtown Manhattan restaurant at lunch-time; in the fatted pages of new and brazenly successful Internet magazines like the *Industry Standard*—in all these places and

7

many more, you could sense the thrilling, oxygen-rich happiness of wealth being created overnight.

My urgency was driven by hunger. Making money seemed a function of quickness, and in the market, more than anywhere else, you experienced time as the instant dead past. The market underlines the mystery and terror of time: It never stops. As I sat there in the kitchen watching CNBC, there was only the next instant, and the next, rushing toward you, and I kept trying to catch up. In Times Square, across the street from *The New Yorker's* office, the news headlines and stock results from Dow Jones— "the zipper"—flashed around the corners of the old Times tower. My eyes would travel with a group of words until they hit the corner and disappeared. That was time, always moving on: No one could pull the words back. Either read them or lose the information forever. The zipper made me slightly ill, and there were much more powerful zippers around. Using the Internet as a speed lane, an ideally informed person would never sleep at all but would trade the markets and chase news and rumors through the links twenty-four hours a day. What bliss! What a nightmare! The market, it turns out, is the quintessence of instability in the Information Age, the perfect paradigm of life as ceaseless change. That is why it is so mesmerizing, so defeating, and, again, so mesmerizing.

I needed to make money, serious money, that year. Not for the usual reasons that prosperous people want to have more cash. I did not want to buy a villa in Tuscany or a BMW 540i or the Lynx $7,692 gas grill with dual smoker drawers. What in the world could you do with such a resplendent cooking apparatus? Barbecue gold-leafed weenies on it? In all, I was quite sure that I was not the patsy-victim of the standard smug liberal critique—*the American who does not know that money can't buy happiness.* No, I didn't want to buy anything in particular. I wanted the money so I could hold on to something very important to me. For I had already lost something of incomparable value — not a possession, but the center of my life — and I was in danger of losing a great deal else.

At the beginning of 1999, a year earlier, my wife, Cathleen Schine, announced that she no longer wanted to be married to me. She had to leave, she had to get away for a new life, for she had mysteriously changed in her affections. Not just in her affections. She had changed in her being, and she was no longer whole, she was broken, and I was not the one to fix what was wrong.

The announcement was not altogether a surprise. She had been slipping away for a few years, withdrawing into quiet or studied indifference. I couldn't get her to talk about it, she was holding it inside. She didn't mean to hurt me, I now think, but sitting in bed at night reading or speaking on the phone, she was unreachable — and then sleepy and irritable. I stood there like a rejected petitioner, chewing on my innards but unwilling to fight.

"I have to go to sleep now."

"But I want to talk."

Talk was the center; we used to talk over everything, endlessly. But in those bad years a polite silence had descended on the marriage, darkened on my side with foreboding and on hers with unhappiness. She was increasingly depressed. Dark circles appeared under her eyes, she became immobile — the bed was her home, her fortress. And then she wanted to get away. "If you really loved me, you would want me to be happy," she said on the day in 1999 when she first said she wanted to leave, a sentence that no lover ever wants to hear. She was sitting in bed, miserable. I was pacing around the bedroom, in a sweat.

"I love you," she said. "But I can't live with you anymore."

For a full year after her announcement, I tried to keep the

marriage together. We continued to live in the same apartment with the two boys, Max, who turned sixteen in June of 1999, and Thomas, who turned twelve the same month. But she was elsewhere, as remote as a beauty queen on a float drifting down the street to the cheers of other crowds farther and farther away.

I didn't break down, or stop working. A shipshape magazine like *The New Yorker* doesn't let its writers fall into the sea. Good words must be written, and I wrote some of them. But there was a gathering heaviness in my chest and a feeling of forlornness, as if the roof had come flying off my head. Over that year of 1999, it came off piece by piece, as in a slow-motion movie of a storm, first the corners flapping and rising, and then the shingles lifting, a few at a time, then a few more, and then the whole thing violently tearing away in a gale. I was in love with my wife, novelist Cathleen Schine, and proud of the marriage, too, which seemed to me an astounding yet permanent fact in the world, like some comet that kept flying forever. It had lasted for eighteen years, and I couldn't believe it was over. I couldn't take it in; I was sure there had to be some mistake, some error, something we had forgotten, some place in the past we could go back to—a niche, a landing where we could reassemble and start again. At night, I paced around the room while she sat sorrowfully in bed. Some pleasure that we still shared, some experience! A moment in the country, a piece of music, an adventure with the kids. We could repeat that moment, rediscover that quality, and remember what we had lost. But she could no longer join me there.

For almost two decades, I had felt that no thought of mine was complete until I had conveyed it to her. A new movie—I was full of news about movies, since I reviewed them for a living. The cost of fish at Citarella, another of the local markets on Broadway. Darwin sitting on the giant tortoise's back in the Galápagos Islands, rapping his stick on the shell to get the beast to move—we had loved that image and had gone to the Galápagos together. What I gave to her and she to me in those two decades is now beyond my understanding and use, like the fingers of an arm that no longer has any feeling.

We hung on for the year, and then she went off at the beginning of 2000, a dreary greeting of the new millennium, and despite my every effort, the marriage had ended. We spoke every day, we were amiable and affectionate, we raised children together. I was in a rage, but I suppressed it. Of what use was anger? I was determined not to become one of those embittered men encountered at work, at a party—men a little too articulate about "women." There was one fellow I knew who carried the legal papers for his divorce around with him. He was arguing the case himself. The papers swung from his neck, an albatross posing as a necessary cause.

We arranged the practical details. And quickly discovered, as does everyone else, that there is no right way of splitting up when you have children. There are only less bad ways. The boys remained at home, in our seven-room apartment on West End Avenue, and we took turns staying with them. We shuttled ourselves, rather than the children, in and out. When I was at home with them, Cathy stayed in a rented studio apartment uptown that overlooked the Hudson; and when she was with them, I stayed in a one-bedroom place overlooking a schoolyard, two blocks away from the big apartment. We both had views. It was a ruinously expensive way to proceed—we were paying for three pieces of real estate in Manhattan at once—but it lessened the wear and tear on the boys. Once a week, we crisscrossed, gathering for dinner on West End Avenue. Max would cook a steak on the stovetop grill, and the kitchen would fill with smoke. We chewed up a good dinner, and no one got angry, no one wept. Still, it was over, and when I looked at my view from the little apartment, watching the neighborhood kids tossing a basketball at a rim without a net, a claw grasped my chest and throat and stayed there until, hours later, I tranquilized myself to sleep.

And then there was talk of selling the big apartment. A grave matter, selling a piece of real estate in Manhattan. We were told the place had become valuable; it had reached a giddy boom-times market value of $1.4 million, a lot more than what we paid for it in 1986. This was serious money, and by the coldest calculation, it made good sense to sell the place, retire the mortgage, pay the taxes, and then split the proceeds and start over, each buying a smaller place. But I couldn't do it, and my mind went blank whenever the subject came up. I couldn't see my life beyond the apartment, and over and over I said dumb things to myself like "I've lost my wife and I'm not going to lose my house." The closets were stuffed with my dead father's suits. My mother's fancy silverware lay (unused) in a cabinet. It was the place in which we had written books and articles and raised the boys and entertained friends and held family parties. The bookcases were fronted with family pictures — you couldn't reach for a novel without knocking one of the pictures to the floor. It was a writer's apartment, dowdy, comfortable, packed with photographs and CDs and magazines stacked in corners — it was home, and I wouldn't let her deprive me of it.

I conceived a simple plan. The market was booming. We had some serious resources, and I would throw those assets into the right things and make money quickly. I would try to make $1 million in the market in that year of 2000 — yes, $1 million — and then I would buy her out. We had agreed that when we divorced, we would split everything down the middle, and I would give her half the value of the apartment, and it would be mine.

A million dollars! Coming from a journalist on a salary, this thought would have seemed utterly absurd only five or six years earlier. But in 2000 it would not have seemed absurd to the ladies and gents having lunch in fashionable downtown restaurants. It would not have seemed absurd in Silicon Valley, and particularly not on Sand Hill Road in Menlo Park, where many of the venture-capital companies that had funded the tech revolution were housed, and the most fantastic fortunes, instantly assembled, were commonplace. The figure itself, I knew, had no particular meaning—would I not have been thrilled to make $700,000? — but I seized on it because it was the essential round number, the symbol of economic liberty in the common American dream of glory. Whatever else I needed, I needed money—a man facing divorce needs money—and I saw that having lost the greatest thing in my life, I was about to lose another thing, and then, no doubt, another; a loss of substance, a loss of estate, a loss of status, well-being, and peace. Our social life had shredded; our place in the world as a couple, which I had enjoyed more than I had known, was now ended. Extra money wouldn't bring my wife back, but it would help stem the tide of losses. And though it couldn't buy happiness, it could certainly buy pleasure; it could alleviate shabbiness and discomfort and provide, in their place, the consolations of order and quiet, the balm that soothes the welts rising on the surface of the middle-aged ego.

For a period back there in the summer of 1999, six months or so after Cathy's announcement, but some months before I decided to charge into the stock market, they were all gone. Cathy was in Italy; Tommy, our younger son, was at a camp in the Adirondacks; and Max was working and playing in the Caribbean, lucky boy. I did my work, but I had little desire to go out with anyone or even to leave the apartment. I was disgusted and pulse-less, and after doing it three or four times, I could no longer face the women I saw for dinner, friendly and sympathetic all of them and more than willing to listen. You had been left, you had been stranded, the roof had come off—it's not much of a pitch. You had been betrayed. Such a sweet, consol-

13

ing idea, betrayal! It fills the cup of rage right to the lip. Except that what happened to me was not betrayal, exactly, but my wife's escape into a new life. *Keep your head clear!* I shouted at myself. *Otherwise you are lost.* Anyway, what I felt, after the first tumults, was not rage but grief.

For the most part, I stayed home in the apartment that I loved. And instead of going out, I entered in that summer of 1999 a dark and empty tunnel, an enclosure illuminated along the walls by a flash of naked men and women. I had discovered porn on the Internet. In the solitude of night, and in my little study at home, where mighty volumes of Plato, St. Augustine, Hegel, Montaigne, Nietzsche — hardly my regular reading but a recent obsession — loomed over the desk, the kneeling young women awkwardly turned their eyes to the camera. They often had long and beautiful hair that they must have laboriously cared for; they looked for approval not from their partners but from the camera, which I thought was the true object of their desire. They wanted to be seen. And the men, ugly and strong, sullen, tattooed some of them, thick-membered, concentrating on their erection and their orgasm, lest they lose either — they were amateurs, not models, exercising the democratic art form of exhibitionism, with me as their willing audience. They all wanted to be seen, but I didn't want to be seen.

"The worst thing that can be said of pornography," Gore Vidal wrote in 1966, "is that it leads not to 'anti-social' acts but to the reading of more pornography." I'm not sure that that's the worst thing that can be said of pornography. But I know what Vidal means: Obsession leads not to satisfaction but to more obsession. Pornography is addictive. And Vidal wrote that sentence long before the development of the Internet, which so easily feeds the desire for more that it seems to mock appetite itself. You enter a porn site, try to back out, and get sent not to the previous screen but spilled sideways to another erotic site. Asian

Frenzy? Latino Studs? Oh, why *not?* At least take a *look.* Even when you get out, mocking e-mails arrive, by the hundreds. The notes were confidential, blunt, chummy. *Hello, Fellow Pervs, Kinksters, and Lifestylers . . . More goodies for you this week. Several new free sex stories are on-line (including part 7 of the* My Wife Stella *series).* Stella! A man who was married to her, or said he was, shared her with anonymous millions. Did it save his marriage?

I had no desire to "chat"; I wanted only to gaze. After a while, as I spilled from site to site, I felt not that I was controlling and discovering porn on the 'Net but that it was discovering me. It was seeking me out, reading me, and it found out things about me that I didn't know. I continued to review movies, I had dinner with friends, took care of the boys when it was my turn. I fed the cat, read the *Times* and the *Journal,* but I felt, at times, as if I were breaking into fragments. I had this appetite and that one, but what held them together?

The Internet is always spoken of as a medium of connection, but it is also a medium of isolation that surfs the user and breaks him into separate waves going nowhere. There was the movie hunger, and the lust hunger, and the early stirrings of the money hunger. But where was the core, reconciling and joining the many elements together? In the tomes above the computer? My book about the classics was devoted to Columbia's version of the "core curriculum." That's why the big boys were up there, in the shelves above the monitor. What would they have said? Plato, observing a man staring at shadows in a cave, would not have been in the least surprised. But Hegel, I imagined, would have been dismayed by the passivity of erotic contemplation, just as he was dismayed by the passivity of religious contemplation, and Nietzsche, I was sure, would have been disgusted by the absence of vigorous, joyful activity — fighting, dancing, revelry, lovemaking — even though Nietzsche, poor crazy bastard, was as terrified of women as any man who ever lived.

I would look up and down West End Avenue, waiting for some fresh breeze to come along and rescue me — it was there somewhere, coming down the block. When I was home with the boys, they provided the breeze. Max, his handsome brown eyes cast down, then flashing at me, ablaze, liked to argue and storm around the apartment. We would go at each other for an hour, two hours, and we became closer, in the manner of disapproving father and rebelling son, by arguing about his behavior; then we would fall into each other's arms and forgive each other. He was a sweet kid, and smart, too, and saw things that other people didn't see. The younger one, Tommy, flopped into the living room, all elbows and knees, gangly, red-haired, hilarious. He was a paleface, rapidly growing tall. A pale, laughing beanstalk. The boys and *The New Yorker* kept me going, but still, I had to get out of my cave or I would have moldered there. And in the fall of 1999 and the beginning of 2000, I did. It was the stock market that pulled me out. And that's when the chattering began.

Investment has been one of the sacred goods of recent American life, and throughout the nineties I practiced it cautiously and with modest success. By degrees I became an investor capable of living with slightly larger amounts of risk, and then, at the end of the nineties, I became excited beyond measure by speculation and by immoderate risk. In the fall of 1999, I realized we would increase our assets that year (on paper, anyway) more from capital gains than from salaries and royalties. An extraordinary realization. At that point, I began shifting some of our liquid assets into mutual funds geared toward technology. By early 2000, as my wife was about to ship out and I decided to go for broke, I stepped up the pace, placing a good 80 percent of our liquid assets in funds geared toward the Nasdaq exchange, and I began looking for individual tech stocks to invest in. I did it with

16

Cathy's permission, for we were still married and it was her money, too, and I did it without fear, in a rush of exhilaration. *Take hold of the tech boom. Take hold and ride it hard! There is a pile to be made, an apartment to be saved — not to mention a nest egg to be enlarged.* In the midst of my excitement, however, I was a little shocked. Not scared, but shocked. A writer with no business experience, a person wary of booms, circumspect by nature, had risked falling among the crumpled tulips and rotting railroad ties of a dozen schemes gone bust. But I asked myself the same question that many Americans were asking: Was risk something I could any longer afford to avoid? The usual grim historical lesson, the cautionary cycle of greed, euphoria, panic, and collapse — did it have any necessary power over me? Or was it not, in fact, a cliché that should be ignored?

For the economic boom was real; the boom was strong as a tree with many new branches. And the bull market had been continuing with only momentary pauses since 1982 — a crash in 1987, followed by a rapid recovery; a dead year in 1994; a scare in the wake of problems in Russia and Asia in October 1998, and then up and away again. The downsizing and restructuring of American corporations had set off a strong period of growth back there in the early eighties. Go, Jack, go! Recently, the Clinton-Rubin economic policies had reduced the deficit and kept markets open through free-trade agreements; globalization was helping the boom. And since the end of 1994, the bull had forged ahead with particular strength, the S&P 500 index going up more than 20 percent a year.

The change was not just financial, it was cultural. Liberals like me had watched with surprise as their residual distaste for capitalism slipped away, turning to grudging tolerance, and then, by degrees, to outright admiration. Some of the tech entrepreneurs and CEOs, men like Bill Gates, Andrew Grove (Intel), and Henry Nicholas (Broadcom), created products and new markets, employed thousands of people. I couldn't pretend I didn't admire them. I quickly add that capitalism's organization of culture, especially the movies, my art form, often drove me and every other movie lover I knew to despair. If capitalism was "creative destruction," in Joseph Schumpeter's famous phrase, destruction, in the age of conglomerate control, had the upper hand in movies. Still, anyone with sense now knew that our economic system was far better than any other. It was certainly making some of us prosperous.

In early 2000, I found myself in an odd predicament. I was obsessed, but I was ignorant. I understood only the most rudimentary things about the stock market; I knew nothing of the new communications technologies. I was pitching my resources, my faith, my future — and my family's future — into a booming market, and I had never met any investment people beyond my broker or an occasional banker. I knew none of the Internet workers in New York; I didn't know a company head or a single entrepreneur in the New Economy. I needed to meet some of them, to see the men and women. I wanted to read some economic history and some literature — that is, the literature of greed — as I shifted the pieces of my little pile around from one place to another.

2

Euphoria

On January 10, 2000 — a momentous day, as it turned out — I stopped at a newsstand at 74th and Broadway and pretended to look for an automobile magazine. I was on the way to the office, but I dawdled at the newsstand when I heard some stock talk floating onto the sidewalk. The Pakistani vendor pushed Ariba, his favorite stock. His Anglo customer touted Vitesse. They repeated themselves, they argued, these two tech aficionados, and when the conversation petered out, I left the stand and walked down Broadway toward the subway at 72nd. Just north of the station, a total stranger, passing alongside, threw back his head exultantly and shouted the name of a Scandinavian telecommunications company at me. "Ericsson!" he said, laughing. He was bald, with reddish skin and flaring nostrils, and he looked like some manic figure in a Dutch Old Master painting. I stopped in my tracks, but he kept on walking and disappeared. I was astonished: Listen, Mr. Tipster, with your face right out of Frans Hals, why throw back your head and shout at *me?* He addressed me as if he had the absolute right to do so, like someone in a dream, and his face imprinted itself on my memory.

Had he seen me lurking at the newsstand, listening to the tips while eyeing *Car and Driver?* Does a fifty-six-year-old man wearing a blue parka and carrying an old briefcase look like an investor hungry for information? What signals was I sending out? Every day, my ears were pelted with stock information. At Upper West Side lunch counters, young men—customers from the neighborhood—boasted to the immigrant Greeks serving tuna-fish sandwiches that they had bought BroadVision when it was new and cheap and then had got out; yes, they had bought and sold Qualcomm, bought this, sold that. Too self-involved to have lovers, they went to the gym a lot and lived alone, these investment studs, muscular young anchorites chained to their computers. And the day traders! Like bats, they came out when it got dark. A few weeks earlier, at my local hardware store, as I went to the cash register to pay the bill for floor wax and furniture polish, two of them were comparing notes. Other customers were handing over cash, receiving change, but the two men talked through the sales.

Shopper: "I bailed on Qualcomm early and got killed." Store owner: "I held it until three and made eight and a quarter."

A few days later, I saw the hardware-store shopper on the street, and I struck up an acquaintance with him. I'll call him Jackie. He was about fifty-five, heavyset, and friendly, and he worked, as it turned out, above the hardware store, as the owner of a telephone-answering service. Bells Are Ringing, it was called. But of course bells were not ringing. No one used telephone-answering services anymore, and the old black phones sat there in a melancholy row, quiet and unmanned, and Jackie spent his time lodged before two computer screens. CNBC was always on, and occasionally he turned up the volume to listen, but mainly he peered at the screens, making maybe twenty-five trades a day. "I'm not a day trader, I'm a *swing* trader," he told me, meaning that he held stocks longer than a few minutes. He didn't "scalp" — go for an immediate trade after a stock went up or down a quarter point. Instead, he was full of tricks. Sometimes he bought a stock just before it split and made a few points on the "bounce," when the price fell by half and other investors, thinking the stock was cheap, sent the price up. There was a European company that he would buy late in the day and then ride up a couple of points as the Europeans bought it overnight; then he would sell it in the morning and buy it again a couple of days later. The rest of the time Jackie took tips from a technical analyst or played his hunches and made or lost a couple thousand a day. "I have the same setup," he told me, "at my house on the west coast of Florida and also at my daughter's house on the east coast."

Two computers and a TV everywhere! Here was a man who followed the zipper around the corner. Jackie got in and got out, and enjoyed the tension, the excitement. He wasn't in the least surprised by my interest in him. In his own mind, he was an interesting figure. I admired his thoroughness, but otherwise I was depressed by him. Was he a free man, as he thought, or was he carrying his cave around with him everywhere he went?

Jackie's life was a form of bull-market retirement. On January 10, thinking of Jackie as I went to the office, I knew it was all bull-market behavior — the stranger shouting the name of a telecom company, the excitement at the newsstands, at lunch counters, and in the hollows of worn-out businesses. My fellow obsessives, *mes semblables*. The big sell-off right at the beginning of 2000 was also a form of bull-market behavior. The hedge funds that beefed up their performance late in 1999 with technology stocks did some of the selling, and so did individual profit takers who waited for the turn of the year so they could put off capital-gains taxes on their winnings until 2001. Interest-rate hikes were in the offing from Federal Reserve Board chairman Alan Greenspan; the hikes would likely drive the market down, and I wondered, Will individual investors buy into this dip, as they have so nobly and resolutely in other dips throughout the recent years of the bull market? Or were we just possibly at the end of the bull, the beginning of a panic?

Entering the subway at 72nd Street, I shook my head. A panic? Couldn't be. I had just joined the tech boom in full force and wanted to get in even further. I looked around for signs of panic and saw none. I couldn't, for instance, see anything comparable to the displays of wealth in London near the end of the South Sea Bubble of 1720 — a carnival atmosphere of giddiness and gross absurdity, with crazily extravagant parties, jewel-embroidered dresses, excited mobs roaming the streets. Excessive expenditure and social turmoil, too much capital sloshing around the edges of a speculative boom — that's what Edward Chancellor, in his superb history of speculation, *Devil Take the Hindmost*, said were the indications of the end. But this period was different.

It's a complicated matter. Certainly the 1990s was a time of enormous wealth in New York. Yet even if the wealth was stupendous, the new fortunes had not burst forth in bouts of outrageous expenditure. Only a fool would moralize about the $250,000 diamond-studded cell phone that I had recently seen at an Internet trade show. Astonishingly ugly and rather dangerous-looking, the phone was too obviously a stunt, an object so grotesque that nothing of interest could be said about it. The cell phone, adorning the display for a site called inshop.com ("Celebrate your inner shopper"), was not an instance of habitual extravagance. In general, the California roots of the Internet craze, with its puritanical-utopian communitarian longings, had produced a softening, even frowning, effect on mere display. What writer Michael Lewis called the "big-swinging-dick" bravura of eighties

Wall Street champs had been replaced by the earnest talk of the hip Silicon Valley entrepreneur with his black turtleneck and jacket and his belief in free information and "empowerment." He might have been just as crazy about money as the arbitrageur and inside trader Ivan Boesky, but he had the manners of a sixties spiritually ambitious guru, not a shark on the prowl.

No, it was the investment culture itself that had been wild and frivolous in the manner of the South Sea Bubble — wealth *accumulation* and enterprise more than expenditure. We were still in an expansionist phase, and there were no signs of panic. A friend engaged in an Internet start-up told me that in the Starrett-Lehigh building, at 26th and Eleventh Avenue, where many new enterprises were located, a female investment banker from Donaldson Lufkin & Jenrette, walking the halls, was recently heard cold-calling the new companies in the building and asking if they needed any money. Now that was extraordinary, because it sounded like an everyday practice. Here was this undoubtedly competent person in her black power suit and her Prada low heels wandering about in that ungainly building, a classic of the 1920s partly renovated for the future, half old, half new, with its raw corridors and exposed cement and its hip-looking offices, and this paragon was looking for twenty-three-year-olds to give money to. One imagined her chagrin when she was turned down, for the most appealing of the start-ups, it seems, were able to *choose* whom they wanted to receive money from — choose the names that would sound best in their résumés. Kurt Andersen, the former editor of *New York* magazine (and my boss for part of my time there as movie critic), had started up his own company, Power Media, and had once told me that there was "literally too much money. You have to decide whose money is better than someone else's. Whose investment makes you look good." And Kurt had said, publicly and notoriously, "Raising money now is easier than getting laid in 1969."

In the subway, I looked at the men and women sitting around me — single women in dark slacks, the men in blue or gray suits; they were whites, blacks, Latinos, Asians, all of them heading to offices in midtown and Wall Street, and also to civil service jobs in the federal buildings downtown. They were blank-faced, their eyes turned to a newspaper, or merely glassy and inward-looking in the defensive style of New York mass-transit riders. Yet these were investors, many of them, ordinary people who had some holdings — a few stocks, a bond fund, maybe a lot more. By the end of the nineties, roughly half the population was investing in equities. Investment had become as much a part of popular culture as baseball, fishing, and bar-hopping. There were strip clubs that ran the stock-price ticker as the girls took off their clothes. People sat for hours in airport lounges, haircutting salons, and hotel lobbies, stoned by CNBC, just the way I was at home. At the same time, pension funds and 401(k) plans had turned factory workers and even university intellectuals into investors. In all, wealth no longer appeared to a great many Americans as a rare goal pursued through entrepreneurial skill or achieved through extraordinary luck. No, in the late nineties, wealth was almost an entitlement. There was a widespread, unspoken belief that you betrayed a character weakness if you were not rich, or not trying to *get* rich.

But that wasn't all of it. What distinguished the period, of course, was its unique character of hope — an ecstatic belief in the future as an enormous ever-expanding bounty of freedom and money. In the subway, people may have avoided contact with their neighbors, but some of these sullen-looking New Yorkers, just trying to get to work, must have shared that hope and wanted a piece of the bounty. In the last few years, the usual desire to make a pile had merged with the sunrise ardor of creating a new way of buying, communicating, and doing business. At its most extreme and utopian, the vision ballooned into grandiose views of an altered reality, a new human being exchanging his soulful essence with spiritual machines. Astonishingly, the sixties counterculture, hiding in disgrace in the seventies and eighties, had re-emerged in the nineties and had contributed for corporate use the old exalted blarney of "revolution" and "community." Third World peasant children smiled at us from a half-dozen ads for fashionable new business-to-business software companies. Idealism and greed were mixed together as never before.

When I wanted reassurance that the boom was genuine, I would get on the phone with an intellectually accomplished friend, Edward Rothstein, who was the "critic at large" for the *New York Times* (i.e., he wrote about whatever interested him). Rothstein was a family man like me, though generally more sober, a serious guy thoroughly rooted in his marriage, his work, his Brooklyn neighborhood. He played Beethoven's violin and piano sonatas with his children, understood abstruse mathematical concepts. But on the phone, all aflutter, he said to me, "This is not just money moving around from one place to another. This is new wealth being created." To which I said, in agreement, "Half the people in the world don't have telephones. What are they going to do in the Third World, put up poles? Lay wire in the ground?" Eagerly we deposited cell phones into the hands of Ukrainian peasants and Argentinean gauchos. We were two middle-aged men long schooled in culture but suddenly all agog over business enterprise. Netscape, the Internet browser, went from start-up to its initial public offering (IPO) in eighteen months, reaching a market capitalization of $2.2 billion the first day it was publicly traded. Four months later, the market cap was over $6 billion. New wealth. And now Rothstein and I wanted a piece of it. For the previous twenty years, we had purchased one computer after another without making a dime from computer stocks, and we were determined, this time, not to be left out.

Another writer friend, whom I shall call James Stevens, had emptied out his funds in 1995 and had made major bets on Microsoft, on Cisco, and, recently, on JDSU, an optical-networking parts maker, and on EMC, a network storage company. "Diversification is for fools," Stevens said, explaining his all-tech strategy. Stevens had unusually large brown eyes and spoke with great animation always. An enthusiast. And a bit of a gambler. In five years, the $200,000 he had invested in these stocks had become about a million dollars. Where was it decreed—on what tablet was it inscribed—that writers should not get rich, too? Or at least prosperous?

I got off the local at 50th and Broadway, picked up *Forbes* at a magazine store on 48th, and walked south toward the office in Times Square. At 47th, I passed the huge electronic signboard on the Morgan Stanley building. I had never really looked at it before—it was just another element in the electronically seething atmosphere of Times Square. On the Broadway side of the building, there were three rapidly moving bands, more than anyone could keep up with at once. The New York Stock Exchange and Nasdaq tickers ran on the lower lines, and along the top ran news of African bonds (African bonds?) and the latest excitements from . . . New Zealand. I stood looking for a while. What was this information doing there? No one standing on the street could use it or even take it in. The information was superfluous, a mere display of the *ability* to inform. Along the side of the building, facing north at 47th, the price of hog futures flashed onto a giant screen, disintegrated into a star shower of moving light, and re-formed into the yield on six-month treasury bonds.

In the last few years, Times Square had become not only the entertainment center but the self-advertised financial communications center of the world. The Nasdaq MarketSite, with

CNBC's reporters on duty as well as reporters from CNN and other networks, was right there on the ground floor of my own office building at 43rd and Broadway. The British news and financial service Reuters was putting up its American headquarters across the street. The giant media conglomerate Bertelsmann was building its headquarters up the block, and ABC's *Good Morning America* was broadcast on the ground floor at 44th, practically on the pavement. Across the way, on the west side of Times Square, crowds of dopey kids waved their arms back and forth on cue for MTV. The *New York Times* and HBO were only a half block away. Times Square had become the blast furnace of communication (eros, the area's former fuel, was now banned). The entire area was one vast zipper, as electrified as Ginza or Vegas but even more centrally devoted to money. For surely entertainment, news, and finance had become a single vast system, forever shaping and reshaping itself in massive configurations of capital and light, as fluid as the crowds of tourists in the square, including little children from Iowa following their dad as he led blindly, his eye plugged to a camera pointed up at some electronic facsimile of Britney Spears's belly button. Mock them not, I said to myself sternly, for they are investors, too.

Exhausted just from walking through all this pulsing clamor, I climbed with relief to my room on the twentieth floor of the Condé Nast building, the new corporate headquarters where *The New Yorker* and many other magazines were published. I was safe inside the quiet, windowless little office. Idly, I turned through stacked-up copies of *The Industry Standard* and *Red Herring* and *Fast Company*. The mags were three, four, even five hundred pages an issue, and spread through their effulgent leaves were all the current mantras: Technology spending by corporations had been increasing at a rate of 30 percent a year; the use of the Internet doubled every ninety days; the computer box was fading, but wireless was taking off like a rocket. The value of a given network—computers, servers, Web sites, etc.—increased *exponentially* as more people were added to it. So the magazines said. Up, up, up; expand, expand, expand.

I heard, I saw, I responded: I was rapidly shifting assets into tech. Such things as price-earnings ratios in the tech stocks had gone way up, but who really knew if a high price-earnings ratio was wrong? Were the common measures, blessed by history, now out of date? A stock's price generally depends on predictions of discounted future cash flow, and I knew damn well that a large part of the current boom, at least in the Internet sector, was sheer desire and abject pleading: *Let them make money! Dear God, let them make money, somehow or other!* But doubt was overwhelmed by hope. The unknown, in its silence, thundered loudly of intangible assets and undiscovered growth. As I learned from the rubble of magazines on the floor, the point for the Internet companies and the new technologies was to get there first, build up share, and dominate their sector, putting other contenders out of business, the way Compaq, Dell, and Microsoft had done in the past. Then, in the future? There may be factors, markets, means, ways of reaching the consumer, the supplier, and the vendor that we weren't aware of yet. Advertising? Fee-based use? There were tech companies whose high price was geared not to earnings but to revenues—Cisco, say. It was one of the new ways of measuring value. As it happened, I didn't own any Cisco directly, but all my Nasdaq-oriented funds had loaded up on Cisco.

I didn't look closely into revenue growth, profits, debt, and the rest—I didn't perform my "due diligence," a close study of the fundamentals. I listened to those I wanted to listen to—the gurus on CNBC, the investment studs at lunch counters, the tech specialists at Web sites. I would listen, then scout a stock or fund on the Internet, then buy it according to reputation and its position in its industry. I wasn't lazy, exactly, but at some level,

I thought the study of fundamentals was a waste of time. Fundamentals for brand-new companies with exciting prospects were virtually nonexistent, and anyway, as anyone could see, investors were ignoring such basics as cash flow and were continuing to drive up prices. If I had been asked to reduce my thinking to a formula, I would have said this: A very fast growth rate in a tech stock can support a higher than normal price-earnings multiple. That's the assumption I was going on. In this low-inflation environment, a stock growing at 25 percent a year was worth a P/E ratio of, say, 65, which is a lot higher than normal. But that's as far as I worked it out, for the market was galloping and I thought there was no need to worry if the harness was a little loose or the bit didn't quite fit the horse's mouth. In such an overstimulated climate, there was a measure of relief in just buying something. Right or wrong, at least it's an act, a *move*.

Over the previous four months or so, from the fall of 1999 onward, we had increased the percentage of our investment in stocks, investing in equity funds mainly, but we bought individual information-technology stocks, too. In the first week of 2000, with Cathy's permission, I bought JDS Uniphase; and Broadcom (chips for the new set-top boxes that handle much greater "bandwidth"); and Internet Capital Group (an "incubator" of Internet start-up companies in the business-to-business area); and Rational Software (integrated software and Web site testing for e-business). Some of these stocks, pushed up by the boom, were priced very high — Broadcom was at 233 when we bought it, JDS Uniphase at 126, Internet Capital Group at 120. Very high, but I was going on the principle that the stock of a growing company would split and continue to appreciate, just as the great stocks of the nineties like Dell and Cisco had split and grown again and again. Was this a false analogy? It had better not be.

I bought Nokia and Motorola, too, the leading makers of cell phones, ignoring Ericsson, so loudly hawked by Frans Halsian tipsters on the street. Buying individual stocks was a relatively rare experience for me, and I felt a slight flutter of alarm, like a kid's nerves when he's out on the diving board for the first time. But how dangerous was it? Internet Capital Group was a speculative play, but the others were great companies essential to the growth of their industries. They made hardware or system software; they were not Internet retail sites selling, for $7,500 a shot, designer dresses that no woman could try on.

One had to keep making moves. I was sure of it, because I had not moved in the past. I brooded over my story, my blunder. It is the primal scene, the type of wound that almost everyone carries around during a boom period. My story takes place in our neighborhood Japanese restaurant, Bon 75, on Broadway, where my wife and I had lunch with our broker in 1986 — early March 1986, just before Microsoft went public.

"There's this stock," I said, holding a piece of sushi between sticks. "Microsoft. It makes the operating system for IBM and all the clones."

"Never heard of it," our broker said, dipping his vegetable tempura in sauce. If his right hand had been free, he might have written down the name of the company. But it wasn't, *his right hand wasn't free,* and the moment passed. I ate my salmon roe and failed to insist that he follow up, even though, at some level, I *knew.* The ten thousand or so dollars that we could have afforded to invest in 1986 would, if left undisturbed, be worth almost $3.5 million by early 2000. At the height of the South Sea Bubble, in 1719, the poet Alexander Pope wrote his broker: "I daily hear of such advantages to be gained by one project or other in the Stocks, that my Spirit is Up with double Zeal, in the desire of our trying to enrich ourselves . . . Tis Ignominious (in this Age of Hope and Golden Mountains) not to venture."

★   ★   ★

I laid aside the magazines in my office and read my screening invitations, and then turned through the newspaper ads for new movies. It was time to change one game of chance for another. A movie critic also hopes to get lucky. But there was nothing. Okay, not nothing, but very little good new stuff. In the dead of winter, a critic is forced to grab at tasty scraps, a documentary about Detroit Tigers slugger Hank Greenberg, a revival of Hitchcock's *Rear Window*. The Christmas movies are still playing off, and the studios rarely release anything important so many months in advance of the awards season. In January and February, foreign films, documentaries, and other kinds of nonfiction films look more alive than the Hollywood "product," which lies dormant before its sudden ascension to quality in the November and December months, when the audience IQ, by some mysterious process, suddenly jumps up by forty points.

Whether we wanted to admit it or not, we movie critics were as much dominated and regulated by money as the workers in any other profession. We were controlled by the yearly cycle of releases, lifted and dropped by the tides of cash sweeping in and out. Often enough, critical practice — the length of the reviews and, for the corrupt, the degree of ardor — was determined by the manipulations of studio marketing departments, which arranged such things as advertising and press junkets. I didn't go on junkets or hand out advance blurbs for the movie ads, but I was caught in the tides of cash, too, and when the new commercial movies were feeble, I felt out of it. I may have hated the way the conglomerates controlled the movies, yet leafing through my screening notices in that dead season, I knew that a critic without a vital connection to the commerce of movies was in sorry shape. You could love art, study film aesthetics, adore the films of Jean Renoir and John Ford, the documentaries of Frederick Wiseman, the most challenging features from Korea or Taiwan or lower Manhattan. But if you didn't feel

31

some connection to the big audience, you were a dry-souled man. The great promise of movies, after all, was that they would be a popular art form, and for decades they *were,* successfully bringing art as well as diversion to enormous numbers of people. That was D. W. Griffith's dream, and Chaplin's, and Orson Welles's, and Francis Coppola's, and, in recent years, Steven Spielberg's and Ang Lee's dream, too. But with some brilliant exceptions every year, movies were now fading as popular art, splitting dangerously into spangled spectacles for the malls and earnest little art films for the class audience.

Looking for something alive on the screen, a critic wants to be more than just a judge handing out grades. I wanted to feel, exultantly, that I was riding the crest of a movement, or helping some new taste or sensibility make its way in the world, or perhaps marking the beginning stages in a great director or actress's career—anything but merely rising and falling, like the cars on a Ferris wheel, through the cycle of seasons and releases. Horrible thought! That kind of reviewing was like investing in—I don't know—in *bonds.* No, critics want to be in the big-money game, though always in their own cranky, outsider's way. Like stock investors, they live on a narrow margin of hope, eager to grab on to a winner—an artistic winner, and sometimes a commercial winner, too, because commerce, whatever my fear of its power, has its own excitement, and movies need a big audience to survive.

So critics were often in a funk, half alienated from their own art form, unwilling to give in to commerce—or constantly to play the scold, either. I had been invited to speak on movies in a few months at the home of a man named Samuel Waksal, a doctor of some sort who was head of the New York State Humanities Council. I dreaded such occasions, because I could not honestly say the movies were in good shape, yet I hated to play the critical sourpuss. I didn't know who Waksal was, or why an official occasion was taking place at his apartment, but I would have to come up with something to say.

I flipped the screening invitations aside. I needed a TV; I needed CNBC. There was a conference room on the east side of the building, usually empty, where, at my high-minded magazine, I could sneak off and watch CNBC. Full of light, it was a spirit-lifting chamber, perfect for a market surge.

The time was almost four, and I watched the Nasdaq index close at 4049. After that profit-taking dip at the beginning of the year, the market had been making a rapid recovery: On that day, January 10, 2000, the Nasdaq was up 167, the Dow up 49, to a record high of 11,572. With good reason. It was the day AOL announced its takeover of Time Warner in a $165 billion deal, and the hills were alive with the whirls of spin: New media buys old, the delivery system buys the "content provider." Play money—America Online's seemingly inflated stock price—buys real assets. At the computer that night, I rhapsodized in my journal.

1/10/00

Casting off doubt, the media and investors everywhere seem irradiated by a sense of boundless possibilities: Yes, there will be dips, corrections, jitters, shakeouts, but the movement will be up, and Alan Greenspan, like the Holy Ghost brooding with sweet wings over the earth, will protect us, measuring out the milk of liquidity, harmonizing our virtues and vices into an orderly progression toward salvation. Hallelujah!

3

Moves

"YOU are going to die slowly, and in great pain."

I stood behind my son Thomas, who was playing Command and Conquer: Red Alert on the computer and would not go to bed, and reaching down, I crisscrossed my arms around his chest and pulled him out of his chair and squeezed, and then I tripped over his legs and we fell on his bed, and he chopped me in the side a few times. When we both stopped laughing, I told him a story that had just popped into my head about a father who loses a diamond ring he had meant to give to his wife. His son, trying to help out, heroically scours the garbage dumps in the Bronx, working there day and night until he finds the ring. Covered with filth, the boy presents the ring to his mother. As the story ended, Tommy conked out at last, and I felt a nasty little cloud pass through my chest. I had lost what it was I wanted to give my wife. And Tommy couldn't help me at all.

In the morning, I pulled both boys from sleep ("Can I have another five minutes, Dad?" "Three minutes." "How about four?" "Three."), and shoveled them out the door. It was my turn to be with the kids—Cathy was away in her little studio. We were better off apart. I knew that now, but I both cursed her for leaving and missed her terribly. She had beautiful eyes despite a slight droop in one lid, which gave her a proud but sluggish air, as of an eagle that had drunk too much from the wrong mountain lake. She was beautiful in her own style: an aristocratic nose surmounted a terrific lopsided grin, and she had a long neck, a long pale body. The great caricaturist David Levine had done a drawing of her in the *New York Review of Books* in 1999, which I had not much liked—he got the lopsided grin, but he hung a curtain of hair over the droopy lid and missed the haughtily aristo nose; she came out looking like a wise guy, which wasn't quite right.

A domestic person, she would take care of the children, read, write, talk on the phone, dither. She would leave her glasses at someone's house, ball up the names of two authors she was sitting next to at a dinner party, mistaking Tom Wolfe for Gay Talese (or the other way around). And then, suddenly, her vagueness would fade, she would snap into focus, and she would be devastating. Her judgment was severe, her humor very sharp. Her writing was sharp, too—precise and terse as it followed a line of wit into description or irony, wherever it had to go. The author of *Rameau's Niece, The Love Letter,* and other books, she was naturally and easily a comic novelist. In argument, she cut through tangled issues and located the core; she was stubborn as hell. She figured out how to help my elderly, seemingly half-mad mother when I was at my wits' end, saving my mother from a mysterious illness that was not madness at all. She read difficult books with naive excitement and puzzled them out. She was a birder, and she told me about birds, and early in the marriage, holding cameras and guidebooks, I followed her into mosquito-laden Maine swamps as we searched for Lincoln's sparrows and palm warblers.

The investment moves I made with our money were not just for myself and my apartment. They were for her, too, and for the kids. Separated or together, we had to increase the family holdings, increase family wealth, take hold of the future. That meant taking risks. In a minor act of defiance, during the first week of 2000 I liquidated our holdings in two bond funds and put the money in stocks; and I canceled part of my life insurance. We had other insurance, anyway, and since we had accumulated some money since we took on this policy in 1992, we didn't seem to need it as much. As it happens, we were $11,000 in arrears on the premiums. I hated the idea of insurance so much that I unconsciously rebelled and "forgot" to pay the premiums. The policy had built up some dividends, which I could invest, and that was part of the attraction of canceling the thing.

Ending that policy had produced an enormous burst of excitement. Trust the market to build a sufficient nest egg! Trust the *market!* Trust life, not death! I would keep up, follow the zipper, anticipate the future as it came rushing into the present, and Max and Thomas would inherit enough money to pay the funeral costs and then some—they don't need the policy. I sang these things to myself over and over. I was investing for *them,* for the boys. My course was risky, but I would deliver the goods to them in the end.

All this came as the culmination of other serious moves. In 1998, I had shifted jobs, leaving *New York* magazine after twenty years there as film critic, settling in at *The New Yorker,* and I had lodged my 401(k) money in an S&P 500 index fund offered by Condé Nast, the *New Yorker* parent company. But then in October 1999, kissing caution good-bye, I moved the 401(k) money—all of it—into a fund that invested in Nasdaq companies, the Fidelity OTC Fund.

So there you have it: Over a period of a few months, from October 1999 into early 2000, we had liquidated life insurance, sold out bonds, dropped value and index funds that were moving slowly, and built up our "exposure" to aggressive growth, technology, and biotech. *Exposure?* Are you kidding? We were naked. I had become that journalistic cliché, the momentum investor who loads up on a hot market sector. But pile on! Pile on! and farewell to diversification. I wanted to keep my apartment. I wanted to build that pile not just for the sweetness of life but to hold on to what I already possessed. As Thomas Hobbes said in *Leviathan*, men expand their domain as a way of preventing the loss of what they already have. Anyway, the lure of big gains was too strong, and since the Nasdaq had been going through the roof since October 1999, we had done very well, our portfolio going up over 30 percent in just those few months. The 401(k) investment, Fidelity OTC, had gone up an astounding $120,000 in a single quarter. We even had a runaway biotech stock, ImClone, which sat in our portfolio for years and suddenly took off in the fall of 1999.

At times I wondered, Am I mad? Half mad? I have put my retirement savings into a Nasdaq fund. But at least we carried no credit-card debt, and our mortgage was only about one twelfth the market value of the apartment. After all the recent moves, we took out a home-equity loan and line of credit at the bank, increasing our liquidity, but I vowed not to invest the borrowed money in stocks. There had to be a limit, and that was it. But still, my heart fluttered in my chest, and every night I felt as if I were sleeping on a bumpy Greyhound (sleep . . . wake up . . . sleep . . . wake up). To calm myself down, I had to power-walk around the reservoir in Central Park for an hour or more, for with these latest changes, almost 80 percent of our liquid assets were in stocks, and perhaps 80 percent of *that* money was invested in the New Economy, and this was living dangerously indeed. But to live dangerously is very much to live.

By the winter of 2000, the young men and women had retreated from my screen, frozen in their thick, swollen happiness, un-watched, unattended, like paintings on a cave wall after the dwellers have left. I still received friendly e-mails, especially from a persistent erotic shadow with the *nom de Web* of Heather. I was flattered to be so singled out, Heather, but as I lost you, I gained back myself. By breaking the link between the voyeur and the exhibitionist, between me and you, I willed that you didn't exist, but more to the point, I willed that I *must* exist. No more gazing at porn. Yet I was willing to give obsession in general its due as a driving force. Shifting from one mania to another, from porn to CNBC, and accepting greater risk in the market brought me out of despair; it roused me to the tides and fortunes of life — I had placed myself in danger, and the blood was racing though my veins. I buy, therefore I am.

Odd, this speed fetish of mine, the chattering and impatience. Only a few years earlier, I was trying to slow down. Struggling with Hegel, Montaigne, and Nietzsche for my classics book, I slowed myself down to a walk. I would read five or six pages an hour. In the end, I may have done more for myself than for the classics — it's not for me to say. But I had escaped, at least for a while, the constant need to *keep up,* that bizarre torment of the age which produced, in secular personalities, a fretful irritation not altogether different from the anguish of the religious and the harrowed who knew they could never, never be pure enough. For many of us now felt overwhelmed by what we could not master, and this sense of never being quite on top of things — at work, in consumer behavior, in technology — nagged at our self-satisfaction like a persistent cough doubling up a healthy body. After a while, the cough of displeasure hinted at a larger disturbance: A radical revision of time was under way. It was so radical that such standard integers of pleasure as the casual saunter and laze of a long day in the park; the slow, soft reiterations of a daydream; the lengthy evening with friends at a restaurant in a quiet Roman square — all were harassed by the new common tempo of life. The stock market annihilating time was only an exaggeration of time's common fate. Everything was annihilating time.

Slowing myself down as I did the reading and writing for my book, I relished the memory of such things as the lingering images of John Ford's or Michelangelo Antonioni's mournfully beautiful movies, the shots that seemed to breathe a long plaint of melancholy; and I loved the Rolling Stones songs that seemed to go on forever. I loved a long afternoon spent lolling with a book on a friend's lawn up in the country. I adored the unfolding power of duration, repetition, even attenuation — the summer light that began to wane at six and was still waning, two glasses of wine later, at eight-thirty.

But all that was over now. To re-create that earlier sense of time, I could summon no greater power than nostalgia.

4

The End of Golf
in Bulgaria

IN early February 2000, at *The New Yorker* office, the magazine's economics writer, John Cassidy, turned slightly in my direction and hissed, "You're going to lose your money."

John is a Brit of Irish descent, from Leeds, a tough industrial city in the Midlands. He speaks curtly, in newspaper shorthand, turning sideways as he speaks, so he always appears to be confiding some forbidden or subversive information out of the corner of his mouth. He's actually a very genial man, so I was startled when he let me have it. At *The New Yorker,* politeness, collegiality, and discretion are valued more highly than cleanliness at a silicon factory. Heaven forbid — no, heaven *forfend* — that anyone should get publicly angry in those civil halls. A blunt personal remark seems a surprise; a threat, even an impersonal one, comes as a slap.

John Cassidy did not wish me ill, but he thought that the booming market was a bubble and nothing else, and that people like me had lost their minds. In any case, he had just been talking to Federal Reserve chairman Alan Greenspan, who was determined to bring the soaring market down. Well, let's say, more accurately, that Greenspan wanted to cool off the economy, which he feared would overheat — expand at too rapid a rate and then collapse — and he thought the runaway market was part of the problem. The week before, on February 2, the Fed had raised interest rates 25 basis points, or a quarter of one percent, to 5.75 percent. As it happens, having chewed the rate increase over for weeks, the market didn't even burp. The bad news had already been digested. On the day that Cassidy spoke to me, the Nasdaq, after that early January sell-off, had completed a more than 9 percent rise, more than 300 points for the week, and stood at over 4300. Yet Cassidy, speaking softly but with great intensity, was making it clear to me that Greenspan was not done, that he would *bring the market down.*

I nodded, sighed, and did not listen. As the market soared all through the late nineties, Cassidy had been making bearish noises. *Hates the market,* people said. *Keeps his money under a mattress.* Bears! Had they been right over the last five years? They had not been right. If you had listened to them, you would have missed the incredible surge that began in 1995. But in the office Cassidy wouldn't stop. Suddenly intense, he turned sideways again and said it was a bubble, a classic bubble, just look at history, it had happened again and again. . . .

History, yes, *history.* I longed not to look at it. Like a dark, ranting prophet, it called us fools. The paradigm of greed and speculation, of course, is the *tulpenwoerde,* or tulip mania, in Holland, in the 1630s. In the midst of the bull market, bears mentioned it all the time, and one was irked to be reminded of it — irked by the perfection of the didactic lesson, the story of the dandy little trading empire going mad. Yes, the superb equipoise of the banking and shipping power collapsing into near chaos, and over what? — over *flowers!* Hateful, damned story! The financial press was always dragging it out.

I knew the story well. The rarified taste for these flowers became a marketable commodity, and in the fall of every year, a kind of "futures" mania developed. People met in "Colleges" (i.e., taverns) and traded contracts for the bulbs that would emerge in spring. Sometimes they offered paper attesting to their credit, sometimes real assets, like oxen or furniture or tools or even farms. A mortgaged farm for a few bulbs! Eager to trade, some of the buyers delayed payment, offering as "collateral" stock which they had paid for only in part. The trades were sealed with wine. Madness! A significant part of the sanest, cleanest, most orderly society the world has ever known got caught up in *windhandel,* or airy trade, i.e., speculation. For, of course, money, not flowers, became the point for many people. Speculators traded their paper upward, until the whole thing collapsed, in early February 1637, when delivery of the spring bulbs was looming and no one believed prices could go any higher. Late buyers were ruined, and the Dutch magistrates moved in hard and began to regulate the flower trade.

The tulip has a modest "present" value; most of its value is ascribed to it by sentiment, taste, and fashion. The *tulpenwoerde,* then, is a case of "pure" destructive speculation, and as historian Simon Schama explains in his study of Dutch culture in the seventeenth century, *The Embarrassment of Riches,* the mania was quickly followed by an outpouring of satirical tracts and disapproving graphic allegories in which demons, asses, and victim-fops played the leading roles. The man in a fool's cap—the speculator—is a frequent figure. The Dutch humanists, as well as the clergy, preached against a period of madness in which "the gullible masses [were] driven to folly and ruin by their thirst for unearned gain."

Yes, it was an instructive story—very interesting, no doubt. In his 1989 book, *Manias, Panics, and Crashes,* the economic historian Charles Kindleberger draws on it as he sets up a model of financial disaster. Kindleberger has traced a deep structure common to all speculative manias. In any bubble — tulips, railroads, computers, etc. — at first there is a "displacement" in the form of a new species of investment. This is followed by "positive feedback" as inexperienced investors throw money into the market, followed, of course, by "euphoria" as prices rise and common sense disintegrates. In this period, the speculation spreads to different kinds of assets. New companies spring up and are floated in the market, and investors leverage their rising assets. You know the rest: overextended credit, swindles and frauds, and eventual collapse.

But how much of that described the current moment, February 2000? We had certainly gone through "displacement" in the form of the Internet and fiber optics and other new or newly developed inventions in information technology. In the mid to late nineties, venture capitalists and investment banks had sent start-ups and initial public offerings flying through the system, and then institutional and individual investors had rushed in to buy — that was the "positive feedback." And we were nothing if not "euphoric" at the moment. Between October 1998 and now, early 2000, the Nasdaq composite index had tripled. *Tripled!* But were we condemned to fill out the rest of the paradigm as well? Was it a prediction of the inevitable, or a witches' brew of irrelevant fatalistic pronouncement? The fatalists were sure of the collapse. Were they right? I suspected that God might know the future but Kindleberger did not. We weren't fated to fill out the paradigm, *no, not if new wealth was being created in massive amounts.* My own portfolio was going up brilliantly, and I would be damned if I would don the fool's cap in some allegory of folly. I had read the flagrant historical examples, listened to Cassidy and the bears on CNBC, and I wanted to say to all these people, Let the market *run.* Just let it *go!* Stop questioning it, criticizing it, harassing it with conventional measures of value!

Still, I was nervous, I was sleepless, and when I was lying in bed, I would see the face of a man with flaring nostrils leaning back and laughing. I sighed at my own corny portents — so like a bad silent movie from about 1925 — but there he was, that madman on Broadway shouting "Ericsson" at me. What bothered me was that I knew madmen on the street and investment champs at lunch counters, but not any of the new Internet workers. I had hardly *seen* them.

Rising at the extraordinary hour of 6:45 A.M. (film critics usually rise at ten or later, and more slowly than the Sun King), I made my way on February 10 to a conference center on Desbrosses Street, in the lower-Manhattan neighborhood known as Tribeca. One leaves the heavy brown nineteenth-century cobblestones, noisy with trucks thudding along, and enters what looks like an old loft building. On an upper floor, the landing opened, astonishingly, into a large conference space with a glass roof and brilliant light. It was like walking into a sound stage on the Paramount lot in Hollywood and finding an enormous movie set within — Tribeca re-industrialized by the Internet boom and opened to the sunlight of advanced capitalism.

There was a long, long table covered with Evian water, freshly squeezed orange and grapefruit juice, pastries and bagels — this last a New York touch, perhaps. The attendees, about three hundred of them, had shown up for the monthly meeting of a group called New York Infotech Forum, one of many such groups in Silicon Alley, where conferences seemed to take place every day. (So much for the ubiquity of e-mailing. Serious exchanges of information, not to mention investing, still required a firm handshake and a look in the eye.) I entered a dense crowd of people, though I immediately realized, to my relief, that the scene was not what New York journalists call a "ratfuck" — a packed gathering (book party, awards party, promotional event) of like-minded media workers, an experience that can pass, according to whom you're pressed up against, from deep pleasure to intense misery. No, the overall tone was one of bounding, thriving conviviality. People introduced themselves without hesitation and whipped out their business cards. The pitch for the service, the Web site, the venture-capital company came so fast and unapologetically that it felt less like a hustle than like a new, entirely candid way of presenting oneself. Modesty and circumspection were a mere irrelevance to these men and women, most of whom, at a glance, I judged to be in their thirties. Here were the true fast-talkers, harbingers of the revolution. Even as a mere listener, I couldn't keep up with them. They were lawyers, accountants, bankers, venture capitalists of all sorts—all ready to finance, promote, and service the new Internet start-up companies in New York. Some of them appeared to be escapees from journalism, broadcasting, and advertising. The old media professions were draining out fast. These people at the Infotech Forum were in a high state of transition, electrified and jubilant as they buttonholed me with their projects. They would link up buyers and suppliers; they would "tie in" with a company's internal applications; they would provide a "space" to auction off the toenail clippings of Madonna's masseur. They fixed me with their eyes, waiting for a sign that I got it, that I saw that the idea had . . . *scalability*.

We settled down for a speech from Mark L. Walsh, CEO of VerticalNet, one of the new business-to-business software Internet companies. B2B had captured the imagination of investors; we were told it was the hottest of the new Internet sectors, potentially eight times the size of business-to-consumer sites (eBay, Amazon, etc.). Tall, forty-fivish, with wire-frame glasses and a full head of curling gray hair, Walsh, who had a background in advertising and cable TV, spoke in a tumultuous rush. This man was not a babbling brook, he was a torrent of claims, boasts,

45

promises, visions. His company, VerticalNet, establishes separate Web sites, or separate vertical portals—Walsh calls them "vortals"—for such unglamorous industries as poultry processing or waste management. He has, for instance, a site called solidwaste.com. He has fifty-six of these sites, gathered in twelve business sectors, or silos, and each site brings together buyers and suppliers, offers trade news and gossip. The site is an exchange, a marketplace, a club. He establishes a place for the waste-management heavies to shmooze. Among other things, he wants to eliminate the executives' date on the golf course, and if he can, he will put the three-day Vegas trade show out of business. The duck farmers won't have to leave their places in East Moriches, Long Island, in order to talk with suppliers, customers, rivals. He described VerticalNet as a "poster child for what the Internet can do," and he told us that his company, which had gone public roughly a year earlier at $16 a share, closed at the end of the first day's trading at over $45, and subsequently climbed to a split-adjusted price of $400. He insisted that even though VerticalNet had a "history of losses," the company, with its $9 billion market capitalization, was undervalued. The whole point is share of market, not profits—not now, at any rate.

"If you knew in 1979 what you know now about the development of cable," he said, reaching the clincher, "wouldn't you have borrowed every dollar you could, mortgaged your house, maxed your credit cards in order to get into cable?"

Well, yes, that was the spirit of the moment: We were to take on faith, on the most fragmentary evidence, that in 2020 it would be clear to the entire world that Mark L. Walsh had figured out one of the most profitable uses of the Internet for B2B software. We were to project ourselves into a future from which we could look back to the moment—*the* moment—at which enormous wealth was generated. Essentially, we were *in* the future, if only we had the courage to admit it and to become rich from it. But didn't every Internet entrepreneur believe some version of this about his own company? And how could more than a tiny fraction of them be right? I had a moment of furious doubt. I wasn't so sure how Walsh's "vortals" could generate big fees. His panache was exciting but unnerving. How many such projections that sent up stock prices were as unverifiable as his?

Was I the only skeptical one, or did they all think it might be a put-on? I asked a few of the highly transitionals, and they just shrugged. They were caught. Why not go *with* it? Walsh's business might have sounded shaky, but the capital markets were supporting it. They wanted to join up. After the speech, many of them gathered around for a personal chat. Walsh was the man, at least for the moment. He was seductive, provocative, expansionist, soaring. "Bulgaria leaped to digital without copper wire," he told a group of us, and he assured us that golf didn't stand a chance in the Third World, which would jump into B2B without the intermediate step of developing a time-wasting culture of business sociability. But what if Bulgarians preferred links to links? As he talked, I sensed that he might be more than a little contemptuous of the businesses themselves — that is, he was amused by the contrast between the homely nature of poultry processing and the amazingly clever, odorless thing he was going to do for companies cutting up fowls. And I thought, This guy can't be straight, can he? Find me a real entrepreneur, one with a real product!

But afterward, as people milled around, I eased up on him. I admired the way he listened intently to each person and then made an even, copious response. These New Economy people had something fine and free about their manners. They exuded enthusiasm; they were open, generous with themselves, not guarded or haughty in the old big-business style. Like revolutionaries everywhere, they were fervent and self-propelling, and they wanted to erase all doubts in their listeners. A few days later, the *Wall Street Journal* rather airily referred to Walsh's company, VerticalNet, which had a price-earnings ratio over 300, as a "concept stock." That did not have a good sound. But I was provoked by Walsh's talk, by the deep appeal it made at that amazing moment when some of the Nasdaq stocks were going up five, even ten points a day. In his attention to these lesser mortals, Walsh was a prince, and the business cards flew back and forth like pictures of Sammy Sosa on the rear seat of a school bus.

5

My Hero Wants to Slay the Bull

AT the office, on February 17, I retreated to the sunlit conference room facing east, eager to see Alan Greenspan make his annual report on the state of the economy to the House Banking Committee. As he began, I gazed with adoration at the television set, which was perched high on a stand. An acolyte looking up at a holy man, I was in love with Alan Greenspan — a balding, seventy-three-year-old Republican banker. He had been so effective, this man, so good, flooding the market with liquidity at just the right time, tightening at the right time. I admired his gravity, his civility, his realism, his springing step when he walked into the Fed with his slender briefcase held tightly under his left arm. Looking neither to the left nor to the right, he would not reveal to the press what he was thinking. The mystique of his power depended on circumspection, on habits of quiet, calculated boldness. The only American intellectual universally admired, he was, by nature, dry, respectful, formal — a highly plausible, explanatory man. Yet, when it suited his purpose, he could be cagey and circumlocutory to the point of opacity. He seemed to be in supreme possession of a *secret*. Yet that secret, I imagined, was no more than the labyrinthine skepticism of his intelligence, his habit of considering many factors at once. The secret was also his weapon: The polite mock courtship of grand-standing senators and ignorant congressmen revealed (if you listened very closely) a withering intellectual contempt. Oh, I was in love. I was even willing to forgive him his language, the endless, boxcar sentences whose clauses banged awkwardly into one another and whose rhythmless prolixity only he — reading slowly — could render into sense. In his grim and gummed-up way, he was highly articulate. He *had* to pack so many clauses and references into each sentence, I told myself. In economics, everything is connected to everything else.

The economy, he told the Banking Committee, was good; it was very good. Gross domestic product was up, productivity was up, corporate profits were booming, living standards were up, there were no discernible signs of inflation. He praised a performance "unprecedented in my half century of observing the American economy." Yet he was troubled, even miserable. And he explicitly said that higher productivity, of all things, was threatening to bring on inflation. But why? Well, high productivity was encouraging hyperinvestment, and therefore net asset values were rising fast from the bull market. He mentioned the "wealth effect," a rough calculus that for every $1 rise in household assets, there would be a four-cent rise in household expenditure. But the increased asset values would not lead to a corresponding rise in goods and services, he said, and eventually people would spend their winnings and drive up prices. There would be an imbalance between supply and demand. Inflation would result.

I was stunned. Why make productivity the villain? In standard theory, an increase in productivity, by generating more value out

of a given worker's time, yields more goods without a corre-
sponding increase in prices; it allows profits to rise, that is, by reducing unit costs, and so it's a *counter*inflationary indicator.
Obviously, he knew this, but he was worried—the previous rate
increases in the federal funds rate (the short-term rate at which
banks lend each other money) hadn't had the dampening effect
he wanted. Yes, but so what? The market had been booming for
years, and he admitted that there were no discernible signs of inflation. So what he was he talking about? Why hadn't the
"wealth effect" created inflation *before* this?

I knew his caution was virtuous. It was more than virtuous, it
was morally beautiful, and as close to a tragic sense of life as anyone in this pagan media republic was likely to arrive at. He was
telling us that human felicity has its limits. There is always a
reckoning, always a price for "exuberance." He was virtue itself—he would suffer while others played. But I feared his sorrow; I feared the burden of his pessimism, the vigilance so acute
it started at barely noticeable shadows in the midday sun. Why
had inflation become such a bugaboo, anyway? It was his job to
watch over it, but must everything be sacrificed to his fear? Inflation ran so wild in the 1970s that Paul Voelker, Greenspan's
predecessor, raised interest rates drastically in order to throw the
economy into a recession and bring inflation under control. But
we were nowhere near that situation. In an economy growing
more than 5 percent a year, couldn't we stand a little bit of inflation? Was there any reason to think that the market in a roaring economy with its new wealth-producing industries would
come crashing down if he didn't *bring* it down?

When Greenspan finished, I got up from the light-filled room
and went back to my office. I was furious. Whatever he might
say, he was aiming his remarks directly at the stock market. The
bull, which was making me prosperous, climbing almost every

week, had to be brought to its knees. My hero was going to slay the bull, slay *me*. Cassidy, damn him, could be right, and for the first time I was afraid. And then, sitting there, kicking the New Economy mags on the floor, I thought I understood. Was Greenspan angry because he thought he let the economy over-heat in 1998 and 1999? Yes, he believed he let it get away from him, and now he wanted to bring it to heel. This was a horrify-ing idea. If true, he would overreact. He would kill the expan-sion in order to save the expansion.

6

NyQuil, Nyquist, Blodget

AT the beginning of March 2000, the Nasdaq composite index was at an astronomical 4700, up over 15 percent from the year's opening at a little more than 4000. I was chasing the zipper, trying to stay up with it, but my heart was in my mouth half the time and I couldn't sleep worth a damn. No, that's not quite right. I could *get* to sleep. On a typical night, I would pull the lids down by taking a Xanax, a beta-blocker, and a swig of the cold-and-flu remedy NyQuil, which has an alcohol base. Charming medicine: a green, slimy, licorice-tasting liquid that produced an instant of nausea and then, ten minutes later, ten-pound lids. I also read a bit of *The Fountainhead*, a work by Alan Greenspan's mentor, Ayn Rand. That always helped. (How did this woman get a reputation for writing page-turners?) Pilled, potioned, and Randed, I passed out, sleeping bumpily for a few hours — and then woke up, when the drugs wore off, my stomach fluttering from the NyQuil. In the darkness, I stared at the ceiling and listened to the occasional car passing by. The bedroom at the big apartment was lodged at the corner of 76th Street and West End, and in the middle of the night, you could hear a car coming from blocks away, then passing and fading into the distance. *WsshhSHHHwhssssh* . . .

Ten minutes of this incomparable entertainment, and then into the kitchen for CNBC. The boys and girls of financial reporting went on the air early. Mark Haines, lips pressed together, always evocative of the Mock Turtle, made his dry, quizzical remarks. Later in the day, Liz Claman, whose raised eyebrows suggested a sharp edge of wit, would flirt with Joe Kernen's sexy hair, and Kernen (who did not speed-talk) and his skeptical partner, David Faber ("the Brain"), would slow things down as they observed the idiocy of some worthless company. They . . . paused . . . to . . . consider it. . . . The seconds of ironically tinged dead air built up tension like a moment of hesitation in a classic Laurel and Hardy routine. But that was later in the morning. What to do at 5:30 A.M.? Take another swig of NyQuil? And wind up groggy half the day?

Anxieties grow worse at dawn. Rumors were hitting the press of start-up Internet firms running out of cash, of publicly owned companies also suffering from cash "burn." If the public companies couldn't get more financing, their market value could drop precipitously; they could get swallowed up, disappear. Yet investing remained active. Many tech and aggressive growth fund managers might have been wondering if the valuations could be justified, but if they wanted rapid appreciation, they couldn't let incoming cash sit around—they had to invest it. On what basis were they choosing stocks? In the April 2000 *Red Herring* (which came out at the beginning of March), Jeffrey Wrona, manager of the successful PBHG Technology and Communications Fund, was asked this question: "Speaking of valuation, 75 percent of your holdings are in the industry that's hardest to value. How do you decide what to buy?" Wrona answered as follows:

54

We try not to value them. That's a simple answer. We're interested in business momentum — with the Internet or any other subsector of the tech world, we ask, "Are business conditions today getting better or worse than what they recently have been for this company?" For the Internet world, the answer is that they're getting better. . . . We focus on the key metrics that drive business momentum, such as the reach the companies have across the Internet, and the contracts they're signing that will give them additional reach. . . . When conditions turn negative, cheap stocks get cheaper, no matter how the stock is valued. The same is true when conditions are favorable. An expensive stock will get even more expensive.

Good, Jeff. That's very good. Value, in other words, has nothing to do with it, just potential and momentum — you go with the market, with "favorable conditions." Was this man *paid* to think this way? I had to admit that my own way of thinking wasn't much more solid than Wrona's, but he was a professional, for godsake. Reading Wrona's remarks, I realized why some of us were drinking slimy green liquid out of little cups in the middle of the night. It was not just because the people speaking like Wrona gave you nothing to hold on to as an investor. Such language gave you nothing to hold on to as an American living in the year 2000 and wondering what the country *made* anymore. It was as if industry and agriculture no longer existed, as if the country were being de-materialized. In the New Economy, or at least in the rhetoric of the New Economy, the actual goods — metals, minerals, chemicals, rubber, gypsum, and whatnot, and all the finished goods, too — had receded so far into the background that they seemed like abstractions. The process of communicating about these things, and the co-ordinating of them in supply and delivery chains, was now what was real to people like Wrona or Walsh, with his "vortals" for the poultry processors.

When you read the tech rhapsodists like Nicholas Negroponte (author of *Being Digital*) or George Gilder (*Microcosm*), you sometimes sensed that they had been liberated, yes, liberated from the muck and odor of materiality, the tyranny of *things,* the goods that are the terrain of modern life. The astonished young Karl Marx, writing in the 1840s, realized that in the previous few decades manufactured goods had begun to fill up the spaces between people. Now, in 2000, those goods had been assimilated so completely into our lives that they seemed an extension of our being, and the spaces, conceptually speaking, had been re-opened and turned into conduits of connection. What interest had Mark Walsh in poultry parts? None. For these people, capitalism had become electrons and flowing light pulses, a central nervous system without much reference to the body controlled by the nerves.

As the light came up on one of those early mornings, I would return to bed for an hour or two with a groan. The ground under our feet was changing. I was excited, nervous, dazzled, and scared, and early in March I had a laughing fit, to the consternation of friends, over a weird and frightening thing. I laughed over the awful fate of Nyquist, the day trader—John Nyquist, a former chemical engineer, who chucked his job in the late nineties and moved with his wife, Kate, from Chicago to the edge of a golf course in South Carolina. There was a story about him in the *Journal*. After moving to South Carolina, Nyquist spent his mornings day-trading, his afternoons playing golf; Kate Nyquist looked after her mother, who was dying of cancer. John Nyquist told Kate everything was fine, and one day in April 1999, quite early in the morning, he asked her to come out to the balcony of their bedroom to look at some birds—egrets and herons, he said. When she leaned out, he threw her off the balcony and then hastened to the ground to finish her off, his hands around her throat, only to fall back at the last minute. He confessed to her that he had lost $780,000 of their money—virtually all their assets, it turned out, including her retirement account, which he had raided by forging her signature. Some people said that he wanted to kill her so he could collect on her life insurance and pay off his debts. Whether that was true or not, he couldn't go through with it. He took his hands off her throat.

Paradoxical thoughts: Nyquist must have loved his wife. He committed an unforgivable act of aggression against her, but then he pulled back. Shame over the blown money turned into rage against Kate, which was overtaken by the greater shame of hurting her. Were not his hands, gathered around her throat, loosened by a wave of love? Kate Nyquist recovered, and was trying to get on with her life. Nyquist pleaded guilty to charges of assault and battery with intent to kill, and was serving five years in a South Carolina state prison.

The story was some sort of omen, wasn't it? A warning, a sign in the sand? I read it over and over, imagining the stages of it: Nyquist's glee as he realized he had *so* much more money to invest than he originally thought—all he needed was to get *at* it! And then the mad lunge at the money, the bland way he must have reassured Kate as he grew desperate and threw more and more money after investments that were failing. And then the intermingling of contempt and disgust, the shame, the grasping at hope, the avoidance of what was happening, on and on, until it was gone, all gone, and he attempted to kill her in an act that almost annihilated himself.

It was a few days after reading the piece that I woke up laughing. The affair of the day trader and his wife was a horror story, but it was also—God forgive me—funny in its way. Nyquist's mania was a rushed, violent, silent-comedy version of what some of us were doing with our lives. Nyquist was our fool, our scapegoat, and it was impossible not to feel a kind of relief over the dread that his act released. Oh yes, definitely a lot of dread released there, since my wife was a birder, too, and I had watched egrets and herons with her, though not in South Carolina. Nyquist got so caught up in investment folly that he lost himself; he not only lost his money, he lost him*self*. And he tried to lose Kate; he made her lean way out, and then pitched her over. Dostoyevsky might have said that every man wants to kill his wife. I didn't know about that, but I had known grief after my wife left, and despair, too, and I had invested money recklessly in order to pull myself out of despair, and I had watched birds, and I would not watch them anymore.

With Nyquist in mind, I fell on my knees before my ambition, not as a worshipper but in propitiation of some jealous god. I made the obvious vows: I will not invest in hedge funds, derivatives, futures, or anything I don't understand in at least a minimal way. I will not buy stocks on margin; I will not short-sell declining stocks, since that operation would take full-time vigilance. I will not become a day trader. I will not lie to anyone about what's going on. I will not murder my wife. But I also wondered, rising, how many of these promises I would have kept at the end of a year or two.

Booming portfolio or not, guides like Walsh and Wrona were not aiding my sleep. I needed reassurance. After a lousy night in early March, in which the NyQuil wore off and I had trouble closing my eyes again, I sought proof once more that I hadn't invested in a mirage — I attended another New Economy conference. Of course I realized that no one at such a place was likely to acknowledge doubt. The point of these prayer breakfasts was to keep salvation on track. Still, I needed to see the people.

I was a semi-participant in these affairs — an observer, an eavesdropper. Often I felt like a spy. But a spy for whom? A spy, I suppose, for another self that was hidden from view. I have always loved to observe without being observed — anonymity in the dark is the film critic's chosen paradise — and here I needed only ask questions to maintain my invisibility. No one questioned *me,* or wanted to know why I was interested. Suited up, a tie unaccountably grabbing at my throat, I enjoyed being with these people, *of* them for an hour or two, indulging my private fantasy. I was a financier, a man of money, making deals. At home, at my computer, wearing jeans and an old shirt, I was at work. Putting on a suit and tie—my disguise—I was on holiday.

The conference was a three-day affair put together by the magazine *Silicon Alley Reporter,* which covered the Internet action in New York. Again, the groaning board of bottled water, freshly squeezed citrus, and bagels; again the throngs of the eager, the almost-started, and the up-and-runnings, as well as venture capitalists and bankers. Inside a given company, you could probably tell who mattered and who didn't easily enough, but not at one of these affairs. The sallow droopy kid with a thin, vaguely disgusting beard might be a tech genius, and the white-haired elder in a three-piece suit might be starting all over as an angel investor, amazed at his own foolishness yet excited— he's doing it for sport, for a last shot at a pot of gold. The older guys stood around shyly like voyeurs at a disco; they knew what the dance was about, but they no longer knew the steps. Modestly, they were willing to learn.

I raised my notepad and was quickly accosted. A Web site, a Web site, forsooth! A young man told me of a site devoted to grandparents. It would go after "mature demographics" and would address such issues as how to establish a "dynasty trust," and it would set up discussion groups for such subjects as what to say to your kids if they are getting a divorce or adopting a child. But I wondered, Couldn't the mature demographics figure out these last two things on their own? It sounded a little dicey, though I could be wrong—there are seventy million grandparents, the young man insisted, with some heat, glaring at me when I seemed to hold back approval. He was dark, insistent, passionate, and as other people crowded around, he made his pitch again. In the nineteenth century, men like him must have dominated the American frontier, selling land, railways, patent medicines; men convinced of their own rectitude and use: pioneers. But how to tell the future builders of towns and schools from the snake-oil salesmen and the merely self-deluded? Doesn't the successful con artist always begin by conning himself?

I was listening to dreamers making wild claims — impostors and fakers, some of them. Much as I wanted to believe, I knew that some of these men were nuts. In this same period, Howard Morgan of Idealab, a California Internet incubator, ruffled the tassles of more than a thousand investors at the Waldorf-Astoria by announcing that Idealab "wanted to do one hundred companies in New York in the next five years." Ideas, *ideas!* Morgan spoke of them as if they were as readily available as pigeons in Central Park. "We do a prototype, a few screens, drive a little capital. If it doesn't work, we do another idea." The more the better. Oh yes, certainly. But there was a depressingly familiar sound to his "ideas." He mentioned shopping.com and flowers.com and weddings.com. — the very type of e-commerce niche sites that were beginning to crumple and fall into the sewers of Silicon Alley.

Lord, cure me of my unbelief! I was lost, and I needed to hear something solid — a sign, a voice. And, finally, I did. At the *Silicon Alley Reporter* conference, Jason Calacanis, the editor of the magazine, introduced Henry Blodget of Merrill Lynch, whom Calacanis described as the "most well-respected Internet analyst in the world." Blodget evaluated stocks for Merrill's clients, and when he spoke, the market jumped. His most renowned call came on December 15, 1998, when Amazon was at $242, a price he then characterized as "incredibly expensive." Nevertheless, he set a target price for the stock of $400. In less than a month, Amazon, which had just split three for one, went over $400 on a pre-split basis and soon went to $500. Blodget's career took off. He moved from a relatively small brokerage, CIBC-Oppenheimer, to Merrill Lynch, and was in demand everywhere as a speaker and media guest. He was famous.

"He's been at it longer than anybody," said Calacanis. Yes, but he was still very young. He looked to be in his middle thirties (he was thirty-four, it turned out), and he had blond hair and high cheekbones and a handsome jaw. He was good-looking enough to be an actor—not a leading man, perhaps, but a supporting player who appeared as the heroine's no-good brother in a fifties Western. Standing on a stage, Blodget took off like a shot and never stopped; his voice was strong and clear, and he talked in bursts, which were outlined, in a Power Point presentation, on screens to the left and the right of him.

He did the big picture. There were now three hundred or so publicly traded Internet companies, and he told us right away that at least 75 percent of them would disappear and never make money. They would fail or get bought up. Still, he said, "we believe the Internet stock phenomenon thus far is mostly rational." It was not a land boom, it was not the biotech bubble of 1991. "Amazon's mere existence makes Barnes & Noble worth less," he said. AOL's subscribers were spending sixty-three minutes a day online, which makes media companies like Disney worth less. A "transfer of value" was going on, and prices were so high not because investors were irrational but because lots of capital was chasing a relatively small number of shares. "The leading stocks are proxies for the growth of the Internet," he said, getting to the point. He moved his hands in parallel as he spoke and pressed forward over the lectern. "If you don't invest in the Internet, you're not hedged against the impact of the Internet on the rest of the economy." Each Internet stock may be overvalued, but the Internet itself is undervalued. At some point, there will be a "rebalancing of supply and demand," and Internet stock values will move more in line with historical norms.

His manner was strenuously earnest, his mind quick-moving, powerful, inclusive, consecutive, but not monochromatic. He seemed to have taken into account the likely disasters in the game without losing his taste for victory. No one, he said, should put more than a small percentage of his portfolio in Internet companies, and even then buying individual Internet stocks in a "pure play" might not be the best strategy if you wanted to sleep. A pullback of 20 percent was normal with these stocks, and some of them could go down as much as 40 percent in a day. You needed a basket of stocks, in which the likely result was that two would go through the roof, six would do okay, and two would flop, leaving you with a healthy net gain. He was, in effect, advising us to act like venture capitalists: *We* would take the risks that the professionals alone once took. It was the brave new world of investment. The investor pays for product development.

Stick with the market leaders, he said, particularly if they are gaining share in a given "space." They will grow more slowly than they have in the past, but they will last—that is, as long as someone else doesn't come along with a better way of doing whatever it is they do. Technology is a winner-take-all game. In all, he expected trouble ahead. But he thought the wealth of the New Economy market would survive, at least for the near future, and we pikers and opportunists who had been bidding up prices were not necessarily immoral fools who deserved punishment—not unwitting players in Charles Kindleberger's paradigm of folly.

The individual stocks I owned were mostly in tech hardware, not the Internet. I was wary of the Internet as an investment, but this was the closest I had heard to a coherent justification of the sector. At the end of his talk, as the meeting broke up, Blodget, still standing onstage, crouched and leaned over so his head was at the same level as the people below him. He smiled nervously as people grabbed his hand. Many wanted to touch, to come close. An interesting face: There was something mysterious in the long plane between his eyes and his jaw, something unfinished, inert, as if the sculptor of his character had left out an element that might reveal all. Of course he was young, and faces take time to come into focus. Now and then, he broke into a charming, toothy smile. That ended one's doubts (he could be charming when he wanted to be), though only temporarily, for his face recomposed and the mystery returned.

I took one of his business cards, and we agreed to meet for lunch. He had the aura of a winner, a guy who understands which way the wind is blowing. I liked his tone, his manner, his words; I wanted to hear more from Henry Blodget.

7

On First Looking into the "Wall Street Journal"

How did I get to this point, this obsession? There was nothing extraordinary in what happened to me, but I set it down anyway, because this commonplace American journey may cross paths that others have traveled; they may recognize common stopping points and junctures.

I can't say that in the past I was ever an active investor. For years, I wasn't in the market at all. Before the nineties, I had little extra money to invest, and I figured, like millions of others, that I didn't know enough to take chances. In truth, I was unwilling to learn what I needed to know. Out of pride, or snobbery, or mere laziness, I refused to get absorbed in investment thinking—the grim perusal of charts and averages, the daunting minutiae of interest rates and price-to-earnings ratios. Why bother with it? John Maynard Keynes wrote that investment is "intolerably boring and over-exacting to anyone who is entirely exempt from the gambling instinct," and for years I was exempt from that instinct. My job was to build a career, build a family.

The sane approach to life, I told myself, was to find something that you were good at, something that gave you pleasure and was useful to others, and then discover a way to make a decent living out of it. This seems obvious enough, but I was always meeting young men and women in New York who had headed straight for lucrative jobs in banking or corporate work, and had then discovered after a few years that they didn't really like what they were doing. They dragged themselves through work waiting for weekends, drank a lot, did a lot of drugs. What was that remark of Dale Carnegie's? "Success is getting what you want. Happiness is wanting what you get." Pretty good aphorism for a second-rate popular success guru. Not bad for anyone, in fact.

Okay, I wanted happiness in work, and I believed that both journalism and intellectual ambition, in the end, would be rewarded—if not as well as corporate or Wall Street work, then, at least, well enough. American capitalism was elastic. There was always a way to make money if you were willing to work extra hours and take on new jobs. In the early eighties, Edward Kosner, then the editor of *New York* magazine (and recently editor of the *New York Daily News*) and my boss, acquainted me with his 10 to 15 percent rule. Kosner has a tendency to gruffness and a dark reddish complexion that makes him look permanently embroiled, but we got along just fine. A few years after I began working for him, I walked into his office seeking reassurance; my wife and I were about to buy our apartment and take on a mortgage. He let me know that I was not in any danger of being fired. And then he explained his prescription for success in New York. "You've got to take on 10 to 15 percent more," Kosner said, his voice rising. "More work, more obligation, more debt than you're comfortable with." He enunciated the trio of responsibilities with great intensity, making a crescendo out of it. And then, after taking on more, according to Kosner's law, you would expand your capacities to meet the added demands. After a while, the "more" would seem natural; you would get on top of your life and you'd be willing to take on still another 10 to 15 percent. And so on, forever and ever.

I came out of his office reassured, but also a little over-whelmed. *Expand, always expand.* I knew that Kosner had just enunciated—in New York journalism terms—the essence of capitalism, for individuals as well as for companies. Expanding, you would be rewarded. Stay where you were, and you slipped behind. That was the obvious meaning. For individuals, then, earning was the central issue. And back there in the eighties and early nineties, as Cathy and I earned, from jobs and freelance work and book royalties, we invested, when we could, in the standard way, taking money out of my salary at *New York* maga-zine and putting it in a 401(k) plan, which offered both stock and bond funds; and we put Cathy's book royalties in tax-free municipal bonds and in conservative large-cap value and growth funds.

I didn't study, I didn't learn; I didn't even check the results. I was unconsciously afraid, I now think, that I might have to take some responsibility for the results if they were bad—or partic-ularly good. I thought of the funds as tubers, growing under snow. Let them grow out of sight. The intimidating subject of investment was covered with feelings of dread and avoidance. We were raising children, writing some good things, living a de-cent life—that was the important stuff.

"How are they doing?" Cathy would ask from time to time.

"I guess they're doing okay," I would respond, hoping that the investments would take care of themselves—maybe even dreaming that, with luck, they would do better and better. But I certainly didn't expect to get rich from investing.

Neither had my parents. In the 1950s and '60s, when my mother and father came home from work, they would pour themselves a double Scotch and settle down in a couple of club chairs in our East Side apartment. They never sat in the lavishly furnished "parlor" — the sacrosanct parlor of the old genteel middle class, only to be admired, never to be used. That's where expensive coverings and complicated standing mirrors and very fine teacups lived, the cups lodged in a pale green, faux-antique cabinet that I can't remember ever seeing open. Instead, they sat in front of a television in a little space created by the complicated mirrors, where the J&B on the rocks was the center of their pre-dinner ritual. The stock market was not. "How did the market do today?" one or the other might ask, but it wasn't a very important question, and it often went unanswered. My mother and father had some individual stocks, and participated, in a small way, in bond funds and investment trusts. When they bought stocks, they depended on brokers and on tips from business friends, and they tended to be loyal to their buys for years. General Motors — that's what I remember hearing about in my childhood. General Motors, DuPont, other blue-chip stocks. Long Island Lighting, because of the alleged unlimited growth of the Island. A few oddities, like Yonkers Raceway, because my parents knew the wealthy New York family who controlled the racetrack. When they spoke about stocks, a lot of the talk was about dividends, not price appreciation. *Dividends!* Who invests for dividends anymore? Back in my parents' day, dividend yields used to be 4 or 5 percent. In 2000, companies were plowing earnings back into the business, and dividends were usually below 2 percent, if they existed at all. Except for the elderly living on fixed incomes, who even *took* dividends? Everyone wanted growth.

They kicked off their shoes and had their drink before dinner. Yet I never saw them drunk. Steady, steady people, regular in their habits, rarely altering in mood from one night to the next, one year to the next, my parents were quietly triumphant survivors of the Depression, hard workers who had blossomed in the postwar American Eden. They *earned*. They earned perhaps $50,000 or $60,000 together, which was good money in the late fifties. That Scotch before dinner, with the afternoon papers sitting on their laps, was their early-evening time to talk things over and pull together the elements of their lives.

My mother was the bigger earner. Short and peppery, she was a great success as a buyer and informal designer for clothing chain stores. At work, on Seventh Avenue, she bossed people around, shouting to the men in the other offices or to the designers and fabric cutters in the back. Her voice had developed so strident an edge that she could have trimmed the hem of a garment or the fat off a lamb roast from ten paces. But at home, amazingly, she calmed down. She modulated her metallic attack and spoke softly to my father, a dapper, self-contained man, kindly and quiet, an elegant dresser — Fred Astaire was his hero, though I think my mother was his only real hero. He adored her, and she repaid his love with that mysterious gentleness at home. He ran the Fifth Avenue showroom of a costume-jewelry firm (baubles, bangles, and beads), while his partners ran the factory in New Rochelle. As a double-income couple (Seventh Avenue division), somewhat rare in those days, they were certainly prosperous, though they weren't wealthy. An only child, I was spoiled not so much by their money as by the miraculous absence of worry. They simply didn't talk money and business at home. They wanted to talk about politics, sports, the new Broadway play.

Is it possible there was some hidden flaw in their happiness? A strain of disappointment in my mother's goodwill toward my mild-tempered father? And did he fear his high-achieving wife? I can only guess, because people who survived the Depression didn't speak much of their personal problems. They didn't, as a rule, admit that they *had* personal problems. By today's standards, my parents were repressed and evasive and refused to face their demons, whatever they were, but as a child I hardly minded. Children are selfish, and intentionally or not, my parents did an amazing thing for me, creating a zone of safety that I knew even then was a good place to be. Since they built that zone not out of inheritance or class privilege but out of hard work, I admired them more than I had the courage, as a child, to express. They were businesspeople, and I wanted to be a writer, so I didn't tell them very much of what I was thinking. Kids didn't spill to their parents in the 1950s; I never fought with my parents the way Max fought with me (or me with him). The mood was more civil but less open than now. I kept my thoughts to myself, but I knew even then that I had stumbled into the right family.

These two sober Scotch drinkers paid their bills and, beyond a mortgage, carried no debt that I was aware of. Yet they moved all the time, making a triumphal journey down Manhattan's East Side, from Park Avenue and 92nd Street to a flooded-with-light apartment on the East River at 82nd Street, and then to a fabled New York address, Sutton Place, and finally to a still-more-fabled address, Beekman Place, very close to where Henry Kissinger, Greta Garbo, and other notables lived. Why would the children of displaced immigrant Jews want to move so often? They were so restless! Yet their real-estate ambitions issued from no greater imperative, I suppose, than to find living quarters that represented their income to the world. They certainly spent a great deal. Their closets were filled with shoes; they ate well, shopped well, got dressed up and went out on weekend nights to the theater and nightclubs. Holding a history book as I studied for some exam, I would salute them as they swept out the door in their evening clothes, off to El Morocco or the Copa. They traveled to Rome, Paris, and Palm Beach and stayed at the best hotels. Saving and investing were simply not very important to them. People didn't climb into their eighties and nineties then as they routinely do now: The long years of retirement were not the obsession they have become.

My father, his heart weakened by angina, died in 1980. He died right next to me, suddenly, in the vault of a New York bank. We were going through some papers, sitting at a desk in one of those closed little rooms they give you in a vault, and he had a moment of hesitation, a forewarning of what was about to come. "Not good," he said, taking a deep breath. "Let's go on with our business." I should have insisted we leave, but no, he wanted to stay, and a few minutes later, without another word, he frowned, closed his eyes, and slumped forward at the desk. I held him, called to him, but he was away somewhere—and then he was gone, as quiet and self-effacing and circumspect in his dying as in everything else he did. It all happened in less than a minute.

After I recovered, and my mother recovered, I realized I did not want to inquire closely into how she was handling the family finances. She was a proud, accomplished, and ignorant woman, and she repelled inquiry the way a taloned bird repels a net. (When she flourished in business—from the forties through the sixties—you could be both ignorant and accomplished.) I loved her, but in old age she was difficult and demanding, and increasingly, I couldn't talk to her about anything that mattered except the impossible question of whether I loved her *enough*. She had a broker who placed her in conservative investments, and since she seemed to have enough money, I never bothered to get the specifics of the investments straight. In 1991, she died, too—also suddenly, at home, where I found her, three New York cops at my side. We had been away, in California, and she had died alone. I have told parts of her story in the chapter of *Great Books* devoted to *King Lear*, whose great, ungovernable hero she resembled all too fiercely in her later years. She was then, and always will be, the source of my strength, my will, my ability to love.

★　　★　　★

My mother left me about \$325,000. Not a fortune, but not a pittance, either. Certainly it was something substantial to play with. For months I grieved, and I procrastinated as I grieved, guiltily pleased to have the money, but also, as I remember, vaguely annoyed by the new burden. Finally, under advice, I invested the money in municipal and corporate bonds and a few funds. I put the money to work, thinking all the while, The hell with this; it's a waste of time.

But during the summer after my mother died, the summer of 1991, I went one morning to the newsstand — later the gathering place of ardent tipsters — and bought a copy of the *Wall Street Journal*. It was a newspaper whose peculiarities I had never regarded with anything but amused disbelief. I had the liberal humanist's prejudice against it. In the past, when I had read the paper at all, I ignored almost everything but the feature piece, which began every day on the front page, third column from the right, a space that had become legendary for its journalistic originality, even eccentricity. Crackpot inventors, weird collectors, the mating habits of orangutans and cormorants, entrepreneurs who gathered the manure from the rodeo in New Mexico and converted it into something or other — who could remember what the articles were about? I made up that list, but the tenor of it is accurate. The choice of subjects was determinedly local, specific, and offbeat. The point, I believe, was that the American business class could afford to enjoy such humble and bizarre goings-on as examples of the manifold variety of the capitalist paradise. These curiosities were no more than happy sport to the readers of the *Journal*, men and women who knew that the country's real business, as the man said, was business.

As I read the paper in 1991, my eye still bounced off most of it, though I noticed, of course, the pinstripe chic of single-column heads and long blocks of type. The gravely circumspect nineteenth-century style of the typography announced all too loudly the paper's ethos of silence: The *Journal* had no need to draw any-one's attention to what it had to say. The attention was *there*. By degrees, one got used to the archaic look, and to the lack of insistence, and one appreciated the *Journal*'s deadpan manner as an elaborate irony that embodied the paper's worldview. The fury of enterprise was actually the great stabilizer of American life. Enterprise had the true dignity that government did not have. So why change the typeface to represent the twentieth century? Business, investment, the market—these were the elements of order. The formality was vaguely British and clubby, and impishly proper in the way of establishments everywhere. It was the very sign of power.

My curiosity aroused, I bought the paper day after day. I would read it in the subway, folding it in quarters (it was a highly vertical publication), as if I were heading down to Wall Street rather than to a screening room to see some Sylvester Stallone movie. The reporting, I discovered, was always thorough, the pieces often well written (I hadn't known). So much for liberal-humanist prejudice! The *Journal* was a great resource of information about our national life, and second only to the *Times* as a daily journalistic event. And then there was the financial news, which fascinated and baffled me. As the stations went by, I would try to puzzle it out. The lingo had a kind of cryptic but soothing charm. What was "call money"? Who was "testing a high"?

Reading the *Journal* seriously in that summer of 1991, I found myself feeling—of all things—a slight tingle of pleasure, an emotion not all that different from the happiness felt by a young man who goes to his first job in a new suit. "Beware of all enterprises that require new clothes," said Thoreau, but new clothes usually mean new fortunes, and why should one beware of them? Yes, I knew that Thoreau wanted a new man—a naked angel—underneath the new clothes, which he regarded as mere meaningless coverings, but, still, I was enraged by this brilliant literary man's contempt for enterprise. What need had he of new clothes in the woods around Walden Pond? *None,* he would say. *That was the point.* Sorry, but I think Thoreau missed the exhilaration of new clothes. Extracting information from the long columns, I felt, at the age of forty-eight, properly dressed for adulthood. No doubt about it, this was serious. The *Journal* was fluent, but it did not jabber; it had the silencing dignity of big money.

I sensed that I had joined a modishly demanding and high-spirited club open to anyone who applied for membership. For all its sophistication, the paper does not hesitate, on the financial page, to return to first principles, and so, in the early part of the nineties bull, in 1992 and 1993, I learned the commonplace gospel of *diversification* and *asset allocation* and the inverse ratio between a bond's price and its yield, a simple-enough idea that three people out of four can't seem to get the hang of. We invested in funds and in bonds, and we had pleasant modest returns, and as we made money from book royalties, I gathered boldness through the accumulating bull market in 1995 and 1996 (the market took a pause in 1994), and I added small and mid-cap value funds, overseas funds, and so on.

Through all this, I stupidly missed the surge in computer stocks — Dell and Compaq, say — because I thought it would end, and I didn't see the Internet coming at all. I simply wasn't aware of it, and later, I didn't want to learn about it. I was paying no more than half attention, and I was too scared to buy individual stocks anyway. But still, we did all right; even well. Our funds rode the bull, and our pile grew steadily. Back there in the mid-nineties, as the market continued to rise and risk seemed more and more appropriate, I shifted all the 401(k) money — I was then still at *New York* magazine — into equities. It was a large-cap value fund, and I remember, as I made the phone call to the fund family, the tiny thrill of going beyond received wisdom. I was no longer balancing the pile between stocks and bonds. But why be frightened? The market as a whole was growing at a rate of 20 percent or more a year; the game was afoot, and it was liberating to make that telephone call.

Overall, about 60 percent of our liquid assets in 1996 were in equity funds. A broker bought bonds for us, but otherwise I handled the finances myself. Everyone his own financial adviser! I had begun keeping a list of our holdings and I updated it at the quarter, and each time I looked at it, I felt that slight tingle of pleasure I had first noticed when reading the *Journal's* financial page. That tingle was itself a payoff. I was "managing" on my own, devoting maybe an hour every month to it, moving money in and out of funds. A well-informed person could have gained much more, I'm sure, but I was pleased to have joined the American investor class — it was fun holding the tiller, occasionally catching the wind and turning the prow this way and that. And so I continued, with steady, moderate success, until the tech boom gathered me up into its sinewy arms and deposited me into the land of triumph or folly.

8

Nasdaq 5000

THE Nasdaq was just soaring, crashing through roofs so high no one could see them—4900 on March 6 and then 5000 on March 9. On the ninth, as the Nasdaq raced above 5000, I watched for several hours at home, in a trance of pleasure grazed by spells of disbelief. The kids were at school, Cathy was working in her little apartment, and I was glad to be alone. I didn't want anyone to see me like this, seared with pleasure and fear.

The index had almost doubled since the previous August, and had gone from 4000 to 5000 in just forty-eight trading days. The top ten stocks in the exchange had a combined market capitalization of $2.4 trillion, more, as some newspaper said, than the gross domestic product of Germany, which was the third-largest economy in the world. Could this be right? The half-dozen top companies specializing in optical networking alone boasted a combined market value of $200 billion at a time when the most optimistic forecast for their revenues five years from 2000 was $20 billion. Sixty-one percent of Nasdaq stocks were up for the year, 39 down. A lot of the market capitalization was new. More than 20 percent of Nasdaq's value was made up of companies that had gone public only since the beginning of 1999. Creation of wealth! Creation of something where before there had been nothing!

On CNBC, celebration and amazement competed with warnings of a coming collapse. A sell-off will punish overweening ambition—that's what one heard from the bears, old-timers mostly, who were angry at what was happening. They seemed to believe in the market as a teacher of morality as well as a place to make money, and they were sure that what was happening was immoral. Buyers were driving prices way beyond any conceivable notion of value. I listened, swallowed hard, and before leaving home, I made the rounds. Checking online would have been faster, but I wanted to hear a voice, so I called up fund families just to make sure I wasn't imagining the balances, I checked stock prices in the newspaper, and so on. And then I wrote down the figures on a piece of paper and looked at them, so to speak, through my fingers, both seeing them and not seeing them. Two of our funds—Van Kampen Aggressive Growth and Fidelity Select Biotechnology, were up over 50 percent for the year. Fifty percent in ten weeks.

I was on track to make that million. We had done very well in the last quarter of 1999, and in the ten weeks of the year 2000, our portfolio as a whole, which still, of course, included some bonds, had gone up more than 20 percent.

We could have gotten off the ride then, sold out, and rediversified into a saner mix. But who wanted to? At that moment, water seemed to be running uphill, plants were growing in cement, and ginger ale, shaken once or twice, poured out of the bottle as champagne. In brief, we tech investors were counting on continued rampaging growth in the tech sector and an end to the business cycle, which, in the previous six months or so, had frequently (though not universally) been declared dead. The economic expansion was almost a decade old.

But then, after leaving home and walking to the subway at 72nd Street, I had a moment of panic, my knees shaking a bit as I went down the short staircase to the tracks. Is there something about entering the subway that brings on bad thoughts? Bubbles, bubbles. I got on the express, closed my eyes, and recalled what I knew about the South Sea Bubble, one of the greatest and most extensive devourers of value in human history. The basic story goes like this: The South Sea Company, which was formed in 1711, agreed to take over £10 million in British government debt — annuities owed to war veterans, mostly — in return for which it received a 5 percent interest payment from the government and monopoly over Britain's trade with Spain's colonies in South America, including the slave trade. It turns out that the company never did much trade with the Spanish colonies. The trade monopoly was a lure, a mask, a commonly agreed-upon illusion. The real business of the company was selling itself as an investment. It offered to convert the annuities into shares in the company, bribing members of Parliament into acceptance and even celebration of the idea.

An odd case: The South Sea company converted illiquid debt into tradable shares. There was no fixed price for the conversion, and the price floated upward on fanfares of nonsense. Many of the annuity holders converted their shares, and freshly issued shares were added in a series of public "subscriptions." In 1720, the company issued stock and began to manipulate the stock price. Everyone, it turned out, had a stake in a rising share price — the annuity holders who converted their shares; the public at large, which subscribed to the new issues; and the directors of the company, who secretly issued shares to themselves and periodically sold them at market price. The price of the South Sea shares went up in 1720 from 128 pounds to 1,050 pounds. And yet through all this rise, the company's only serious revenue was the government's 5 percent interest payments.

I opened my eyes. The train was almost at 42nd Street. What a pack of scoundrels! I meant the managers of the company, not my fellow passengers in the train, who looked blankly ahead. I closed my eyes again. My daydreams were stronger than reality. The managers had got caught up in a kind of primitive amazement over the mere mechanism of the market. Everything they did drove the price up. Opening my eyes again, I looked down the row of seats in my car, and on the other side, facing me, there was someone familiar. Who was he? I couldn't quite place him. Not another journalist, certainly. He was ruddy, balding — oh, God, it was the tipster from Broadway with the Frans Hals face, the man invading my sleep. The train was pulling into 42nd Street, and I went over to him.

"Weren't you the guy who shouted 'Ericsson' on the street at me a couple of months ago?"

He looked at me in consternation. Then he smiled. "I saw you at the newsstand," he said.

"The newsstand?"

"Yeah, I went to buy some cough drops, and you were standing there listening to those guys talking about Vitesse."

"Did you actually buy Ericsson?"

He hesitated and then shrugged. "No, I bought Nokia."

Wise guy. He didn't even believe in the stock. Here was a guy haunting my dreams, a nightmarish face acting like a portent in a silent-movie melodrama, and the son-of-a-bitch was just a bluffer and a tease. Of course I bought Nokia, too. Concealing my annoyance, I told him this. By the time we got done talking, the train had left the station, and I had to get out at 34th and come back uptown one stop. In the new train I thought of the Bubble again. What happened to it? Back in late 1720, the directors of the South Sea Company started to overreach them-

78

selves. They got their allies in Parliament to pass an act against rival speculative companies; they announced a patently un-payable 50 percent dividend. Opinion turned against them, credit tightened, and the company simply ran out of momentum. Since momentum was all it had going for it — the rest was humbug — there followed a wave of panic selling, and the whole affair collapsed in a tragicomic rout of all hopes and desires, followed by a flurry of bankruptcies and suicides. By September 1720, the stock's price had fallen to £135. The Duke of Chandos lost £700,000, an inconceivable amount of money in today's currency. In the wake of the disaster, there was talk of divine wrath. Public fury against the company's managers led to the confiscation of their profits and imprisonment in the Tower of London.

The clickety-clack of the subway wheels hitting the joints in the rails sped the disaster along, and at Times Square, as I climbed up from the tracks, I dragged a heavy question with me: Does speculation like this, including jokers like my street tipster, do any permanent damage to an economy? Or is it, despite the ruin it sows among the unwise, a useful and socially benevolent event in the end? And the lesser question is: Must speculation always be accompanied by fraud? Is there something inescapably criminal in the process of quickly raising money for some new enterprise? Bizarre questions for a day of celebration. But I was built that way.

Upstairs, in the magazine's office, I started to work, but my resolve lasted about a half hour: I stayed away from the TV room, but the fear on the subway stairs returned. The possibility that one might lose one's gains, heckling as it is, is accompanied by still another complication, an inability to sell and calmly accept that someone else might make more. Why not sell now? Just get out! Book the profits, put the money in corporate bonds! In his column in *New York* magazine, and on the Web site

TheStreet.com, the excitable hedge fund manager James J. Cramer had been screaming at people to lighten *up,* take some of their winnings off the table.

But I would take nothing off the table. I didn't even consider it seriously. I had only recently gotten into this area of investment. Anyway, I don't believe in "getting out." Cramer, in his hedge fund, held stocks for a few days, sometimes just a few minutes, even though holding them for a year or two would net him more. He operated, at times, like a day trader with a few hundred million dollars at his disposal. But I was a buy-and-hold man.

Since calm was not possible, I had no choice but to live with the results of obsession — a ceaseless, restless, almost shaming agitation, a pounding heart, and a compulsion to rattle on at people. At night, alone in bed, I was as dry as a dead stick, as romantically active as a hermit in a high mountain cave. I was developing all the habits that lonely people develop to prop themselves up and kick away the blues — exercise and work, dinner with friends and more work, ceaseless watching of CNBC and TV news. Self-sufficiency! The proud shield of the single man or woman. But self-sufficiency enwrapped obsession, and I was less frightened of greed, I realized, than of the fading away of other passions, the emptying out of life. I spent my day-dreaming time — essential to any writer — thinking of stocks, of sums rising and falling. There were also absurd fantasies, onanism for the investing class, dreams now almost humiliating to recall: A time machine brings me back to the 1950s, at which point I begin moving forward, buying and selling the most dynamic stocks — one at a time — at just the right moment. Let's see: Buy Warren Buffett's Berkshire Hathaway in 1956 and hold it until Cisco emerges at the beginning of the nineties; then, after holding Cisco through most of the decade . . . You certainly do get rich playing that game in your head. Dear God, had it come to this? Instead of writing my review, I wrote in my journal.

3/09/00

Sit in a field somewhere and just take it in. Read poetry, look at pictures. This trembling impatience, as if every second has to be filled with productive or pecuniary activity, is completely crazy. You know perfectly well that the words not spoken matter just as much as the words crammed into overloaded sentences. Struggle against the absorption into the market. What I want is to experience *duration*, in which life does not dissolve into nothing as Auden feared it did ("In headaches and in worry/Vaguely life leaks away"), but passes slowly and steadily with both momentary and cumulative magnificence. In this moment of moment-to-moment excitement, how do I get back to that?

Well, you can't get back to that. Do your job, then. After much starting and stopping, and considerable shifting of clauses, all the while watching the Nasdaq run up above 5000 on the CNNfn Web site, I put together the following as the opening of a review:

In *Erin Brockovich,* Julia Roberts appears in scene after scene wearing halter tops with a bit of bra showing; there's a good bit of leg showing, too, often while she's holding an infant in one arm. This upbeat, inspirational melodrama, based on a true story and written by Susannah Grant and directed by Steven Soderbergh, has been brought to life by a movie star on a heavenly rampage. Roberts swings into rooms, ablaze with indignation, her breasts pushed up and bulging out of the skimpy tops, and she rants at the people gaping at her. She's a mother and a moral heroine who dresses like trailer trash but then snaps at anyone who doesn't take her seriously—a real babe in arms, who gets to protect the weak and tell off the powerful while never turning her back on what she is.

Nothing great, but not bad either. I was reasonably happy with at as a lead—it moves, it's active, it conveys a little of my pleasure in the picture. I got up and walked around the outer perimeter of the twentieth floor, looking west, looking east. Writing about this strong, simple movie, I felt an immense sense of relief. I had been reviewing movies for thirty years, and for periods of every year it seemed a strange, furtive occupation. We are creatures of the city, we critics. We dip in and out of shadows, seeking enchantment through long periods of disaffection. We slouch and vegetate, waiting for a good movie while cultivating endless memory and odd loyalties — the Westerns directed by Anthony Mann and starring James Stewart made in the early fifties (*Winchester '73, The Far Country*), Philip Seymour Hoffman's acting right now in small roles. Part of the time, we fight off the blahs or cynicism. In America, six conglomerates controlled eight production companies, and the conglomerates were squeezing the companies for revenue flow. In eager response, the studios hoped to make as many blockbusters as possible — "franchise" films like *Batman* or *Men in Black* that could be repeated as sequels and marketed through all the units of the conglomerate, not just as movies, but as videos, DVDs, books, toys, games. In the most cynical provinces of Hollywood, a given movie was just so much software, a collection of manipulable digits.

There were spoilsports like me (and a good number of others) who refused to be controlled by the tide of releases, the wash of money in and out of the season — we did nothing heroic, but we pissed people off. We didn't seem to get what was going on. We didn't understand that the thriving movie business paid everyone's salary — the employees at magazines and newspapers that took movie ads, as well as the people working at the media conglomerates themselves. People working in the media were not upset if you attacked this or that movie — in fact, they enjoyed sharp attack, since they agreed with it half the time — but if you raised the question of whether the whole system

82

wasn't rotting, season by season, year by year, movie by movie, they rolled their eyes in exasperation. You were coming a little too close to the knuckle.

I hated what the conglomerates were doing to movies, but at the same time, I enjoyed the commercial triumph of a good movie as much as anyone. Not that *Erin Brockovich* needed help from me or any other critic, but I was glad that I would play a tiny role in launching it. For the first time in the winter, I felt a moment of peace. I may have longed to slow down, but another part of me wanted to be in the swim, to find the winners, find the vitality—Julia Roberts busting into a room. Finding the winner was the great excitement of American life.

9

Seven Sins, One Deadly

HE started as a journalist, of all things. The star Internet analyst Henry Blodget graduated from Yale in 1989 and, after teaching in Japan for a year, tried, and failed, to publish a novel based on the experience and wound up as a fact checker at *Audubon* and an intern at *Harper's,* and then as a freelance writer, the most desperate of all literary occupations. He had been one of us! I couldn't believe it. In his mid-twenties, he trained as an investment banker at Prudential Securities, but when Netscape went public in 1994, he became an Internet analyst overnight. He did this by knowing slightly more about the new field than the people around him, who knew nothing. At lunch on March 10, 2000, at Judson Grill, a busy fish-and-sparkling-water establishment for midtown honchos, Henry Blodget was as bullish as ever and as relentlessly vivid about everything that could go wrong. I was a little in awe: Here was a realist of the boom, the most valuable kind of man, because he appeared to have the capacity to say "invest" without harboring any illusions. At that moment, Blodget was the champ of the new high-wire act of projecting value for companies showing little or no current profits.

At least, I thought he was good at it, there being no proof, no proof at all, that many of the companies he recommended would survive. As he expounded relentlessly during lunch, I realized that I wanted to believe in him, that I needed to believe in him. I was at risk, not in his sector, but nearby, in tech hardware and systems software, and my success, in my mind, was in some ways tied to his. At that moment, he was like an explorer who sets sail with more courage than certainty and who carries men of lesser conviction along with him. The rising stock prices certainly confirmed his judgment.

I was impressed again by his gravity, his candor, and his way of addressing intimately the person he was talking to, his long face turned down slightly so that he needed to open his eyes fully to look at me across the table. The expression was almost lugubrious in its seriousness, but then he would break into that awkward and charming smile. I still found something missing in the stretches between the blue eyes and the wonderful smile, something calculating and withdrawn. He was aware of himself as having an unusual authority at a very young age; he was a harbinger of the New Economy without the long preparation usually thought necessary for wisdom. He was aware of the risk, too. He had extended himself so far he might not be able to retreat. So I had to ask — I wanted the reassurance of seeing him engage failure so cleanly that he could trumpet success again — "Do you ever feel like a man riding a stallion to the edge of a cliff?"

He leaned over the table, and his mouth drew down farther. "I feel like a man riding a stallion across an endless plain, and someday the horse will begin to slow. Growth at this rate over a long term is unsustainable."

No doubt about that. "Look, you have to develop calluses," he said. "The most successful way to invest in this thing is to have core holdings you know well. You establish a basis. Say one hundred shares of a great stock. When it goes up, you hold it, because if you sell your position, even if you call the top correctly, you get into a debate with yourself about when to buy it back. Instead, wait for it to go *down*, and then buy more. And when it goes up again, you sell off the extra shares. But you always have that core."

He was speaking of still growing but relatively mature companies like Yahoo! or AOL; you couldn't do this with a little firecracker that goes public, flies through the roof, and then, twenty weeks later, falls through the floor. You couldn't do it in a falling market, either. But as a recipe for a rising market that undergoes occasional dips, it was very appealing. I would say that he was swinging from a vine rather than riding across a plain, but I liked his style of somber resolve as the air whistled by his ears.

Vibrating a bit as I left the restaurant, I took a long walk home, first going up Sixth Avenue and then turning west, across the bottom of Central Park. What is this thing called greed? I knew that I had my legitimate need, my serious reason to make money. But I also knew that my hunger had grown larger than mere rational need; my hunger never stopped, it had taken over my mind. At home, the night before, on my olive-drab couch, where I had once tried to think seriously, I imagined this or that stock taking off (JDSU? Global Crossing?). Nothing strange about that. Everyone who invests probably does it at one point or another. But then there was another daydream. I imagined a sudden bequest landing on my doorstep out of nowhere. A wealthy person has recognized my value and given me a gift. And now I will spend the money wisely. Oh yes, very wisely, and generously. I will endow a school, I will help the needy, I will aid medical research! Oh, I will be good! This wet dream of wise expenditure was the way I dealt with these fantasies of sudden riches, which I knew put me in the same league as every sucker on the street with a lottery ticket.

As I walked home, I told myself that I had to try to reason. Get on top of this thing, think it through, work it out. What were greed's components? For many people this may be an absurd question: Someone is either greedy or not, and why bother to define it? But definition has a peculiar interest during the dislocations of a boom period. I needed to understand what had seized me if I were not to lose myself like Nyquist, who developed itchy fingers and got his wife to lean way out over the balcony.

All right, then. I was sure it was meaningless — mere cliché — to speak of "pure greed." No great emotion was purely one thing or another. A beginning answer, perhaps, was that greed melts all fixed principles. Even Pope, the sternly witty satirist of follies, the author of "The Rape of the Lock," behaved with considerable irresolution in the South Sea affair. He kept changing his attitude. After his initial enthusiasm, he warned friends against the scheme. Then he decided to buy stock. But once the whole thing came crashing down, he reverted to hostile judgment, while congratulating himself that he had not been among the most unscrupulous of the investors. He announced that "God has punished the avaricious as he often punishes sinners, in their own way, in the very sin itself: the thirst for gain was their crime, and that thirst continued became their punishment and ruin." His imprecations recall Dante's *Inferno,* in which the avaricious are punished in hell by having to roll heavy balls with their chests halfway around a circle, only to meet their opposite numbers doing likewise, at which point they turn and push the ball again, and so on, forever and ever. The punishment for greed is the physical realization of the emotion itself. But here's the interesting part: Dante, a master psychologist, suggests in the *Inferno* that people are deformed by their sins *before* they get to hell—in life, the greedy are pushing weights with their chests. In Dante's terms, my anxiety, which was screwing up sleep, forcing chatter, killing all thoughts of sex and love, was itself the punishment for greed.

So begin with the obvious: Greed dissolves the foundations of character. Nyquist, whose loosening hands suggest that he still loved the wife he almost killed, was probably not criminal by nature; he had nevertheless lost his balance as a wage earner, a father, and a husband. Was greed, then, a soul-destroying force, a canker wearing away one's innards and shredding one's relationships? A purely negative energy? The gnarled reflection of man's noblest faculty—reason—as a destructive madness? This is what religious, political, and economic moralists have always said, particularly after the end of a boom or the collapse of a speculative bubble. But isn't that sort of description much too grand, too apocalyptic? Doesn't it make more sense to speak of greed as a silent, stealthy, unappeasable longing?

The Freudians speak of it as the infant's unwillingness to give up the breast, followed by the savage memory of the breast's withdrawal. In the Freudian account, greed is an infantile passion. But this is not very illuminating. Just as a cigar is sometimes just a cigar, a dollar is sometimes just a dollar. Greed may contain nuances and levels—a lust for power or a pasha's greasy dream of an endless banquet—but it was unhelpful, I thought, to view it as a stand-in for some other, hidden desire. On the contrary, the longing for riches is perhaps the most transparent, lucid, and self-sufficient of all passions. As I walked across the bottom of Central Park, past the luxurious apartment-hotels, I was quite sure that the people living above, with their matchless views of trees and fields, knew exactly what they wanted.

At that moment, greed was two things—the same old breathless longing for personal riches that people felt at any boom time and also an eagerness to be part of a social organism growing at enormous speed before our eyes. One more time, damn it. We were not just tapping a tree in order to catch the milky substance in a cup or gouging the ground for some mineral or metal—gold, diamonds, uranium—that will instantly be consumed. No, we were taking part in a social transformation akin to the metamorphosis wrought by the . . . Well, you know the mantra. I left it this way: Greed, at that moment, was fired by hope and seared by risk. There was some glory and more than a little danger in it. Whatever shape it took as fantasy, greed could not be altogether pathetic or ignoble.

I arrived at Columbus Circle. Donald Trump's International Hotel & Tower, with its gleaming exterior of dark burnished gold, loomed over the open space. The building looked like a deluxe cigarette case. Plenty of greed there. Wasn't greed actually one of the seven deadly sins? Yes, but the Church calls it avarice. The list originated in the sixth century, with Gregory the Great, and the whole point to the classification was that the sins did not exist in isolation; they were meant to be the root of still other (presumably lesser) sins. Besides avarice, the others were pride, wrath, gluttony, lust, envy, and . . . and . . . *sloth* (hard to remember that one). Along with lust, avarice was certainly the most active, the most outward-reaching. No one could say, after all, that Trump did not get a great many things *done*. Before he took it over, the structure now housing the hotel was an office building owned by Gulf & Western. When Gulf & Western controlled Paramount Pictures, I used to go to the building for screenings, and it was a menace for years, with glass windows falling down on people's heads. Donald Trump, whatever I thought of his taste, turned the old horror into a functioning luxury building. Avarice, then, is clearly directed toward mastery. Frank Cowperwood, the supreme operator in Theodore Dreiser's fascinating 1912 novel, *The Financier,* is certainly greedy, and Dreiser meant Cowperwood to be a hero. How deadly a sin *is* greed? The list itself, a product of the early medieval religious imagination, required modern annotation, or else we would never understand avarice's role within it.

Many of us would consider lust not a sin but a sign of life in all but the violent and the perverted. Nor is pride a sin, at least not when justified by skill or accomplishment. Gluttony can be destructive and gross; it can also be fine-tuned into taste, the delicacy of a connoisseur's palate. Is not gluttony a lovable sin, a sign of indestructible curiosity and temperament—an embrace of the variety of life? Falstaff was a glutton, and so was Orson Welles, both great entertainers who brought others alive.

I walked up Broadway, past Lincoln Center and into the domestic reaches of the Upper West Side. Not much sin around here, I thought. Everybody works hard, raises children, obeys the law. If you're not a solid bourgeois, you don't live around here—you live in the Village or SoHo, or, at the upper rungs of the income ladder, with the Europeans and the corporate executives and bankers and surgeons, on the East Side.

It was a comforting thought, and it warmed my insides for a block or two, but by the time I got to 72nd Street, the true beginning of the Upper West Side, I knew it was rubbish. There is evil everywhere, just as there is goodness everywhere. Sin lurked in the familiar old buildings. What about wrath? Well, God is wrathful in the Old Testament; and so is Achilles, the first warrior hero of the West, in the *Iliad*. Wrath may be divine or heroic; it can also be futile or murderous. In itself, wrath is morally neutral. As for sloth, it is comical and commonplace, though it has sinister overtones when it yields mere indifference, a sliding acceptance of one's own death or the death of others. Indifference to mass suffering is the most destructive form of sloth.

I had reached my own neighborhood, arriving at the Fairway Market, at 74th and Broadway—Fairway, whose folkloric depths contained hundreds of elbowing people in pursuit of cheese, vegetables, olive oil, and fruit. Ambitious, hardworking people, very knowledgeable about pickled fish and artichoke hearts in sealed jars, people out for themselves, of course, but useful, many of them. They worked in law, advertising, medicine, finance, corporate management, the universities, the media, journalism. My neighborhood, my peers, the professional class of Manhattan, one of the many driving pistons in the engine of American success. Could these medieval categories contain them? They could not. In the modern world, we had too rich a sense of the intermixture of good and bad, the possible complicity of evil with virtue; we noticed the slippage between intent and result. We knew what *crime* was and we knew what *wrong* was, too, but sins, as we understood them, were full of ambiguities, pardonable flaws, even a few hidden strengths. Greed brought on the Trumpian acceptance of risk and change as well as mere hunger for wealth. Was Fairway an example of greed? The management certainly stuffed a lot of shoppers into the store and extracted a great many dollars from their pockets. But Fairway provided an incomparable selection of cheese and coffee and olives. Seemingly chaotic and unworkable, the store was actually well organized and easy to shop in (once you knew it), a perfect metaphor for New York. Greed built hotels and filled up produce counters with endless variety. It was the fuel of capitalism's creativity.

No doubt it is better—or at least safer—not to speculate during boom times in equities, even in equity funds. But was there any great *moral* value in resisting such acts? There may be commonsense value, but how much of common sense in such a case was loathsome timidity and hopelessness justifying itself as wisdom? It's far too easy to moralize about greed, and when one does it, one has no assurance of having said anything one wouldn't take back in a rising market. Pope, after all, did make money in that South Sea mess.

How about envy, then? Among the seven deadly sins, envy is pure, and it interests us morally, because it may be one of the doorways to the complexities of greed. Unambiguously nasty, a low, despicable emotion, envy is the sour land in which Linda Tripp resides. It is familiar to all of us at our worst, for it motivates a part of our conduct, and I was sure, for all the neighborhood's virtue, that envy ruled the Upper West Side of Manhattan.

And so I reasoned, all the way to 76th Street and West End, a street bleakly handsome in its dull-brown way. It was winter, and the trees were bare; the avenue had a severe dignity. A good place to live, West End Avenue has physically changed very little since the 1930s. It was one of the most stable neighborhoods in New York, but why, I wondered, had this apartment in particular become so important to me? As I went upstairs, I thought it was a great joke that there was nothing special about the place. Yes, it was a sizable piece of Manhattan turf—seven rooms. But none of them was particularly large, the light wasn't good, the closets were shallow and cramped. The building was put up in 1924, the work of an architect named Emery Roth, who designed some genuinely grand New York apartment buildings, including the Beresford and San Remo on Central Park West. The apartments in those buildings have enormous entrance halls and high ceilings, and almost all the rooms are cavernous. Roth was obviously working on a more modest scale on West End Avenue, though he did some nice things with the exterior of our building. The outer brickwork was unusual—a yellowish gold rather than the usual West End Avenue sludgy gray-brown, and with French limestone for trim. Here and there, odd, repressed balconies, sticking out no more than a foot from the façade, in vague imitation of the balconies of Venetian ducal palaces, broke up the monotony of the exterior. Nice. Still, the apartment lacked the amenities of light and quiet that many middle-class people all over the country, living in suburban and country houses, took for granted.

I went upstairs and kissed the boys, both home early from school. In the living room, steam rose through the pipes, which issued dolorous groans and knocks. Daphne, a cranky old girl with marmalade fur, waking from a nap as I came in, thwapped her tail, in syncopated rhythm with the radiator. Clang-thwap . . . clang-thwap. We were on the second floor, in the corner of the building, and the brownstones and high-rises around us partly cut off the light, but there were compensations for being low to the street. The trees outside the windows waved in the breeze coming off the Hudson. Mothers and children on the sidewalk sang back and forth to each other. Couples wrangled drunkenly at two in the morning (I prized the nuttiest insult lines), their voices reaching a crescendo as they passed below the living-room windows (*I don't give a damn how many times you slept with your sister-in-law* . . .), then fading away to curses or a giggle.

From my older son's room—an unaccustomed silence. Had he begun working? Max was almost seventeen, still skinny, dark-haired, getting tall. He moved quickly, despite baggy pants—the jeans hung low on his waist. The new fashions derived from hip-hop had made adolescent awkwardness almost cool. Tommy was reading in his room, and he was quiet, too. All New York apartments can be judged by the hums they give off when they are still, and once the radiator calmed down, I enjoyed the hum of this apartment—a steady surf noise of traffic from West End Avenue, brightened by the sound of someone practicing the violin somewhere.

Amazing how much emotional space this issue takes up, but it was my home, and I was comfortable there, burrowing in the dowdy rooms with their books and records and pictures and bits of pottery. The kitchen, expensively redone, was splendid, and I had become addicted to such minor comforts as a bathroom shower with a thermostat — so easy to get the water to the place just under scalding hot. The place had lost a little of its life and color since Cathy left — now it was really drab — and we seemed to have acquired a family of waterbugs in the kitchen, under the sink. Tommy tried to train Daphne to take care of the pests, bringing her close, prompting her, but she meowed and rubbed against his leg, giving it up as a bad job. The sound of the cat knocking something off the dining-room table, the boys playing rap or Dave Matthews in their rooms, the ocean sigh of passing cars, the super, a Hungarian, shouting in his staccato Budapest style at some delivery man on the street who was blocking the entrance — what I could hear every day blended with what I had heard before, creating a kind of frame around all the life that had been lived there at home, at home.

10

Tremors

Quarterly Report, April 1, 2000
Cumulative Net Gain $237,000

THE day I had lunch with Henry Blodget, when we ate fish and drank sparkling water and Henry leaned across the table and spoke so seriously of the stallion running out of turf—that was the day of the Nasdaq high, March 10, 2000, when the index closed at 5048. The *Journal* ran an article that morning that asked with a straight face which stocks would be the ones to "carry the baton" up to Nasdaq 6000.

But there was trouble after March 10—not just a dropped baton but, in middle March, skittishness, minicollapses, sessions in which the Nasdaq index would fall by 200 points on rumors and misunderstandings, only to recover over the next couple of days. Just as I feared, my hero Greenspan appeared to be ruining me. Initially, his blow at the stock market hurt the Dow alone, which went down as the Nasdaq went up. The split between the two indexes reached its extreme point also on March 10: The Dow was down 13.64 percent for the year, the Nasdaq up 24.07 percent. What was he doing except punishing the Old Economy stocks and creating a weird atmosphere? Now he was knocking down the Nasdaq, too.

Also on March 10, the day of the Nasdaq high: On CNN's *Moneyline*, the after-market show hosted by Stuart Varney and Willow Bay, Professor Jeremy Siegel sounded dubious about the Nasdaq's run-up continuing. Siegel, who has square glasses and a big smile—a charmingly gawky professorial manner— teaches at the Wharton School of Business and is the author of the classic *Stocks for the Long Run*. Siegel pointed out that the Nasdaq "has almost doubled in the last five months, but I don't see any change in earnings projections"—by which he meant that there wasn't any defensible reason to expect stocks to continue to rise at this rate. And Siegel said that, on the contrary, there could be a sudden and violent downdraft.

3/16/00

A rising pressure in my esophagus, as if a Spalding were being driven up a garden hose. It felt like a mild heart attack, but then I chewed a couple of Tums and it went away. Acid reflux, or influx, or deflux, or whatever it is called. It returned a few hours later. A sharp pain that rises and makes your back teeth ache, a referred pain. My entire body is a referred pain—headaches, stomachaches, odd things pulsing here and there in my chest, in my temples, in my ankles. For weeks, now that I think of it, the simplest digestive event has been an adventure, and sometimes a disaster. I have spent more time on the toilet than Martin Luther or Portnoy's father—their problem, however, was constipation, and mine is diarrhea. I sleep in periods of three or four hours. In my dreams I no longer see that rascal tipster from the street—meeting him in the subway expunged him from my mind—but I do see Nyquist now and then. And sometimes I see Cathy, and I do my damnedest to wake up when those two get anywhere near the same dream. I am NyQuiled at night, fogged and raw during the day, and my thoughts, like negatively charged electrons, race away from one another into fragments and fancies. I can feel an artery throbbing near my ear, like a steady Indian drumbeat heard softly through the woods.

There is no way out of this; one can only go *through* it. At the end is success or trouble. At the same time, I have begun to hate the spiritual price of my desire. What started out for me as a practical and emotional need has transformed itself into obsession, and when I reach out at night, there is nothing there but thoughts of money. One cannot live this way. But do I know anymore—do I know what love feels like? Do I know what it is to spend some time with a woman? Has the body memory faded? For almost twenty years, I lay next to my wife. It is hard to think of another woman, though I know there is at least one, R., who has eyes that see much.

The last week of the quarter was vicious and frightening. Earlier in the year, the Nasdaq dipped and came back three times, and then reached new highs. At the end of March, another correction got under way—a nauseating drop of 700 points in a few days, then a partial recovery, starting around three o'clock on Thursday, March 30, and continuing on the last day of the quarter. Still, the index was off 7.9 percent for the week, and some of the drops were extreme. For instance, Mark Walsh's B2B company, VerticalNet, with its clever, odorless way of handling poultry parts, and its solution to the problem of business sociability in Bulgaria, dropped $15 on March 31 alone. Another tremor, on a larger scale: The giant hedge-fund firm of Tiger Management LLC announced at the end of the month that it would close much of its operations and would likely liquidate the bulk of its $6 billion in investments. Julian Robertson, Jr., the value investor who had started the fund in 1980, and who was routinely described as "legendary," couldn't hack it anymore in this volatile market. He was sixty-nine, and there was a note of bewilderment in his remarks.

We were rapidly losing gains, and as the investment giants buckled and second- and third-tier New Economy stocks like VerticalNet plunged, the scolds and moralizers came out of their corners, heroically mounted the desks at CNBC, and hurled dead tulips at the believers. Their message: The speculative boom is over. Investors will buy only those New Economy companies that show solid profit.

What to do? The ground was shaking all over the place, and I was unsteady but still standing. For the quarter, our portfolio went up about 17 percent, which, of course, would be an extraordinary return at any time, but the gains had fallen from the high point on March 10, and I was exhausted, drained, and, despite the great quarterly returns, disappointed. It was dangerous and mean out there—treacherous, unknowable. And there was no way of avoiding the obvious: My dream of increasing our assets by $1 million could slip away if the situation didn't reverse itself immediately.

But I was certainly not about to sell. The gross domestic product had increased for the last quarter of 1999 by a fantastic 7.3 percent. I knew that Alan Greenspan, trying to slow the economy down, would raise interest rates again in May. But the American people were flush, and Greenspan couldn't stop them from pouring money into the market.

What was a real entrepreneur like? A genuine financial mind, I was sure, would operate with total disdain for fantasy—and with disdain for my kind of nerves and disgestive flip-flops, too. I admired Donald Trump, hero of the burnished cigarette case in Columbus Circle, because he got things done, but I hated Trump's taste, his ruthlessness, his sneer, his destructive passions.

I admired Henry Blodget, but he predicted the likelihood of others' success; he did not risk his own capital. Tired of my own floundering, and in despair of finding anyone sensible at the investment conferences, I turned to fiction. In his portrait of Frank Algernon Cowperwood in *The Financier*, Theodore Dreiser was insistent on coolness as the dominant attribute of his ideal capitalist. His hero, the son of a bank clerk, grows up on the streets and in the marketplaces of mid-nineteenth-century Philadelphia. He becomes a broker and then a banker, and Dreiser, clearly in love with his creation, tells us that Frank exercises power without flaunting it, spends money without vulgarity, courts women without coarseness. He is always straightforward and bold — in the words of an opponent, "suave, bland, forceful, unterrified." Well, that certainly isn't me. Reading the book, I was abashed. For a while.

Cowperwood is essentially egotistical, a man too concerned with immediate advantage to notice either social rules or the powers arrayed against him. His amorality is presented by Dreiser as a form of strength. His motto is the Nietzschean "I satisfy myself" — by which he means "To hell with conventional morality." Having discovered that money is an amazing tool for making more money, he perfects the art of "pyramiding," or what we would call "leveraging" — making a given asset serve multiple uses as a source of credit and fresh investment. But in the end, bribing a city official and misusing municipal funds, Cowperwood overreaches himself. He runs afoul of powerful people who work together to bring him down and send him off to jail for fraud. So Dreiser's praise of Cowperwood would seem to be a trap. The superb capitalist male, triumphant in the stock market and in bed, a master of accumulation and lavish expenditure, becomes by inevitable steps a crooked operator. The complete capitalist is necessarily a criminal — that would seem to be the meaning of the book.

By the end of *The Financier*, my chagrin regarding Frank Cowperwood had vanished. I knew that I did not adjust quickly from moment to moment, that my confidence, putting it mildly, was shaky. By contrast, Cowperwood's readiness for action, mirrored in so many successful men of business, never flags. But whatever Cowperwood's qualities, and whatever Dreiser secretly thought of him, Cowperwood was not in the end someone to emulate. As the market buckled and recovered in March and April, I felt more than ever that I needed to encounter someone who *made* something—a man or woman whose achievement would last beyond the ups and downs of the Nasdaq composite index. Such men created the prosperous society in which I practiced the craft of film criticism, a craft that floated as a kind of luxury item on the sea of general wealth. I wasn't grateful to the entrepreneurs, but it would be nice to know what was *in* such people.

II

A Thing Is Itself and
Not Another Thing

On April 4, 2000, I was talking to a fellow CNBC watcher on the telephone around 1:15, and the Nasdaq index was down 575 points. Not the Dow, the *Nasdaq*. "It's a crash," we agreed solemnly. What else could you call it? I hung up, went to a doctor's appointment, returned a little more than an hour later, and stood in the kitchen blinking at the screen. The Nasdaq had come back about 450 points, and it closed down only 75. The total swing, from top to bottom, was 25.4 percent. One of our stocks, Broadcom, was down at one point by almost $94 before finishing down by a little more than $15. The market had been shaky all month and was convulsed, absolutely convulsed, in the wake of U.S. District Judge Thomas Penfield Jackson's ruling on April 3 that Microsoft had violated antitrust laws. By the end of the day, I was relieved, of course, but still, three-quarters of our gains for the year had been wiped out in recent weeks.

On paper—or, if you like, onscreen—we had lost around $200,000 since the peak on March 10, and I was overwhelmed by feelings of helplessness. "We're all fools, no one can control or predict the market." And then disgust: Why the panic selling? I repeated the mantras: The means were in place to transform this society through . . . Nothing had changed. Still, I was beginning to fear that I was seriously out of my depth. There was no safety for me, or for anyone else. I didn't understand this thing, yet I was at the mercy of it. I could only hold on and hope that it would not betray me.

With my welfare in mind, a friend, H., told me a curiously self-punishing story. His clever older brother had called him in the early fall of 1999 and tipped him off to a pharmaceutical stock called LeukoSite. The price was $7. My friend bought the stock, and after a few months, when he noticed that the stock had more than tripled, he sold it and made a nice profit. His brother called again in March. "You haven't sold LeukoSite, have you?" My friend allowed that he had. A dead silence followed. LeukoSite had been taken over by Millennium Pharmaceuticals, and the stock was then worth $300 a share. If my friend had held on and sold at the peak, he would have made about a million dollars before taxes. There it was: a million, not *my* million, but still, a million, and it was unreachable.

By selling when he did, my friend showed neither weakness nor poor judgment. He tripled the value of his investment, and regret over his loss would be absurd at any time except at this incredible moment, in which multiples of forty, in a period of seven months, do occur now and then. So he did feel regret, even chagrin, though his sorrow over the lost money was mixed with something else — relief that his whole life was not tied up in investment. He had a good job; he had friends, a love life, people who depended on him. What he meant to convey, I think, by telling me *his* primal story, was that an obsession with money is disfiguring. Obvious enough, but he thought I needed to hear it. He was telling me that one has to breathe, one minute after another, one day after another. I had to slow down and breathe.

On April 14, as the Nasdaq was again dropping through the floor, this time without any signs of an immediate recovery, I took my friend's advice. I got out of town — with R., whom I had been seeing the last few weeks. We had been talking about going away, and this was the time. Relief, an enormous relief in just fleeing the catastrophe. Just pick up and go. As we drove north, I saw a cartoon in my head: The two of us were beating a path over a hill in a large red car with rounded fenders, while behind us the metropolis glowered and people in despair threw themselves out of skyscrapers. An unimaginative cartoon, as it turned out — what was actually happening wasn't all that different. Back there, in the real city, there was wave after wave of selling — the index dropped 355 points by the end of the trading day.

In Massachusetts, still bleak but beautiful in early April, we took long walks and drives, and listened to torch singers Ella Fitzgerald, Sarah Vaughan, Jo Stafford, and Peggy Lee on a tape that R. had lovingly put together. They sing of love hoped for, love lost — lambent, honeyed, bittersweet songs, the kind of songs that have disappeared forever from our raucous culture. R. is a disillusioned romantic; the music suits her low voice and sultry looks. Like me, she wanted to stretch out time and savor what was rich and resonant in the moment. At an inn in Stockbridge, we ate a long dinner and afterward conversed gravely in the lobby with a great-looking but boring couple from Amsterdam. The part of me that cared about the market was away somewhere else, and I felt relieved that boredom was permissible, even something to be cultivated. Boredom! How nice! What a relief to feel time passing, purposeless, empty time, our little defiance of eternity and of efficiency, too. R. was also fascinated by the couple, and together we went deeper and deeper into the purposeless conversation. Boredom was one of the possibilities of life, like trees and road maps and oil stains on Massachusetts tarmac. Sitting on the porch of the inn, earlier in the day, I had stared at the bare trees and the discolored spots and cracks in the road, grateful for the things of the world.

In bed, a numb, numb body (mine, not hers), inert, though hot and flushed with the fever that I must have brought with me from town. I sweated out my unhappiness, but it was no go. Those six weeks or so of porno back there in the summer seemed to be exacting their toll, the young men and women in my head drawing strength from my body now. I thought they had ceased to exist when I stopped looking at them, but now, just when a beautiful woman lay next to me in bed, they claimed their revenge. St. Augustine, in *City of God*, says again and again that Adam and Eve, having disobeyed God in Eden, are cursed with the loss of control over their organs. Man disobeyed, and so, as punishment, his body disobeys *him*. I was cursed by living too much in dreams, a sin against God in the flesh. As my inability to make love spread through my limbs like acid — one can feel it everywhere, not just in the nether regions — I began to wonder if I would be punished for dreaming too much of money by losing the money I already had. This was the wrong time to have such a thought, and I cast it away and turned to R., who was silent and gentle, and it was a long evening and she was kind, and I came out of it at last, and felt her flesh, and my own, too.

We drove around the next day and had a fine time in the chilly New England spring. The Berkshire resort towns and the immense lawns of Tanglewood were empty, and I was glad, so glad I was not *there*, back in the city. R. was the first woman I had been close to since my wife and I separated at the beginning of the year, and I was relieved and happy, but R. looked at me strangely, as if I had changed in some way. She was sick of hearing about the market; it interested her, but not as a steady companion. She had known me for some years, and it was obvious to her that I had become a transformed person. As she looked me over, I noticed something new — a curiously dead feeling inside as I thought of the possible mess engulfing me, not calm exactly, but a hollowness and the sense that despite every protest and failure of my body, this financial minidisaster was happening to someone else.

A million in gains! What idiocy! A *million!* I wouldn't see it, I couldn't see it, I would never see it, and this thought got mixed up in my head with the soulful regret of the torch singers on R.'s tapes. "The million that got away." I felt the hope for it leave my body physically, an ache in my chest that got dimmer as the day went on and was just a soreness by nightfall. But all this was not happening to someone else: I had gone dead inside as a form of protest against the remarkable truth that it was happening to me.

In the morning, waiting for R., I sat on a bench across the way from one of the hotel buildings and tried to remember the things that had amazed me the day before — the grass, the trees, the cracks and even the oil stains on the roads. Today I was transfixed by the rotting wood of the bench, and a bud on a nearby bush, and then some sparrows hopping on the lawn. I stared at them for a long time in a kind of trance, grateful for the duration of nothingness. Everything in this world was itself and not another thing. Knowing that was true was the beginning of sanity and all morality, for if one recognized that everything was itself and not another thing, then one might begin to recognize that people were each separate, too, and treat them as such. The zipper didn't move there, in the Massachusetts countryside. Matter, and flesh, unlike economic data, did not immediately change into something else, or mean two things at once, or the opposite of what it seemed. These were solid things, and my concentration came together and stayed together and demanded nothing more, and I was still.

12

Fog and Clarity

BACK in the city, hope drained away, and I felt my brain slipping through my fingers. The Nasdaq index dropped all through May, reaching a low of 3164 on May 23, a fall of 1900 points in two and a half months. As the index fell, I was beginning to get seriously hurt. From day to day, I struggled for clarity. The million . . . I kicked it loose as savagely as I could. I was in the office in mid-May when I let it go for good, staring out of the room with the great view east and the strong light. It was a joke, the million, and I had to rein in my fury, because I could do nothing with it but destroy myself. There it was: The Nasdaq was now down over 20 percent for the year. Greenspan, it seemed, was trying to slow the economy so it would continue to expand at a sustainable pace. To that end he raised interest rates again, by 50 basis points, on May 16. But wasn't there a potential danger in these moves? Slow the economy by how much? For if the economy slows too much, profits go down, too, and what good is that?

This stuff was maddening. I read the papers every morning and listened to CNBC, and I had never felt like such an outsider. But perhaps every investor at times feels like an outsider, for the market is remorseless, a storm that favors or spares no one. The Fed action that produces a good result may produce too much good, at which point it suddenly becomes a bad result; the momentum either way, for good or bad, takes on a life of its own, until extreme measures are needed to reverse it, and these new measures, in turn, become a danger, and on and on, forever and ever. In the market, you never come to stable point, or even an entirely comprehensible point. A given fact (low unemployment, say) determines a mood, which mood produces new facts, and these facts further enforce the mood. Causes become effects, which turn into new causes, and so on. There is a lurching, self-fulfilling logic to it that always makes sense in hindsight but often seems arbitrary and unnecessary at the time.

I began to realize what a strange thing I had gotten into. My everyday assumptions of how the world works — everyone's everyday assumptions — depended on a reasonably straightforward relation between effort and result. In any given project, you study, you work, you put something into play, and you risk approval or disapproval, acceptance or rejection. This is true for teenagers taking tennis lessons, for writers, for most professionals, for most companies of any size. If a little luck enforces your best efforts, you can expect, more often than not in America, to come out all right. But playing the market is not a set of problems that can be solved through mere application. It's not a subject, not a *field,* for heaven's sake, that you can *master.* It's not biochemistry. You can learn a great deal, you can find support levels, establish a pattern of resistance to new highs or lows, cheer or moan when those levels are broken, and you can minimize your chances of failure or risk by hedging your choices with contrary choices. But all this effort can be rendered useless by some additional element that falls outside your view — or by too many people sharing the same view. Often enough — not always, of course, but often enough — mood and fashion determine the direction, and then the direction itself determines the direction. Crazy, man! And then the perversity of human ends, the sheer perversity! Bad economic news, like an increase in unemployment rates, makes the market go up, because it suggests that the Fed is likely to decrease interest rates. Thus the interests of investors run against the fortunes of the most vulnerable part of the working class. Yet too much unemployment could lead to a drop in consumer spending, at which point the market will fall. And so on.

Any market professional hearing these cries would probably say, "You expected this to be *easy?* You thought you could just climb aboard and you would be safe, you would just make money forever?"

I had to admit that at the beginning of 2000, I did feel something like that. And now, as I jumped from one extreme to the other, the fog of the market seemed so thick that I lost the will to take any action at all.

It's because of the fog that so many people "diversify," spreading risk around among many kinds of investment. It is hard to see many things clearly, so they let the market do their thinking for them. But I had committed myself to technology, and I could not, at that point, in May 2000, go back to diversification. I just couldn't do it. Where would I put my money? Technology still had the most spectacular growth potential. As pessimism battled against optimism in the press, in the financial community, and in me, I could do nothing but wait. I didn't have the will or the cash to buy, or the desire to sell, and I said nothing to anyone but Cathy, who was calm and philosophical — "It will come back," she said, trusting me, which hurt more than a howl of protest. She raised the issue once and then let it go. The silence of my wife and the silence of the children, too, who knew nothing of these events, at first made the slide easier to bear. But then made it worse, because it was their money, too.

Tech was still powerful, growing at 25 percent a year. So what had been bringing the market down? Collective skepticism? Warren Buffett, who had been noisily contemptuous of companies with indistinct earnings? The Fed? Abby Joseph Cohen, the Goldman Sachs equity strategist and longtime bull, who had recently recommended that clients allocate a mere 5 percent less of their portfolios to stocks? The collapse of Julian Robertson and the subsequent sale by George Soros's Quantum Fund of massive tech holdings? All these things? People had been saying tech was overvalued well *before* this collapse, but despite certain pullbacks, tech roared all through the late nineties. Starting in late March, however, and then even more so in April and May, there had been a wavering, a wilting, and now a mysterious turning, as if a grove of poplars, unforced by the wind, had suddenly leaned in the same direction. People had begun to look for a reason to sell. But this was irrational. And surely it was temporary. Wasn't it?

Money had become important to me in a way that it never was years earlier, when I worried about my writing and out of sheer gratitude simply accepted whatever small sums I was paid for the pieces that got published. I had been schooled in idealism by the decade of the sixties. In those days, thinking about money, among liberal-arts types in college and graduate school, was very much infra dig. No, you were supposed to discover your soul. I was out in California, a graduate student at Stanford, and I took all the soul talk seriously. I couldn't have cared less about LSD and acid trips—at parties, I was a boozer—but, along with friends, I tried, yes, we tried hard, some of us, to make new American lives. We hated the corporation, and we disdained mere careerism. In those days, one could live in Palo Alto, Berkeley, or Santa Cruz on a few thousand dollars a year, sharing an apartment, driving a patched-up Datsun, and wearing as little clothing as possible. Taking a pass on the drug culture, I still got high from the atmosphere. The free concerts in Golden Gate Park, for instance, the Grateful Dead and many other bands — a lot of things were free back then. However solemn and self-important the quest, we searched, we questioned, and, for a while, idealism and nihilism, fear of the Vietnam war and a mad excitement of defiance, alternated as violently as the moods of a schizophrenic. In that maelstrom, success wasn't important; success was an embarrassment. The general sixties prosperity helped make disdain for money a lot easier, and we were confused, a lot of us — too literal-minded to understand that discovering your soul and holding a job were not always incompatible. Yet I will always value that tender, earnest, and pleasure-soaked time. Making fun of the sixties, as nearly everyone did in the seventies and eighties, was no more than a rancorous mistake.

A bit later, as a young movie critic in New York, I lived simply and plainly and never thought about money. I was protected in this, I admit, by my parents' generosity, which established a net under me and allowed me to get my act together. It was only much later, as I married and had children and crossed forty, that I began to feel a delight, mild at first, then greater and greater, in expansion and in prosperity — income growing, household growing, investments slowly increasing in value. I still wanted most of all to write, to learn, to be published, to be quoted, to gain a little notice, a little power; and to be a husband and father. But by degrees, rightly or wrongly, I began to associate money with freedom. And for the middle-aged, money is like a coat you wrap around yourself in winter — literally so, for as you cross fifty, the fear of bad food, shabby surroundings, landlocked circumstances crowds in on your morale with a presence that is almost physical. Robert Frost wrote his shuddery poem "Provide, Provide" about that fear: "Die early and avoid the fate./Or if predestined to die late, / Make up your mind to die in state." Very bitter stuff: "Better to go down dignified/With boughten friendship at your side / Than none at all. Provide, provide!" Well, boughten friendship certainly isn't "dignified," so there's a mocking hardness in the poem, a jeering bleakness and mystery, too, but it touches that fear of being poor and landlocked, of not being able to just get up and go somewhere.

There was nothing in the least ignoble in the drive for family wealth, the desire to protect children and to protect oneself, too, in old age. What is ridiculed, in its excessive form, as greed, can be seen as the devil-eyed exaggeration of a most respectable passion, the desire to expand, and as the perversion of a lovely emotion, the warmth of orderly increase — increase of children, land, goods, flocks, houses, even furniture. I knew one place where that passion came from.

The pleasure in abundance and the passion for increase is right there in the text that generated our civilization. At the beginning of Genesis, God produces an illimitable treasure, the elements of existence conceived as gifts: air, earth, and water; grass, seed, and plants; herbs, fruit, and beasts. These are gifts without number, and God places man in dominion over everything, the beasts and the verdant growing things. Man is master of the illimitable Garden from which, when he disobeys, he is expelled, losing the plenitude for all time. In the Flood, the fruits of existence are restored and then taken away again, and thereafter human life becomes an endless struggle. People move from place to place, eager to escape famine and plague. The fear of expulsion, of being left outside, without tents and blankets and sheep, haunts the entire book of Genesis, a book burdened by the specter of loneliness. God has granted existence and may take it away again, and in the midst of this fear, some are blessed and some are cast into the nowhere of the desert and poverty.

I read the Old Testament in the spring of 2000 with that peculiar mixture of awe, fear, and comfort that the book always produced in me. Awe, fear, and comfort — these were also the central emotions, I realized, of the family man and householder.

God promises his servant Abram (soon to be Abraham) that he will have descendants as numberless as the stars. He rewards him for his loyalty and goodness with "flocks, and herds, and silver, and gold, and manservants, and maidservants, and camels and asses." The covenant is renewed with Isaac and Jacob, and at each moment of reward there is a gathering of goods against the emptiness of the wilderness. "And the man waxed great, and went forward, and grew until he became very great" — this of Isaac, who piles up more than his share of ewe lambs and servants. Genesis and Exodus can be seen as setting up a plane of action in which the chosen, awaiting their promised turf, move ceaselessly about and sojourn in alien lands (amid Philistines and Egyptians), where they receive material signs of blessedness. Surely no reader can miss the bodily comfort of the old patriarchs lying in their tents at night with their wives and slave mistresses. The earth is theirs.

The goods in Genesis have a tangibility, a solid weight, both as the means of healthy survival and as physical tokens of God's esteem and the virtue of his chosen servants. By saying this, I don't mean to suggest that the plenitude can be taken as some early version of "Greed Is Good." Yet, as anyone can see, there is no demand for austerity, no indifference to the gathering of goods, in the five books of Moses. Instead, one sees an acknowledgment of the sheer virtue of increase as a passion. When the Hebrews leave Egypt, they take with them, adhering to God's advice, Egyptian gold, silver, jewelry, and clothing.

13

Faith: Sam Waksal

I found the kind of entrepreneur I was looking for.

In May 2000, I entered the home of a wealthy Ph.D., Samuel Waksal, who threw his arms around me as if I were an old friend. I was a little baffled, since I was there to give a talk about movie criticism, and who loves a movie critic? No one but a director whose film the critic has just praised. I had been invited by the New York Council for the Humanities, an organization funded by Congress and individual donors; the Council gave out money to museums, cultural groups, and artists in New York State. Waksal, a man of parts, was the chairman of the organization, and once a month, in his loft in SoHo, he put on a kind of soiree. Forty or fifty guests would eat and drink well, and then gather around and listen to an informal talk from someone who had written a book or done some interesting research. Sam Waksal used these events to raise money from his wealthy friends for the Humanities Council. At the same time, he liked to hear good talk and get others to hear it as well; he was interested in what people had to say.

But he didn't embrace me because I was there to talk. He threw his arms around me because in a recent article in *The New Yorker* I had mentioned in passing a biotech company, *his* company — ImClone, it was called, an outfit based in New York. He was Im-Clone's CEO. I mentioned it in the article only because I owned some ImClone stock, which had been going up. When I received the invitation to speak, months before the article came out, I had no idea that Sam Waksal had any connection to the company. My speaking at his swank pad was sheer coincidence, and I decided that our meeting was fated in some way that was bound to be interesting.

In 1984, Sam Waksal left his teaching post at Mount Sinai Hospital, where he was doing research in leukemia, and raised $4 million from venture capitalists to start ImClone with his brother, Harlan, a doctor. The brothers Waksal took over an old shoe factory on Varick Street, also in SoHo. Sam was maybe one part researcher, two parts financial guy. For a few years, ImClone fooled around with various ideas — diagnostic kits, gonorrhea vaccines, AIDS drugs — and went public in 1991. But the company was stumbling along, surviving only because of Sam's social and entrepreneurial skills — until 1992, that is, when Sam latched on to a cancer researcher named John Mendelsohn, who was doing work on monoclonal antibodies. Mendelsohn had developed a molecule that would target specific kinds of cancer cells in the body and leave healthy cells alone. He was now the president of the University of Texas M. D. Anderson Cancer Center in Houston; Mendelsohn had done the first work on the idea in the early eighties at the University of California San Diego, but had never marketed the idea. Not until this dynamo from New York came along.

I bought some shares of ImClone that year — 1992 — on a tip. My friend Peter Ranier, a film critic then writing for the *Los Angeles Times* (he's now at *New York* magazine), was receiving news about biotech from a doctor in Los Angeles, a doctor who, in turn, was close to still *another* doctor familiar with the latest research. Who was this enlightened person, twice removed? I never knew. To this day, Peter and I refer to him as "Deep Genes." In general, taking tips is a terrible idea, but Deep Genes seemed to know what he was talking about. In 1992, he recommended Amgen, which had taken off the previous year and has since become a biotech stalwart; he recommended a few other stocks, and also ImClone, a new company with an interesting idea about cancer. No doubt Deep Genes knew about the Mendelsohn-Waksal connection. I had bought some of the stock at $22, and it had languished at the bottom of my portfolio for years, falling, in 1995, to 69 cents a share, and I had more or less forgotten about it. But then, late in 1999, it began to stir, and I bought some more. There was talk of a promising new therapy for advanced colorectal cancer, of preliminary trial results—the usual biotech rumor mill grinding away. Deep Genes's hopes for ImClone had taken a while to bear fruit—more than eight years. But in the end, the tipster had planted well.

The SoHo pad appeared to be one of the happy results. It was no ordinary home. Sam Waksal lived in a loft on Thompson Street, just south of the Village. You entered a hallway which led to a large square living room, with a grouping of couches and chairs in the center and lots of space around the sides. The wall facing Thompson Street was given to a solid bank of windows—the setting sun made the room orange the night I was there. Paintings by the New York abstract expressionists Mark Rothko and Franz Kline and some sort of nineteenth-century epic canvas of storm and shipwreck all hung on the south wall. Everything else was painted white—the floors, the walls, and the fluted columns that must have been part of the old loft construction.

Candles glittered on the windowsills and on the groups of dining-room tables, which were positioned near the windows and surrounded with chairs in gold trim. White and gold, enhanced with little bursts of flame—these were the colors of celebration, rich yet subdued, an anticipatory promise that if one had something interesting or witty to say, it would be admired. In Sam's loft, one felt as actors feel on a stage, warmed by attention. In an enclosed dining area beyond the big square living room, there were more tables and chairs, and beyond that a bedroom that was virtually unfurnished and a bathroom furnished solely in marble. It was an odd place, lavish yet unconventional, a rich man's whimsical urban palace; it seemed like a party space, yet in the dining room, on a large, dark credenza, groups of family pictures stood mounted in frames—parents and two boys and their sister in solemn formation. They were an immigrant Jewish family, serious people—Sam's parents, obviously, and their promising American children.

The loft, it turned out, was indeed intended as a party space. Sam Waksal was a man who liked to have people around him. Before my talk that night, the champagne and wine had flowed liberally; the crowd had flowed, too, an interesting mix of Sam's friends and wealthy people interested in the arts, some writers, professors, and educators, a film director or two, professional women with a taste for fashion, the former mayor Ed Koch, and some finance guys. The evening was gilded by self-approbation and money. I aired my hopes for movies and my doubts about the current system, and at the end of the talk, there were heated arguments—Sam liked a contentious atmosphere, he liked introducing people with power to personalities from the intellectual and journalistic world and watching the two groups go at each other. He talked easily and well on many subjects himself.

A man in his early fifties, not too tall, but strong and slender, he had a swarthy complexion and dark, very bright eyes. His re-

117

ceding black hair brought out a prominent forehead. Thanks to his dark coloring and the sparkling eyes, the balding forehead looked forceful and serious. As he talked, he laughed frequently — he was full of gossip and jokes — and he moved his arms, which were unusually long, up and down in parallel, sometimes letting them drop and then reaching out, as if he were gathering something in. I don't know what I expected in a medical entrepreneur. Greater measure, perhaps. Was that a prejudice? In entrepreneurial medicine, measure may have mattered less than this quick, darting attentiveness. The lean, rangy, mobile style of movement and the steady laughter, which warmed the rooms — it was his welcome sign as much as the food and drink — made him one of the most animated men I had ever met.

I was an investor in the company, so my interest in Sam Waksal, I suppose, was not exactly pure. But what of it? My little investment (it was 800 shares) made the connection more alive, more emotional. Sam Waksal and his brother, Harlan, the other boy in the serious family picture, now ImClone's executive vice president and chief operating officer, had built up ImClone from nothing. Some might have said, in May 2000, that it was still nothing. After more than fifteen years of existence, and almost ten as a public company, ImClone had earned hardly a dollar. But it was running trials on Mendelsohn's anticancer therapy, C225, it had other drugs in the pipeline, and it had built a market capitalization of roughly $2.5 billion.

ImClone was as good an example as any of the new nongovernmental way of advancing research. For years research and drug development was done by the king's minions — the Royal Society of this, the Royal Society of that, the National Institutes of Health, and so on. We would lick cancer with centrally directed research. But now comes the shocker: The government-led War on Cancer declared by President Nixon in 1971, and

118

administered by the new National Cancer Institute, had not been a success. For years, much of the research was devoted to a theory of cancer—that the disease was caused by retroviruses—that turned out to be false. Thousands of patients had undergone trials, sometimes with painful side effects, and not much was developed in the way of serious new therapy. In a given year, about a million new cases of cancer were diagnosed in America, and about 550,000 people died from the many forms of the disease. The numbers were growing, and centralization of research and development had come to be regarded as a mistake. The NCI still funded a lot of primary work in the universities, but the enterprise of discovering and marketing drugs was increasingly decentralized and capitalized—a series of calculated risks on the part of entrepreneurs, scientists, and investors, a sport of the profit system. In brief, greed had been placed in front of the cart and had been asked to pull the load faster.

For biotech CEOs like Sam Waksal, the drill went like this: Develop or license a promising therapy; exploit the capital markets for support; test the drug rigorously under FDA guidance; and then, after it had passed all the tests and fail-safe procedures, get it out to the public as fast as possible. Thanks to this new arrangement of science and capital, Sam owned a loft filled with art and gave serious dinner parties. He had been a wealthy man ever since his company had gone public in 1991, wealthy in advance of having a drug to sell. His success, his warmth, his chairmanship of the Humanities Council—it was all, so to speak, a claim on the future, a payment he had drawn against that time when he would actually have drugs under manufacture and heading for hospitals and clinics.

Was he a hustler? Or part-hustler? Hard to say, but whatever the state of his science, he had placed himself in jeopardy. One of the trials could fail, the FDA could disapprove. A biotech analyst that I had met, Matt Geller of CIBC-Oppenheimer, told

119

me very plainly that investment in companies like ImClone was "all based on stories—what the company says it can do. Some people make things up, sell you on nonsense. Stupidity can run for a long period of time. Eventually you run into the FDA, and their decision becomes a 'binary event'—either they approve or turn it down, and if they turn it down, the stock loses 80–90 percent of its value overnight. Or they demand more trials of the drug, which can set a company back for years." Such things happened now and then, Geller said.

Preparing trials to submit to the FDA, Sam's company was now in that position of risk, and I wanted to hear what would happen next. Here was a guy operating at the top of his game, a wealthy man who clearly enjoyed the well-being and freedom that wealth can bring. He had a purchase on the future. He was my entrepreneur. Maybe he would lead me into part of that future.

I walked out of his loft and then west along Houston Street, the dividing line between the Village and SoHo, and in the cool night air, I had a fanciful thought: I wondered if this unconventional researcher-CEO, with his charm, his animation, his many interests wasn't the kind of man I would have been if I had my choice and could start all over again. I was disgusted by my passivity as an investor; I was looking around for models of someone more decisive. Frank Cowperwood's chicanery was repellent: he was no model. Of course, looking for models in middle age is a vain idea, since by that time we are all uniquely what we have made of ourselves. That was my theology, wasn't it?—"A thing is itself and not another thing, and that is the beginning of all morality." I could not be anyone else. Still, blasphemy or not, I looked at Sam and saw a dream of an alternative life (let's put it that way), and I liked what I saw. Cowperwood's expertise conceals a freezing egotism and nihilistic selfishness, and to become like him—even to want to become like him—

would be an act of self-betrayal. But Sam Waksal, with his vivacious attention flowing all over the place . . . There was merriment in his eyes, an invitation to the fun of enterprise, and, matched to that, an invitation to talk over an idea — any idea in the world. His appetite was irresistible.

14

A Vision—and Its Critics

A brilliant spring day on Fifth Avenue. Blue sky, champagne air, a sparkle embedded in the sidewalks at Rockefeller Center. And then something out of the corner of my eye, shining in the sun—an impression of rich dark blue, one of the many things on Fifth holding the light. It was a car. A *car?* Who cares? But I recognized it, a midsize Audi, the Audi A6, with that peculiar glowing dark-saturated paint job that German sports sedans alone seem to have. I stopped on the sidewalk and turned fully to face it. It was astoundingly beautiful. A graceful, long, sloping form that just pours, *pours* from front to gently rounded rear. It bulges, but only slightly; no one could call it muscular-looking or bulky in the brutal Wehrmacht style of the big Mercedes. It flows, without an abrupt corner or an awkward joining or transition anywhere. Yet it's not a shape too obviously streamlined, either—there's a definite avoidance of anything overtly chic. The car's somberly beautiful shape has been fashioned by practicality: It would plow through the resistant medium like the rounded head of a dolphin. I knew this car, I had seen it in magazines and passed the A6 on the street, but I had never seen one so highlighted by the sun. Standing there on Fifth Avenue, I was thunderstruck, and I felt a surge of emotion the likes of which I had never before felt toward . . . an automobile.

I hung on for a long time — maybe five minutes or even ten — as people rushed by or banged into me; and when I moved on at last, I was more than a little surprised. I hadn't owned a car since 1978, when I left Boston after a couple of years there and returned to New York in a Volkswagen Rabbit. Happy in a new job — as film critic of *New York* magazine — I kept the Rabbit a few months and then sold it to a colleague. Unless you needed a car for business or could easily afford a garage, an automobile in Manhattan's streets became a set of chains, and for years we just rented cars — plain, dull, square-backed Dodges and Plymouths — when we wanted them in the summer.

Like any other American man, however, I had fondled my share of automobile magazines over the years, and once, in Beverly Hills, I had gone mad from just looking at the beautiful Porsches, BMWs, and Ferraris everywhere. But I had never felt anything like this kind of personal desire for an automobile, and I began to wonder, as I walked away from Rockefeller Center, whether my new passion for money had not roused a dormant interest in possessing beautiful things. The guy who had written a book about rereading the classics in middle age now lusted in his heart not for a woman or a work of art but for a dolphin-shaped thing that cost a fair amount — at least $40,000 — and so I had another reason, suddenly, for wanting to make serious money in the market, and not a high-minded reason, either.

Could I pay for the Audi? The market was deep in bear territory in May, but came roaring back at the end of the month and at the beginning of June, and I was shouting, "A reprieve, a

123

reprieve!" to friends on the telephone and "You go, girl!" at the little kitchen TV when cat-eyed Maria Bartiromo of CNBC reported the results. The Nasdaq was recovering. In one week, the index had risen an astonishing 19 percent, and by June 2, it was down only 6.3 percent for the entire year. For the year, my own investments were as flat—just about even, which meant I was doing a little better than the Nasdaq composite index. But I was exhausted from this ride, and increasingly puzzled by my own hunger, which seemed to be changing into something new. Sitting on my couch or riding to the office, I would add up portfolio holdings in my head, running through my calculations like a neighborhood drug dealer doing his numbers at a corner pizza parlor. *What was moving? What was coming in, going out? Gotta patrol the neighborhood.* How much was I changing? In the fate of the world, it is a tiny question, but we have only ourselves to look after our own souls.

The market was showing some signs of life, but I needed a break from it, some time to sort this out. So I sat down to read someone who had written a famous book about the Audi A6 about a hundred years before the car hit the American market. Thorstein Veblen, the Wisconsin-born iconoclastic sociologist who drifted from one university to another, created a devastating theory to interpret what he took to be peculiar and dismaying in American consumer behavior. He did it in 1899.

In *The Theory of the Leisure Class*, Veblen laid out the anthropology of desire and reward. The society of primitive man, and later, his successor, the barbarian, gives way to more developed societies, and the old rewards in the form of trophies — goods, women, and slaves — are replaced by the accumulation of land and riches. In the modern era, those capable of leisure (by which Veblen meant not idleness but work in government, management, the professions, the church — anything but agricultural or industrial work)—these people long to accumulate signs of culture and distinction, a mark of spiritual worth. Members of the leisure class, Veblen said, set about furnishing their lives with high-crafted goods—not things they have made, but things they assume they deserve. In order to receive the highest esteem, these goods require an element of wastefulness in their composition. Their real purpose is "invidious comparison"—the demonstration to your friends and neighbors that you are slightly better than they are. Hence the desire, in the late nineteenth century, for such things as curved driveways and liveried servants, the cult of candlelit dinners in the age of electricity, the collecting of first-edition books as furniture, and so on. Veblen called it *conspicuous consumption*. By its very uselessness or ornateness, its functional irrelevance to the task at hand, it advertises the purchasing power of the person who buys it.

All that is familiar enough. The woundingly modern part of it is Veblen's grim assessment of human nature in capitalist society. For it turns out we are caught in a trap. It may not be a trap entirely of our own making, but it's a prison with bars nonetheless, and there's no obvious or easy way out of it.

> So soon as the possession of property becomes the basis of popular esteem, therefore, it becomes also a requisite to that complacency which we call self-respect. In any community in which goods are held in severalty it is necessary, in order to [preserve] his own peace of mind, that an individual should possess as large a portion of goods as others with whom he is accustomed to class himself; and it is extremely gratifying to possess something more than others. But as fast as a person makes new acquisitions, and becomes accustomed to the resulting new standard of wealth, the new standard forthwith ceases to afford appreciably greater satisfaction than the earlier standard did. The tendency in any case is constantly to make the present pecuniary

standard the point of departure for a fresh increase of wealth; and this in turn gives rise to a new standard of sufficiency and a new pecuniary classification of one's self as compared with one's neighbors.

What we would call "upscale consumerism," then, is not just the purchase of goods people need, or even the goods they *think* they need. It is the purchase of the things they think they need in order to compare themselves favorably with their neighbors or to imitate their betters. And, of course, the upward movement, once achieved, only puts them at the bottom of a new cliff. By definition, the climber can never be truly happy, because he's always comparing himself with others higher up. In the jargon of today's social sciences, he is caught on the "hedonic treadmill"—the pleasure pursuit that goes nowhere.

An unpleasant theory, very disagreeable, and just true enough to be genuinely upsetting. After a while, Veblen insisted, we work only to earn, and we spend (apart from necessities) mainly to impress others. Activities that don't lead to payment get scorned; expenditure that doesn't impress, or any other activity that doesn't lead to conspicuous consumption, gets dropped sooner or later. And, in the end, the drive to master the art of invidious comparison has all sorts of corrupting effects. The sense of beauty, for instance. We say "beautiful" when often enough we mean expensive, for intrinsic beauty begins to matter less to us than the honor we gain from buying something. In the end, we praise as beautiful precisely what adds to expense, and so, in an insane logic that almost every upscale consumer has understood at one time or another, we wind up paying a high price for the honor of . . . paying a high price. What is called "fashion," Veblen said, is just a pecuniary satisfaction in newness. Things that are not in fashion offend us; they don't look right, and that odd sense of looking "wrong," that disgust for things out of fashion, is created not by aesthetic feeling but by the de-

126

sire for prestige. After all, only few years earlier, the older goods looked just fine.

Is all this true for me? Initially, as I read Veblen, and saw the bony finger pointing in my direction, I thought it was no more than partly true. I thought I had escaped a lot of it. There were plenty of expensive things that I couldn't care less about. I had always, to the despair of every woman I had known, been negligent about my clothes, wearing a pair of pants until it simply clung to my body like a sheath, turning a single sweater into a winterlong garment. When it came to suits, I was a serial monogamist: Wear a suit until it was shiny and threadbare and then throw it out and buy another one. I hated to shop, except for books and records, of which my wife and I had amassed thousands. But there I was on the street struck dumb by an expensive automobile. Later, I wondered, Was my struck-dumbness an expression of grief of some sort? Losing my wife made me want to own things. I would show my friends, and myself, that I wasn't defeated. I would buy something that made me feel good, that advertised my well-being. Greed was therapy, at least for the moment. The idea was grotesque, but Veblen insisted that our common behavior is often grotesque.

All through May and June, I kept seeing the Audi A6 on the street, one car more beautiful than the next—silver and blue and burgundy cars, gleaming in the sun. Once, on Broadway, in my neighborhood, I saw two of them, both dark green, parked very near to one another, like a pair of visiting royalty. The green was deep, rich, saturated, and glowing, and looking at the green royal twins, I began to wonder what was next for me as an object of desire—a $7,000 silver teapot designed by Henning Koppel? I saw it in a shop on Madison Avenue. An incredibly graceful shape. I had never noticed such things before.

God knows there were plenty of people around ready to judge this sort of fascination. It turns out that Veblen's insights, so original, bracing, and mockingly witty in their original form, have given rise, in the last half century, to a whole school of grumpy American moralists—scourges of consumerism, mourners of the spiritual death of the United States. We are wasting our scarce moral resources, it seems, in unappeasable bouts of shopping and insane desires for luxury. Our purses gaping open, we compete with our friends and neighbors, and we are obsessed with the rich, who, with their big houses and cars and vacation homes, are pulling away from us, driving us crazy in the bargain. The chief contemporary exponent of the spiritual-death-of-America school is Juliet B. Schor, formerly of Harvard, now at Boston College. In her books *The Overworked American* (1992) and *The Overspent American* (1998), Schor has put forth a particularly harsh picture of the American personality in the age of consumerism. And yet, because Juliet Schor seems, on the surface, sympathetic and commonsensical, keening with woe over the wreck of American virtue, I could not easily brush her off.

There is a great deal of anecdotal evidence in *The Overspent American*, much of it concerning women, especially the American career woman. From the assembled anecdotes and studies, a negative "ideal type" emerges. Our heroine worked hard in school in order to get a good job. But once employed, whether married or single, she begins spending heavily, immediately passing into debt, haplessly purchasing upscale status items with money she doesn't have. Almost from the beginning of her working life, then, she lives a sort of fantasy existence one level above her actual income. In order to support this dream, she works harder and harder, destroying her leisure and crippling her family life, for she is acutely aware of what her friends have and how they live, and she wants to keep up or do better. She seeks approval from them while constantly risking humiliation—it seems that pulling the wrong lipstick out of her purse at lunch could lead to social disgrace. At work or at play, she constantly thinks about stuff she wants to buy. She always wants *something*, and as her income increases, she accumulates an extraordinary number of things in her house — appliances and kitchenware, also electronic equipment, art and decorative items, closetfuls of clothes and sports equipment — and she spends a fortune on such services and entertainments as child care, travel, restaurants, insurance, and lawyers. If she's lucky, she keeps things going, but if she gets in trouble, she will have to cut back somewhere or fall further and further into debt. She does not save, she cannot get ahead of the game — it is a portrait in which contempt vies with pity, exasperation struggles against sorrow.

How to escape the hedonic treadmill? There are people who jump off. They work less, and they spend less. "Downshifters," Schor calls them, and she is full of praise for them. They move to smaller homes, give up expensive shopping habits, do their own hair; they take walks instead of going to the gym; they make their own clothes, even carding the wool. Like teacher's pets, these people are constantly brought forward in *The Overspent American* and given a nod of approval. But there's something amiss here. The women Schor interviewed work in advertising, computer programming, marketing, or such jobs as registrar at a college. These jobs, of course, are quite good, but Schor's subjects don't enjoy them, they don't find them spiritually rewarding, and that is a social and personal tragedy for which downshifting, I'm afraid, is an unlikely remedy. Buying less is not going to allow people to enjoy their work more. Second, Schor seems not to have noticed that her downshifters are no freer from material obsessions than anyone else. They are obsessed with their austerities, with what they *not* buying. They are not liberated, they merely have less money than they once did and are making the best of it.

I read *The Overspent American* in a rage. I fought with it, writing things in the margins, and buttonholed friends at work, who looked at me wide-eyed as I railed against this slanderous text. Why was I harping on this book? Because the Veblen-Schor critique of materialism and consumerism had obviously gotten to me in this moment of lunging after money. The automobile was as much a symbol of status, taste, and power as it was a good car I would drive on occasional trips to Connecticut and the Adirondacks. I didn't actually believe in Schor's critique: Much in it was creepy and beside the point. It seemed a philosophy suited to an economy of scarcity, not one of abundance, an economy in which morality depended on minimizing desire. Schor's Americans — not just the shawled pilgrims journeying to austerity but everyone — were among the most depressed and defeated-sounding Americans I had ever heard of. These people needed to get better jobs; they needed to do some good work, spend some money, and pep themselves up a little. Downshifting is not a solution, not for me or anyone else. Yet Schor's book still rankled, though I couldn't, at that moment, put my finger on exactly why.

I didn't really know how much fun it was, how good, how transcendently good, until I got up to 168th Street and, thinking I had gone far enough, pulled off the road. I had picked up an Audi for a test drive, at Zumbach Motors on 56th and Twelfth Avenue, right along the West Side Highway. The salesman had given me an A6 with a six-speed manual shift and a twin-turbo engine that generated 250 horsepower. The car was silver-colored, not "Ming blue," like the one I had seen reflecting the sun on Fifth Avenue, but beautiful enough, with a vanilla leather interior. The deal was that I could have the car for only about twenty minutes, since someone else had an appointment to test-drive it. *Twenty minutes?* Where to take it? Manhattan is perhaps the worst place in the world to take a car for a test drive.

There was nothing to do but head north along the Hudson — north on the West Side Drive, which immediately became the Henry Hudson Parkway and was perhaps the most primitive artery girdling a great city in the Western world. It was old, pot-holed, uneven, narrow, without much in the way of shoulders. Oh, but I loved it that day. I hadn't driven a standard shift in years, but I got the car moving north on the parkway, and within a few minutes I was darting around the other cars, changing lanes by downshifting and accelerating. I had never driven a really good car before, and I had no basis of comparison with other exceptional cars. But I knew this was a good car. The Audi A6 is not a small automobile, but when I downshifted (not quite in the way that Professor Schor meant), the turbo engines, after the tiniest of lag, would kick in, and like Derek Jeter coming up to the balls of his feet to move left or right, the car would seem to rise slightly and simply go wherever I wanted it to go.

Frustrated, and hearing the clock tick — I would have to go back to the dealer soon — I got off the highway at 168th Street and wandered around in the upper Manhattan neighborhood of Washington Heights for a few minutes. There was something familiar about the yellowish-brown apartment buildings, and a smell . . . there was a smell in the nostrils of memory that I couldn't quite name. Oh, God, my Uncle Irving, the pharmacist Irving Harkavy and his wife, Kate, used to live here. As a child, I would be deposited at their apartment on weekends. I remembered now: the old buildings, filled with immigrants from Central Europe — escapees from Hitler, many of them — and the smell of cabbage and boiled beef cooking in a half-dozen pots. It was a good forty-five to fifty years ago. Cabbage and pumpernickel and sauerkraut. . . . I tried to hold on to the memory for more than few seconds. Hold *on,* for heaven's sake, defeat time . . . But I had to return to the dealer.

I went back to the highway, crossing underneath it, and

turned onto a downtown entrance ramp that stretched perhaps 100 yards in a steady upward grade. I wanted to see how much torque the Audi had in third gear, so rather than downshifting, I just floored the pedal, and to my amazement, the car took off in a smooth, steady rush, right up to the top of the ramp, and my body was pressed so hard against the seat that I felt as if my heart were going to come right out the back of my chest. At the top of the ramp, going about 70, I had to slow down.

So that was what it was all about. The age of fifty-six was not too late in life to learn something so simple. That feeling on the way up the ramp was the purest pleasure I had experienced in months, and as I drove the car back to Zumbach on the highway, I suddenly knew exactly what was wrong with Juliet Schor's gloomy views of consumerism's effect on the American soul. As it turned out, I had plenty of time to think about it, because the next driver never showed up at the dealer's, so I parked the car, as instructed, on 56th Street, outside the showroom, and just quietly sat there. Schor and the other death-of-the-American-soul moralists left out pleasure altogether. They saw only desperation, but I wasn't sure they had zeroed in on the source of desperation. Schor's interviewees were bored. They were bored at work. They worked to pay the bills, not to fulfill some passion for achievement — they lacked what the Greeks called "spiritedness." They lacked pleasure in work. They were stuck in routine or exhausting jobs and couldn't find the time or energy to learn something new, in the manner of those admirable people — millions of Americans did it — who retrain themselves, going bleary-eyed to community college at night in hope of a fresh start. But if they were bored or stymied, was it any wonder that they devoted themselves to clothes and furniture or household goods or cars and the rest? Consumerism was the displacement of exasperation. You might deplore it, but there was no reason not to regard it with sympathy. There but for the grace of God shop I.

132

Now, it may seem odd, even perverse, that I came to these thoughts while sitting in one of the finest of all consumer objects, a German sports sedan that cost $42,300. But there was some passion in the making of that car and certainly great joy in driving it, and I was sure that a moral critique of America that began and ended with those things in life that give true satisfaction — work and its possible excitements, and consumption as refined pleasure — I was sure that that critique might have a greater chance of accuracy than the sour-spirited stuff I was reading from Schor and the others. I sat in the back seat quietly, but my heart was pounding. The ride, as I remembered it — as I felt it still in my body — was taut and tight, the car was as fit as a great sailing vessel. It doesn't seem to have occurred to Schor and her allies that many people might shoot for the best, according to their tastes and incomes, because they want to lend distinction to their lives. After all, a lot of these people flocking to the malls or to Saks didn't inherit their money; they earned it in a meritocracy, or at least much more of a meritocracy than existed in Veblen's America of the 1890s.

Isn't it possible that some of the compulsive buying is driven not by status anxiety and emulation but by a changing notion of the good life which requires different goods to furnish it, camping equipment and fancy "casual" duds, and all sorts of stuff that doesn't do a thing for me personally but that is nevertheless part of the exuberant comedy of American existence? David Brooks, in his brilliant 2000 book *Bobos in Paradise*, turned upscale shopping into one wild bout of self-expression after another. Brooks wrote about the new educated class, whom he calls "bourgeois bohemians," the Information Age types with one foot in "creativity" and the other in business. These people have guilty feelings about shopping, and they resolve their guilt, Brooks says, by turning shopping into a form of soul massage — buying, for authenticity, an "expedition-weight three-layer Gore-Tex Alpenglow reinforced Marmot Thunderlight jacket." It is a jacket to shame a sherpa. This sort of thing, of course, is what Veblen was talking about. But what a comedy! And don't many of the shoppers know full well that it's a comedy? What pathos of ambition and vanity combined! And whose soul is destroyed by the pathos or the comedy? This is a jacket, not a liveried servant. As it turns out, Brooks himself is no class snob. In his magazine articles, he is equally approving of the eager parishioners at Kmart and *their* choices. Schor and her allies miss all this—the variety and nuttiness of the bazaar, the ironies of self-definition, the trying on of roles and new selves. She would imprison us in her own literal-mindedness.

My long background in criticism, the adoration of art, the contempt for vulgarity all worked against buying an expensive useless thing. Yet I wanted that car. I didn't need it, I couldn't afford it, but the pleasure it gave me was immense, and I couldn't pretend that my desire was negligible. I was pulled in two ways: I had no more trouble than anyone else justifying pleasure, but greed, I saw, had its own momentum. It created new objects of desire. Even as I dispatched Schor's surly critique, I again felt that there was something in it gnawing away at me, something more serious than ill humor, and I needed to figure out what it was.

15

Wavering

Quarterly Report, July 1, 2000
Cumulative Net Gain $110,000

MY affair with R., so handsomely flourishing in the bleak but beautiful early New England spring, did not survive the greening of the landscape. By May it was over. This was no one's fault in particular, though I may well have been too tense, too rigid and spooked to accept the ease of her touch. The failure hurt, however — it hurt her as well as me. After a while, I fell in with T., who was slender as a reed, and intelligent and fine, with a soft voice and a gentleness unlike anything I had ever encountered. But we were not to be a couple. I seemed to want some intensity in a woman comparable to my own restlessness. My wife had it, in her idiosyncratic style, cranky and funny, her dithering ways and goofy smile and ready kindness giving way to the suddenly asserted razor-edged intellect. She was more than capable. Anything she put her mind to do — make a party, set up a trip, write a novel — she would do. But now, at last, she began to fall away from me. She escaped my appreciation the way she had escaped my bed. Divorce was inevitable, and I did the work — hard, exacting, bitter work — of letting go of her, slowly, steadily, letting go day by day, letting go even when I was thinking about her, but only in the past now, as a completed episode.

We were taking our time. We shuffled ourselves in and out of the big apartment where Max and Tommy lived, we kept a common bank account, we hadn't even drawn up separation papers; and in some ways we were closer now, living apart, than we had been living together in the dry and distant end of the marriage. We spoke nearly every day, exchanging confidences; and we took care of the boys, getting them through school, through lessons and doctor appointments, lighting a fire when they got lazy, collaborating on limits and punishments, sorting out their glories and misdemeanors. As the writer Daphne Merkin has remarked, every divorce is a failure of one sort or another. The only conceivable honor in divorce, therefore, is protecting the children from the righteous grievances of their parents.

I had not made the mistake of comparing other women to my wife, since nothing ends a new relationship faster than that. But I had become impatient in general, and even a little overbearing — racing on about the market or technology or whatever else I was interested in. It was money-driven behavior, market behavior, hunger and anxiety annihilating the slow caress of time stretched out, minute after minute.

By the end of spring, I was beginning to understand my time problem a little better. What is time, anyway? Time is a constant, an absolute. The river runs past the fixed observer; it never ceases. That's the usual metaphor. Yet it's somewhat misleading. Time, properly speaking, has no volume, no body; it has no speed (except in a subjective way: "The movie seemed to go on forever"). Time, as philosophers say, is merely the medium in which events take place. Measuring time by the clock in hours and seconds is a convention we have draped onto the actual events of day and night in order to keep track of duration, to compare the length of different events, and to maintain schedules. An hour is an arbitrary measure, for time is a continuum, and a continuum, I was beginning to realize, is profoundly antithetical to human desire. Why? First of all, because we like to think in terms of *instants*. "I stepped out of the subway and I realized I was in love with X. . . . I had to quit my job immediately. . . . I couldn't stand my roommate anymore." But such instants, all those realizations and epiphanies and crystallizations are, as temporal events, something of a fiction. Let us say that a "realization" is a way that the story-making and inference-drawing resources of art and mind superimpose themselves on life: consciousness, we call it. We also like to think of time stretched out or contracted, we think of it as a possible medium of pleasure — or at least I did. Those are all agreeable and fruitful human ways of thinking of time, opposed to the disagreeable inhuman truth that time is a continuum with no fixed instants. It just goes on and on, the future rushing toward us and becoming the past. Or, as the philosopher Martin Heidegger put it, we're "running ahead" to our past.

The stock market was not precisely a continuum. It was made of separate transactions, but there were so many of them, and so many other forces pulling on the market, that the market seemed to be an exaggerated version of time itself, forever moving. In brief, I lived in the continuum like everyone else, a continuum made more unpalatable by my absorption in the market, yet I wanted time to be something that I could apprehend by emotion. I wanted to stop and lose myself in a movie, in a piece of music, in a woman's flesh, or even in the grained and rotting wood outside a Massachusetts inn.

*   *   *

The market was doing okay in July 2000 — treading water really — but I was dry, without spirit. Watching CNBC one day in the middle of the month, I suddenly heard the sound of alien voices rattling my teacups. What were these people doing in my kitchen every morning? What was I doing looking at them? I could be learning something, writing something, talking to the boys; I could be learning how to cook . . . what? . . . I don't know . . . how about a duck cassoulet? It was definitely time the unwilling bachelor learned how to cook a duck cassoulet. Surely there were a lot of things to learn. Instead, I was listening to Maria Bartiromo talking about oil depletion allowances. Bartiromo looked sluggish on that day, her features a little off-kilter, as if someone had insulted her the night before. Tyler Mathisen's good cheer was fatuous, his forehead a slab of granite, his smile radiating all the warmth of the grille on a 1956 Buick. Joe Kernen, a cat lazing in the sun, stretched out his witticisms to an interminable length. David Faber was heavily ironic and vaguely self-satisfied, facetious but not witty. Lord, I was tired of these people.

Only a few months earlier, in the winter and spring of 2000, I had suffered through dead weekends, impatient for the market to open. Yet, in recent weeks, after greeting Monday with relief, I was quickly felled by boredom. The same issues over and over: Will the Fed raise rates? Is tech overpriced? Are we at the end of the bull? Having no reason to buy or sell, many of the traders were looking for rumors, threats, hopes — anything to give them a motive to do something. At bottom, market behavior is often emotional and irrational, built on suspicion, rumor, hope, and dread. Inevitably, a good part of market reporting is like weather forecasting: It's raining today because clouds have gathered. It's cold because there's a low-pressure system coming down from Saskatchewan. The market went down because a lot of people sold stocks. *It happened because it happened.* And then people buy or sell because of these nonreasons, or half reasons, reinforcing the direction in which the market is going. Eventually something serious, or halfway serious—a consumer confidence report, an Intel quarterly estimate, a gross domestic product or productivity number—becomes public, and for a while the movement of the market looks fairly reasonable, but a new momentum may commence based on minimal substance, until the absurdity of a given pattern of buying or selling becomes apparent to everyone, at which point there may be a violent reaction. In general, there's a comical/pathetic disproportion between the amount of intelligence devoted to reading the market and the amount of usable significance that comes out of that effort. Most analysis and prediction is wrong or beside the point, or true so fleetingly that a rabbit's breath has more consequence. Which doesn't stop many of us from listening to it.

An unwilling passivity before my fate, an overall languor. . . .

I neither bought nor sold; I held, merely hoping for fresh gains. I needed a shot of energy, but, in July 2000, entering a three-day venture-capital conference at the Marriott Marquis Hotel on Seventh Avenue, I got exactly the opposite. The glamour, the excitement had gone. What a dreary lot! What sloth and despondency! There were lots of young men, serious-looking Indians and Pakistanis; a few African-Americans; Asians in pairs talking to one another in Chinese or Korean. There were dark and unsmiling Jews with yarmulkes, and many other fellows in dark pants and white shirts, with bad haircuts and bad skin, and they all gathered in conference rooms with rolling walls and dirty crystal chandeliers. The movable chairs with their aluminum frames scraped the spotted and ash-stained carpets. Why are American business hotels so ugly?

Twelve hundred wannabes were there, eager to hear established people tell them how to start up a company. But something had altered in the atmosphere. The bounding, gleeful expansiveness and openness that I had loved was gone. Three months of market uncertainty and some business failures in New York had produced a new mood, pinched, a little dry, desperate even. From the experts up on the stage, sitting in panels, one heard self-conscious joking about "a new concept called profitability," and much talk of "p to p" — path to profitability. Many of the dot-coms already established in California and New York had been having a dreadful time. For the shit had hit the fan and the dot-com boom was rapidly fading. These serious, ambitious, pinched young men had arrived as pilgrims (one changes the metaphor) after the crops had failed. They were too late. But if they were too late, what was I doing there?

Henry Blodget was a more single-minded man than Sam Waksal, whose attention went everywhere at once. During the early summer, as tech stocks began to slide again, Henry appeared on television now and then, and seemed as forthright as ever, smiling and nodding, fielding tough questions without flinching. The CNBC reporters tried to put him on the defensive. He admitted that the top-tier Internet stocks, the dot-coms that he covered, were looking weak, but he also insisted on the bright side. Amazon, he said, looked like AOL a few years ago — that is, it was undergoing transition from a period of hypergrowth to a slower long-term growth. Yes, they had cash-flow problems, as Ravi Suria, the Lehman bond specialist, had said in late June, issuing a skeptical report on Amazon's ability to service its debt (pay its bondholders)—so skeptical that it sent the entire Internet sector cascading down. "Amazon loses money every time they sell me a book," said Suria, a serious fellow, very polite, when I ran into him. But on TV, Henry pointed to the company's increase in distribution and insisted, "They can get a lot more efficient." Their cash flow will continue negative through

2001, but then go up the year after. He was not withdrawing his "buy" ratings for Amazon and other Internet stocks.

I didn't own Amazon, but some of my funds did, and the company was considered a surrogate for the whole Internet sector. Was Henry deluded? The institutional investors loved him, but that might be because his "buy" had consistently driven up the value of their holdings. Parts of the press, however, were beginning to treat him with contempt. His stocks were going down — his magic was fading. Was he a creature of the bubble only?

We kept in touch by e-mail in this period, and occasionally on the telephone. He seemed calm, though he sent me a warning or two not to expect huge returns from the market year after year. "The stock market is not a federally insured savings account that just happens to return 30 or 40 percent a year," he said in July, calling me on the phone at the office. Yet he was still recommending stocks that were rapidly falling in price. Was he sending me a hidden signal, offering his "true" opinion into my ear? I was puzzled, and I remembered my confusion about the long plane between his eyes and mouth, my sense that something was missing or unresolved in him. There was a dead zone in his character that left me baffled.

Hanging up the telephone, I felt a twinge of panic. I couldn't be sure of him. I wanted to believe his ratings and his public reassurances, but as I thought back over his recent TV appearances, his vigorous argument, his earnest address, his lucidity, his sudden smile, it occurred to me that we believe whom we want to believe, that we then invest our own ego — the sense of our own good judgment — in that belief, which makes it hard to evaluate new evidence and see things in a fresh light. If our opinion of that person suffers, our opinion of ourselves must suffer, too. The matter of whom to believe was so damnably subjective, and I knew that I was protecting my fondness for Henry.

I enjoyed his success; I wanted to see him succeed further. Even though I had taken only one of his recommendations, buying Internet Capital Group, the B2B incubator, I had in some way tied my own fate to his: just like Sam Waksal, he would convey me into the future and to wealth. He was one of the people who seemed to understand what was coming. When you listened to him, you felt your tempo increase; you felt you were catching up to the zipper. Until the past few months, the rising market seemed to prove him right, while those in the past who had been skeptical were vanquished—the fund managers, say, who had stayed away from tech and the Internet, and who had shown such mediocre results in the late nineties as everyone else was going through the roof.

In part, a fantasy figure then, a figure in a mirror. What, *another* one? Was I so close to losing myself that I needed, like a lonely hitchhiker, to latch on to whoever was driving by to convey me where I wanted to go? In any literal sense, my identification with Henry Blodget was meaningless, since I was more than twenty years older, dark rather than fair, Jew rather than Christian, writer rather than securities analyst. But the literal truth of it was hardly the point. In middle age I wanted a liftoff comparable in spirit to what he had achieved in wealth and fame in the past two years.

16

Flying . . . and Landing

As a small child I had a recurring daydream just before sleep. I was flying around in my bed. Aloft, I would sweep down to the ground, smack villains on the head with the bed frame, and then rescue certain persons — ladies, usually — in distress. I did not linger in any one place; I moved around. I was only five or six, and I didn't know about Superman, and this was long before Spider-Man became the hero of a popular comic. But children's fantasies in any period are often airborne. In early July 2000, to my amazement, I was flying again. I was at home, working on my review of the movie *X-Men,* in which the characters soar all over the place . . .

Movies may not have become more imaginative but they have definitely become more fantastic. A friend who loves the new flamboyantly aerated style says we have entered an age of "visual rapture." My own ideas of movie rapture center more on a man and woman talking quietly in a still frame, but I know what he means.

The essence of visual rapture is metamorphosis: The old integrity of physical matter and unified space no longer rules the image. Gravity has given up its remorseless pull. Roll over, Newton; computer imagery has re-imagined the laws of time and space.

. . . and as I turned the movie over in my head, trying to find the right way of describing it, I felt myself slowly rise from my desk. The experience was certainly very strange. As I rose, my knees hit the bottom of the center drawer with a sharp crack just above the caps, and then my ankles hooked under the drawer, catching for a second—would I pull the whole desk away from the wall? At last the ankles broke free. Doubled over and reaching down, I flailed at the keys wildly and just managed to type in the last words of a sentence—"*X-Men* pushes a little further into the fantastic . . . than you expect without losing its character-based conflicts and loyalties . . ." but I was pulled away and I passed out the open window. Departing brownish West End Avenue, I took control of the breeze coming off the Hudson and flew to Central Park, and then soared down Seventh Avenue, wandering into Times Square. Film critic flying! What to do? You could spook the kids dancing in MTV's second-story window. Too easy, perhaps. Anyway, they would think it was some kind of weird promotion. Maybe fly right into the lens of one of those tourists with his camera raised up toward the electronic billboards? No, he would never come back to the city, and we needed tourists. What about the zipper? *Of course.* "Nasdaq down by 32.53 points," it said, and I flew by, trying to knock out some of the lights, but the words scurried around the corner. I encircled the building several times, staying up with time, and then, giving it up as a bore (what was so great about *that?*), I scratched at the window of my editor, Virginia Cannon, on the twentieth floor of the Condé Nast building, right across the street. She was intent on her galley pages, reading them, marking them up, just the way she did mine; she looked up and saw nothing (was I invisible? I saw my own body), so I left her, and then, after a tour of the corporate boardrooms, flew home and looked in on the boys from outside as they were playing with friends. Max, now seventeen, was sprawled on his couch, while two other boys sprawled on his bed. Tommy, thirteen, was manning the computer as a friend looked over his shoulder. They were caught in their own dreams.

As I flew around, the sound of people falling could be heard everywhere in the city. Rumors were beginning to circulate of a business slowdown. There were, it turned out, as many as seven thousand Internet enterprises in New York, most of them devoted to content rather than technology. In the previous few months landlords had become unsure that they wanted to continue to rent to new enterprises. Not only that, there had been — oh *no!* — a slowing of the party scene. At the same time, the press was full of stories about capital drying up for new ventures in New York's Silicon Alley. The sell-off in April, and the collapse of many Internet companies, had cooled the venture capitalists' ardor: Suddenly they couldn't see a quick way of taking the companies public. I was a little shocked by this — a little shocked by my own naïveté, actually. I had assumed that venture capitalists really believed in the businesses they invested in. What many of them believed in, it turned out, was the quick rush to the initial public offering that made them rich. They knew as well as anyone that many of the businesses were going nowhere.

The stirring rise in business-to-business stocks in late 1999 and early 2000 had gone into reverse. Big companies like General Motors were setting up their own systems of dealing with suppliers and vendors on the Internet; many of them were not turning the job over to software companies. As for the exchanges, the idea of bringing buyer and seller together — the kind of thing Mark Walsh of VerticalNet was talking about in that rampaging blast back in February — that notion was stalling, too. VerticalNet itself had fallen from a high of over 200 in February to the 30s by early July. Walsh, as I had feared, blew himself right off the stage. I was awed by this — the sheer size of the drop in VerticalNet's price, the emptiness of the pretension. But at least the preening son of a bitch took his risks!

Why was it that I felt no panic — unease, maybe, but no panic? The *Times* had run a piece back in June on how certain baby boomers were rejecting diversification and putting up to 80 percent of their assets in technology. At the breakfast table, I felt a spasm of irritation. I hated being lectured to by the *Times*. And yet they had nailed me. Born in 1943, I was a couple of years older than a boomer, but like the boomers, I had no memory, as the *Times* explained, of the awful 1973–74 downturn in the market. My reality as an investor was the nineties, the years when share prices kept rising and rising. I was psychologically unprepared for loss.

Thinking of the *Times* piece now, I shrugged it off. I would stay aloft. In *The Matrix* as well as *X-Men*, the old integrity of physical matter and unified space no longer ruled the image. One person's flesh can turn into another's, or melt or become waxy, claylike, or metallic; the ground is not so much terra firma as a launching pad for the true cinematic space, the air, where bodies zoom like projectiles. The old rules didn't apply. Fiber optics would enormously speed up communication, biotech would cure diseases and extend healthy life. I couldn't give up on tech; it was too early, and I didn't know where else to put my money.

"I will fly around the city," I said. "I don't believe it's over. I can't believe it's over. I will wait for tech to catch fire again. I will not sell my equity funds and stocks." Returning to the keyboard, I wrote the next sentence: "The rippling muscles and perfect round breasts of idealized comic figures can now be

146

approached by these super-conditioned actors. One element of visual rapture is sublime bodies flying through the air. Eroticism has been replaced by athleticism."

That summer of 2000 I needed to confront fear directly, and therefore to overcome it, so I took up Robert J. Shiller's book, *Irrational Exuberance.* It was a brave piece of work. Much of it must have been written in 1999, at the height of the boom, a time when it was clear that the author's earlier bearish analysis — from 1996, say — had been swept aside by wave after wave of buying. But Shiller was resolute: He faced boldly into the winds of market happiness and spoke what he took to be the truth. Still, brave or not, the book was unpleasant and wearying. Bilious, bullying, even derisive. I hated it.

Shiller's title was, of course, made famous by Alan Greenspan. It turns out that Shiller, a Yale economist, had briefed the chairman back in late 1996, a few weeks before one of A.G.'s public appearances. The market is too high — so Greenspan said in a speech delivered on December 5, 1996. Investors are getting silly; they are demonstrating "irrational exuberance." At which point, after grunting a bit and shifting its weight around, the market went much, much higher — from a Dow industrial index of 6400 when Greenspan made the speech to a high of 11,700 in early 2000, just over three years later. But now Shiller was reclaiming his phrase, which he had used in his briefing of Greenspan, and his analysis.

By any historical standard, Shiller says, what we've got now is a bubble and nothing else — a mad pouring of assets into stocks, the rounds of buying creating still more enthusiasm, and so on. People think their success is proof of prowess, so they keep on investing. Dance, fool, dance! Shiller was outraged that investing had become a part of popular culture — that everyone was doing it, talking about it, enjoying it. He would have been outraged, in other words, by people like me or my friends Rothstein and Stevens or by the investment studs airing their muscles at lunch counters in between successful trades. He thought we were all idiots. He blasted CNBC for cheerleading; stock analysts for making self-serving pronouncements; investors for thinking they could master the world through the Internet. Stock investing is not a *culture,* for pity's sake; it's a high-risk game, and the entire gabby system of market advice—the magazines, newspaper columns, and books, the appearances on CNBC and CNNfn— is fatuous and worthless, a contemptible scam that foists absurd delusions on a gullible public.

For it was not merely the speculator and the day trader who were acting recklessly, Shiller said. No, his censure settled as well on the common investor, the common *virtuous* investor—the model of discipline celebrated by personal-finance expert Suze Orman in her books, the kind of investor I used to be and was not any longer. This steady swimmer puts away, say, 10 percent of her earnings and expects to see a return of 10 percent every year (which sounded like a modest expectation to me). But it turns out that such paragons were being manipulated by the flattery of Orman and the other popular advisers. The praise investors receive for frugality and discipline was dangerous non-sense, Shiller said, because it transformed a mere investment strategy into a moral victory. Basking in approbation and self-approval, the virtuous investor, it turned out, was living in a fool's paradise: She wouldn't get 10 percent anymore. And the sturdy fellows buying on dips throughout the nineties were also deluded; the market would not recover from dips anymore. The hallowed strategy, blessed by Warren Buffett, of buy and hold wouldn't work either: Buy-and-hold would lead to a decline or to stagnant assets. The party was over; the market, Shiller insisted, could only go down.

How could he be so damned sure? The historical evidence,

he said, was incontrovertible. Consider three years: 1901, 1929, and 1966. Each year marked a local peak in price-earnings ratios for the S&P 500. The ratio was 25.2 in 1901, 32.6 in 1929, and 24.1 in 1966, and each peak was followed by a long period of decline. After 1901, the market went into a tailspin lasting until 1920. The crash of 1929 was followed by a long, dull period in the market lasting, despite a few spikes upward, into the war years. The 1966 peak led to another trough, which really did not end until 1982, the beginning of the current secular bull market. Well, in January of 2000, Shiller pointed out, the P/E ratio of the S&P 500 reached 44.3—an all-time high. These prices were insane. What we're heading for, he insisted, was not so much a crash as a long, grinding period of decline or a prolonged limbo of nowhere movement. We were heading for boredom as well as losses.

I read the book in a rage of counter-argument, and I knew that many others had done the same. He shrugged off low inflation and high growth; he ignored the information revolution, with its increases in productivity and profitability. He wanted us all to come to our senses — he talked as if he had just discovered that the market was subject to the vagaries of mass and individual psychology. He seemed to be arguing for a completely rational investor, an investor free of all delusions. I vented at night:

7/21/00

Wait a minute. Just wait a *minute*. There would be no hope, no *market* if people didn't take risks, fool themselves, make bets. What is so wrong with that? People invest, flood the market with money, and the companies expand, buy other companies, put money into research and development and create new products. The market needs liquidity. Most of the companies go bust, some investors lose their shirts, but a new industry is created. What he regards as delusion is the lifeblood of capitalism. *This irrational activity is one reason we have become a wealthy society.* What he calls overconfidence, or the will-ingness to take risks, is absolutely necessary. Its opposite is paralysis.

American enterprise would dry up if his advice was widely followed, though I thought he might be right in the short run — correct about the risks we faced in the summer of 2000. I was scared, just scared enough to hate his book deeply, and my ha-tred made me resolve to find a hot stock — a little-known stock that would take off, as so many tech stocks had in the last few years. I had never yet ridden some big winner from the begin-ning, or near the beginning, and I was dying to find something fresh that I could buy. Yes, this was an "irrational" reaction to Shiller's warnings. What of it?

Movies, that's what he wanted to talk about. At least, at first. Arthur Levitt, Jr., sixty-nine, the chairman of the Securities and Exchange Commission, had a thick neck and thick eyebrows and a fine square chin and short white hair. He spoke slowly and bluntly and looked you right in the eye. It seemed a face and manner almost sculpted for public accountability. His father, Arthur Levitt, Sr., was the comptroller for New York State for twenty-five years, a famously incorruptible man in a highly cor-ruptible profession, and his son carried at all times an aura of stern authority. As a young man, he went into the securities busi-ness, rose high in various brokerage firms, became head of the American Stock Exchange and a power in the Democratic Party. One of the most successful of the Clinton appointees, he was now in his eighth year in office. No one had ever been SEC chairman as long as he, and soon after reading Shiller, I went to see him. He met me in his waiting room, and as he led me into his office, he looked over his shoulder and said, "*The Patriot?*"

"Interesting battle stuff," I said reflexively. "Mel runs around a lot in the woods doing guerrilla warfare."

Levitt nodded, as if he knew exactly what I meant, and then said, "How's *X-Men?*"

Now, really, I'm not a stand-and-deliver critic. I like to take my time, mull it over, struggle to get the words right. But still, now and then every movie critic must answer questions at dinner parties, in elevators, in taxicabs.

"Some of the special effects are actually quite beautiful—almost magical. The best of the comic-book movies since *Batman.*"

Levitt nodded again, and I was nonplussed by the informality of this imposing-looking guy. But I was charmed: He knew there was something else in life besides the financial markets. Was he sick of the market? Sick of the bull, the endless media excitement?

We sat at a marble table at one end of Levitt's office on the sixth floor of the Securities and Exchange Commission building, and he looked at me expectantly, as if to say, "What are you doing here?" I knew damn well what I wanted from him. I was reeling from Shiller's book, and I wanted reassurance from this thick-eyebrowed sibyl that the market would be okay. But I explained to him that I was keeping a journal of my time as investor; that I was interested in how investment had become part of pop culture and had changed individuals like myself. He listened for a bit and suddenly interrupted me. "The amount of leveraging in this country is scary," he said, his eyes burning. Too many people, he thought, were up to their ears in debt and were buying stock with borrowed funds. But there was nothing that he could do about it at the SEC.

"Alan Greenspan said to me, 'Arthur, jawbone the New York Stock Exchange and the Nasdaq. Tell them to raise margin requirements.' " Margin requirements were now 50 percent, much higher than in 1929, when investors could put down as little as 10 percent of a stock's purchase price, borrowing the rest from the broker. But still, a lot of people were buying on margin — that was one reason the collapse had been so severe back in April. When people's leveraged holdings went down past a certain price and they didn't respond to their brokers' inquiries, computers at the brokerage houses sold them out automatically.

He said this wistfully — it was some sort of old joke between Greenspan and him. He had not jawboned the exchanges, and Greenspan himself, who had the power to do so, had not raised margin requirements. Still, Levitt fretted over the common investor. He had, after all, helped bring a great many amateurs and first-time investors into the market. Democratizing the market had been his main achievement in eight years. Levitt believed in transparency and accountability. He was working on a reform that would make the same information available to investors as was available to the analysts of the large brokerages. He traveled around the country facing audiences in small cities and giving speeches with titles like "Renewing the Covenant with Investors," and then answering questions, some very smart, some perfectly ignorant. But now investors were going crazy, and though alarmed, he could do nothing about it.

"Can there be too many investors?" I asked, thinking of day traders, whom I knew he considered reckless.

"Certainly not," he said, bristling. "It's not the government's business to discourage trading. It's the government's business to get investors to protect themselves."

I thought I could see it. At a dangerous moment in market history, at the wavering crest of a long bull market, he was caught between his desire to acquaint people with risk and the American free-market imperative to let them sink or swim. He had done what he could do, but he knew the market could kill you. And of course, listening to him, I had my fear, my fear. Predictions were not Levitt's business; he was a regulator. Still, I couldn't stop myself.

"Will there be a crash in the Nasdaq?"

He sighed. "Prices are out of line with value. People are taking risks they should not be taking. But it won't be a crash. It will be a long, slow, flat period." *Oh God, not him, too!* Had he been reading the gloomy Shiller? Or had he arrived at the same conclusion out of his long experience? "When the market turns down," he went on, "there will be fewer TV shows, fewer publications. Magazines will fail, talk about the market will dry up. After fifteen years, people will give up and put their money somewhere else."

My mouth went dry, and my brain seized up; I forgot the remainder of my questions. It was the answer I had dreaded — and to hear it from Arthur Levitt, too, the chief popularizer of the market! "A lot of people are trying to get wealthy," I said lamely.

He burst out again: "We live in a culture of instant wealth, a more materialistic culture than anything I've read about in the history of the United States. Standards of performance are being measured by how close to a billion you've got." We talked of other things, his failure to get Congress to control the accounting profession, the futures market, and then he ended the interview, abruptly turning his back. I left his office thoroughly shaken up. The interview had petered out because I had lost heart. He couldn't possibly have increased my anxiety any more than he did. His bushy-eyebrowed sternness I took — whether intended or not — as a reproof. Outside the commission, on Fifth Street, I wondered again about his asking me about movies. It's as if he were saying, "What are you doing fooling around with this stuff? You've got your own vocation."

17

The Song of George;
the Song of Sam

DESPITE these rebukes, I couldn't give up the chase, and a few days later, at night, I exhorted myself as follows:

7/25/00

You wanted to avoid self-pity, but you've fallen into it anyway, in the Manhattan real-estate version, and now it's time to snap out of it — time to swallow this wave of panic produced by inevitable departure from a comfortable but unremarkable apartment. . . .

So rouse yourself from this torpor. Concentrate on the new technologies that have been driving the market these last few years, the discoveries, the vaccines and monoclonal antibodies, and the materials, too, that's what you need to know — the fiber, the fuel-cell batteries, the chemicals, and what goes on in the lab. You have to move into the future in order to stay up with the present. The humanist who doesn't understand at least the rudiments of technology will be swamped by it sooner or later, just the way you were swamped by the personal computer in the early eighties. It's time to switch perspective, to move from mere gambling in the market to touching the bricks and mortars of the next world. *Then* invest.

There had been a lot of talk of fiber optics in the newspapers, but it was forbidding-sounding, jargonish, and I hadn't quite taken it in. But perhaps a week after visiting Arthur Levitt, I heard, at a luncheon devoted to the future of the Internet, the following words: "The average packet at the moment travels through seventeen router hubs in getting from one place to another." Yeah, so what? This sentence, spoken into my ear by a venture capitalist holding a muffin in his hand, was nevertheless succeeded by the following: "This current network will not deliver video; it will not perform. It has to be replaced." The cliché of a "dawning" recognition seems laughable, but I understood it then—a sense of change passing through your body as a physical fact, like blood returning to a limb cut off from circulation. By the time the gentleman had finished the second sentence, taken a bite of his muffin, and swallowed it down with some coffee, my brain was on fire. It was big, it was enormous. *This system has to be replaced.* A few days later, I set about reading whatever I could find on fiber optics.

This much seemed clear in the summer of 2000: The Internet system then in place could easily be overwhelmed with data. By some estimates, Internet traffic doubled every nine months or so; by others, every ninety days. Information wasn't flowing through the system nearly as fast as it might be. The system needed increased "bandwidth"—a word that, for all its buzzy, right-up-to-the-minute sound, signified nothing more than the amount of information that can be sent through any given transmission system. Like personal wealth, or thinness among Upper East Side women, bandwidth was something you couldn't have too much of. At home, most of us had modems that could transmit 56,000 bits, or 56 kilobits, per second, sufficient for e-mail and basic Internet traffic, but slow for elaborate Web sites and, more seriously, incapable of accommodating the enormous flow of material that was building up, including the added demands made by the "rich" media—teleconferencing between offices and the transmission of vast amounts of corporate, military, and institutional data (inventories, complex designs, the complete illustrated catalog of the Louvre). And then there were such unspeakably important cultural goods as the complete movies of Annette Funicello and every episode of *Leave It to Beaver*, not to mention such things as the recordings of Muddy Waters and Creem, and Richard Strauss's operas and Jules Feiffer's complete cartoons, material both serious and trivial, the contents of archives and museums everywhere, both the majority and the minority tastes, all potentially available on demand. Like water struggling to get through a clogged drain, the "rich" media were demanding wider passage.

Part of the solution was in place: fiber-optic cables. Magic wires! The fiber-optic cables replaced the old sheathed copper wires that carried charged electrons. Down these amazing cables go flashing pulses of light generated by lasers—photons, not electrons. There were millions of miles of such cables already laid in the "ultra-long-haul" networks that stretched across the country and under the sea. Alas, the photons couldn't go unimpeded from one end of a telephone call or Internet transmission to the other. Arriving at hubs and switching points—after all, nothing flowed from Bakersfield to Buffalo without switching points—the photons, which were hard to manage, had to be turned into the *old* stuff, electrons, and then turned back to photons again; at which point, at last, they could be sent on to the next juncture. Slow, slow—this procedure took whole *seconds*. And the "rich" media could not get through these clumsy switching points at all. The Internet was blocked, stalled, its potential still unrealized. I grew excited: In some ways, we were still at the dawn of these technologies.

There were other practical problems. The wavelengths needed to be regenerated after a while—without regeneration they lose their shape and integrity and the data turn to mush. And to complicate matters still further, we were rapidly adding lanes to the highway. In the late nineties, the accumulating Internet traffic had been sped along by an extraordinary technology known as wavelength-division multiplexing (WDM), which uses lasers and prisms to send wavelengths of slightly differing frequencies down a single strand of fiber *at once*—initially four wavelengths at once, and then more and more, and these multiple lanes were no longer just an addition to the network, they had *become* the network, for they make *light so enormously capacious a carrier that all practical limits on communication disappear.* I said before that the modems that most people have at home could accommodate 56,000 bits per second. If the whole system were "transparent"—that is, if it ran at light speeds from one end to the other—the initial bandwidth for such a system would be something like ten gigabits per second. That's 10 *billion* pieces of digital information per second, all going down a single glass wire. And capacity will only go up from there— forty gigabits per second was the next plausible goal.

There was one last major problem—getting the stuff out of the long-haul and metropolitan (areawide) networks and into the individual home or office, the so-called last mile. Fiber right into the home was too expensive to install, but there were the two "broadband" solutions, DSL and cable modem, both very effective, yet most people were sticking with their old, slow modems. Why? Because, apart from Napster, which was legally in peril, there was not much available—no "killer application"—that required broadband. Not yet anyway. Broadband was rolling out slowly.

But it will come, I told myself, it will come. In the future, if everything goes right, love letters sent by e-mail will arrive before the sender has drawn in his breath to sigh. We shall send the entire Library of Congress, once it is digitized, to Sri Lanka, and in just a few minutes. Of course, if the Sri Lankans started reading it in alphabetical order, in chaise longues and under perfect light, they could read all their lives and probably never get much past Henry Aaron. Maybe they would make it to General Allenby. But so what? The stuff would be available. The simultaneous transfer of enormous amounts of data could change the way we do business and experience cultural goods—it's the ultimate extension of the Internet. Sri Lanka needed to know what we know. And we needed to know what Sri Lanka knows.

Nuts and bolts! Bricks and mortars! These were the materials themselves, though my excitement had been capped by reading some very abstract, high-flown prose—the star-spangled visions of a mesmerizing tech guru. George Gilder is the capitalist ideologue and antifeminist who had written, in 1981, the book *Wealth and Poverty,* which became the bible of the supply-siders in the Reagan administration. After a stint as a Reagan speechwriter, Gilder took up technology, explicating the computer revolution in his 1989 book, *Microcosm.* Eventually, Gilder started a subscription-only report on the Internet (there is a printed-out version as well), which, for a fee of $295 a year, was distributed to some 65,000 eager stock analysts, investors, and the merely curious and greedy, including me. In these monthly reports, filled with jaunty techno slang mixed with religious metaphors, Gilder tracked the advanced developments in information technology. He also recommended stocks.

At times, I had trouble making sense out of Gilder's future-devouring discourse ("Replacing its own PowerFilter with a holographic diffraction grating, its NextGeneration PowerMux will chop per-channel WDM costs by . . ."). But I had no trouble with the eye-ravishing stock tables on the back page of the report. In 1999, many of Gilder's choices had gone through the roof: Broadcom and Avanex and Qualcomm, which last had gone up by a factor of 26 in the *anno mirabilis* of 1999. There were people, once moderately wealthy but now *very* wealthy, who thought Gilder was a genius. By 2000, Gilder would no sooner adopt some obscure fiber-network company on his Web site than the company's price would begin to leap upward, a movement known on the Street as the "Gilder Effect."

At *The New Yorker,* in the summer of 2000, I grabbed the advance galleys of the great man's new book *Telecosm: How Infinite Bandwidth Will Revolutionize Our World.* In this volume, setting out his vision of heaven on earth — the "telecosm" — Gilder delivered a complex argument in a kind of crooning visionary ecstasy. "The telecosm," Gilder wrote, "launches us beyond the fuzzy electrons and frozen pathways of the microcosm to a boundless realm of infinite undulations. Beyond the copper cages of existing communications [i.e., standard telephone wire], the telecosm dissolves the topography of old limits and brings technology into a boundless, elastic new universe, fashioned from incandescent oceans of bits on the electromagnetic spectrum." The new technology, he said, "makes men into band width angels."

Yes, with wings of gold — that was always part of the pitch. George Gilder was the religious troubadour of wealth. I heard his song, and wondered about an immediate gain — an investment opportunity. Many technology companies were trying to build a switch that would not have to transform the photons back to electrons — an all-optical switch. Hewlett-Packard was doing it, and Ciena, and a new company called Corvis that had been spun off from Ciena by David Huber, the inventor of dense-wave multiplexing. But Corvis wasn't public yet. If I was going to play the new technologies, I had to find the right stock to grab hold of before the whole thing dried up. I was electrified all over again by the attraction of speed. Speed was as necessary and as imperious as the quick march of the Roman legions into the future.

For me, fiber optics was one half of the future. Biotech was the other. In late July, while still swimming in Gilder's mad sentences, I met Sam Waksal for lunch. I wanted to get it straight from the horse's mouth. We had hit it off in the last few months, becoming friends, and when I talked with him, I played with the fancy I had entertained on the street after the first evening at his loft, that he was an idealized version of myself, bolder, faster, more free-swinging. He seemed to have things figured out, and had reaped the rewards. He was also great fun to be with. The reasons weren't hard to understand. There are two kinds of egotists in the world: the kind who need so much adoration that they burn up all the oxygen in the room, leaving other people struggling for breath; and the kind whose self-approval lights a fire that shines on others, making them feel larger, more worth knowing. Sam was the second kind. He lit candles in his apartment and everyone felt good in the illumination that he provided. Since he was generous toward me, my admiration for him stopped somewhere short of self-abnegation. He let me know that what I did for a living was worth doing, too.

This mutual admiration society of two convened at an Alsatian restaurant in SoHo — an odd place for an entrepreneurial capitalist to hang out, down there in high-bohemian Manhattan, among galleries and boutiques. But that's where Sam lived and worked. There was nothing of the bohemian about him, but he liked the company of artists, writers, and scholars, as well as his uptown social and financial-world friends. The restaurant was situated halfway between his loft-party-space on Thompson Street, just south of Houston, and ImClone's corporate headquarters and laboratory, on Varick Street, also in SoHo. (Im-Clone's new drug, C225, was manufactured in a plant across the river, in Somerville, New Jersey.) In the summer of 2000, Sam was riding high: ImClone had recently benefited from a burst of publicity when a young Florida woman with advanced colorectal cancer named Shannon Kellum had been given C225 as a case of "compassionate use"—i.e., not as part of an FDA trial but as a personal exception. In April 1999, she began treatment, receiving the drug intravenously along with the chemotherapy irinotecan, and her tumor had shrunk by 80 percent within five months. The tumor was then surgically removed, and the news had burst onto ABC and the pages of *USA Today*. Colorectal cancer was curable if caught early or fairly early. In its advanced stages, after people had failed surgery, radiation treatment, and chemotherapy, it was a dreadful scourge; no one had been able to make more than a tiny dent in its power to destroy. Suddenly, there was loose talk in the media of miracle cures, and ImClone was pelted with requests for "compassionate use" of the drug.

ImClone, Sam told me, had $330 million in the bank, raised through partnerships with pharmaceutical companies and on Wall Street—by issuing debentures through Merrill Lynch, Dillon Reade, and so on. The company was deep in clinical trials on C225 and also another drug, IMC-ICII, that inhibited blood-vessel growth—in effect, cutting off blood supply to the cancerous cells. At lunch, the atmosphere was imperial. We were virtually alone in the restaurant, and Sam's enthusiasms took over the room. News of the sequencing of the human genome was fresh, and Sam's dark eyes shone and his hands moved up and down in his rapid and restless way, gathering in and expelling information.

"If you were to take a map of the earth in 1570—Amerigo Vespucci's view of the world, Africa is known, but we don't know the source of the Nile—well, that map will now be quickly filled in. Right now, we have all the street *numbers* in the human body, so next we have to name the streets. It's like a New York telephone book with numbers but no names."

His entrepreneurial blood was racing. Find a company on every street! He was full of excitement about other start-up biotech companies and such things as Israeli chip makers. Philosophically, he was a vitalist and, personally, a whirlwind who rushed from meeting to conference to social event. Even at lunch, he had a bounding, slinging energy and curiosity, an impatience for news. "We have to define the functionality of the genes," he said. "We know there are tons of orphan receptors on the edge of a cell. But what do they do? Do they have a function in pathology and normal physiology?" Some of these receptors, I later found out, were central to ImClone's drug therapy.

The resourcefulness, the opportunism, the pressing against limits seemed to be a family tradition. His parents—the older folks in the picture on the credenza in his dining room—were Polish Jews who had survived the Holocaust. During the war, his father, Jack Waksal, had eluded the Germans and had fought, while still a teenager, with partisan groups in the woods, sleeping in gravesites during the day and joining the partisans at night. According to Sam, his father, even as a boy, was a tough, wily character. When the war ended, he fled to the west, avoiding the Russians, and fell into the hands of the Americans and the OSS—the precursor of the CIA. For a couple of years, in Regensburg, Germany, Jack played a double game: He helped the Americans identify and round up Nazi war criminals while running contraband goods on the side, selling chocolates and cigarettes to both German civilians and American GIs. According to Sam, his father was in cahoots with an American army lieutenant, and since he was also very useful to the U.S. authorities, they looked the other way. Sam told me all this with great glee.

He was proud of his father's survival skills, which bordered on the outrageous and the criminal.

Sabina, Sam's mother, also a Polish Jew, had survived Auschwitz when her mother gave her a gold ring, which she deposited in her underwear, bribing her way into kitchen duty. For weeks, she lived on potato skins. After the war, she met Jack in Paris, and eventually, in 1951, Jack and Sabrina came here and settled in Dayton, Ohio, where Polish Jews from their village had emigrated before the war. Sam, who was born in Paris, had gone to public schools in Dayton, which is now a sad place, its factories closed, its main streets semi-deserted. Back in the fifties, however, it was a thriving industrial town, and Sam's father had developed a prosperous scrap-metal business.

After undergraduate work and a Ph.D. in immunology at Ohio State, Sam had a research career in medicine at Stanford, the National Cancer Institute, Tufts, and Mount Sinai Hospital in New York. The eighties was a time when the practical applications of genetic engineering became obvious. At first, researchers hoped that they could reach cancer cells with a little toxic package—a guided missile that would explode the cells. In practice this had proved difficult and dangerous, and many of the new therapies had failed. Sam and his brother went back to John Mendelsohn's idea from the early eighties—the use of monoclonal antibodies to repress the mechanism of cell division.

C225, or Erbitux, as it later came to be known (I will call it that from now on to avoid confusion), was a very clever idea. If killing the tumors outright was too hard, or had toxic effects, why not try to block the elements that caused the cell to reproduce itself? On the outer edge of many cancerous cells, it seems, were innumerable little nubs called epidermal growth factor receptors. They worked this way: The cell's nucleus emitted an enzyme—the epidermal growth factor (EGF) itself—which exited the cell, circled back, and latched on to one of the nubby receptors on the surface. At that point, the receptor sent a signal to the nucleus telling it that it was time to divide. This self-generating mechanism was so powerful that it could overcome the assault of chemotherapy, which mucked up the DNA within the cell; instead of dying from the blow, the cell all too often struggled, repaired itself, and continued dividing. But Erbitux interfered with the reproduction process; it latched on to the receptor nub on the surface, capping it, even driving it into the cell, and the signal then failed to reach its target in the nucleus. Without the signal going to the center, chemotherapy could begin to do its happily destructive work. Now unrepaired, the cell would stop dividing uncontrollably and start to fail, and eventually shrink and even die. That was the hope, anyway — the drug didn't work on all patients. The question was: Did it work often enough for the FDA to justify certifying it as a treatment? At least one third of all tumors showed ("expressed," in medical language) the epidermal growth factor receptors — colorectal and pancreatic tumors for sure, and head and neck carcinomas, too. The market for Erbitux was potentially enormous. Therapy for colorectal cancer was just the beginning. Sam was sure of it.

Trials of Erbitux for colorectal cancer were now under way in consultation with the FDA — that was the standard procedure. After lab work and animal trials, you went through three trial phases with patients, testing first for side effects ("toxicity"), then for the efficacy of the drug itself, and then, in a paired set of trials, for its efficacy both in combination with and isolated from the treatments that were already available. But there was a catch: In order to be ready to sell the product quickly, you had to "ramp up" for production of the drug — perhaps investing $50 or $60 million doing so — *prior* to the completion of trials and FDA approval. Only by doing that could you get Erbitux or any other new drug into the hospitals and clinics within days of the

FDA saying yes. Capitalism! No one could say that its procedure for developing drugs lacked drama.

"If you start out with a great product," Sam said to me in the restaurant, "and a product that serves an unmet need, and you put together a good team . . . After that, after the good science, it's a matter of finesse—how to move the science and maximize the market possibilities at different periods of time."

His dark eyes sparkled as his hands moved restlessly on the table. Getting the drug out there was a financial as much as a medical challenge—he made no bones about that, and I was impressed. Writing well was hard, but writers rarely took risks that lasted for fifteen or more years. If Erbitux was approved by the FDA, it would get to the market maybe six and a half years after the first clinical work was done on it, and almost twenty years after the first theoretical work. Yet even though he had no drug to sell, Sam floated in the upper echelons of New York, the benefactor of a mere *possibility*. Cancer therapy was the real issue here—I knew that. Still, I was fascinated, I admit, by his loft, his paintings, his abundance. At his monthly soirees, which I had been attending on a regular basis, he made you feel you were part of some elite emboldened to hear and say only the very best things. He venerated anyone with talent or knowledge, and he gleamed with money. ImClone and fortune-making never came up at his social evenings, but there was an implicit promise— hadn't I detected it, responded to it, gloried in it?—that he was going to lead us all on the great adventure of wealth. But not *only* wealth. His parties were impossible without cash, a great deal of cash, but he embodied romantic hope—the dream of the future as an opening to glory, a limitless possibility. We were going to name the streets and say who lived there; we were going to pull all of knowledge together and understand the human body at last.

He was a mixture of idealism, ambition, and guile the likes of which I had never encountered before in a single man. He confided to me that ImClone was rushing ahead with trials of Erbitux as a treatment for colorectal cancer before trying the same drug on head and neck cancers. Colorectal cancer was a bigger market than head and neck, and it was also a disease that had a certain cachet in the media. Katie Couric of NBC News had publicized it after her husband had died of it, and colorectal patients in general were seen as innocent victims. Those suffering from head and neck cancers were seen as not so innocent; they were heavy smokers and drinkers, most of them. Yes, there was a degree of calculation, perhaps even cynicism, in ImClone's moves. Did not all cancer sufferers, I wondered, deserve equal treatment? Well, perhaps they did, but it was not possible to make trials in all varieties of cancer at once, and the point, I could see, was to be effective and get the drug approved as quickly as possible. If everything went well, the head-and-neck patients would get their treatment, too, in a few years, and so would the more rare sufferers from pancreatic cancer. ImClone was a case of science supported by Wall Street and sold through marketing savvy.

Sam quoted philosophers like Ortega and Camus, but he also loved gossip, even of the most commonplace kind — his eyes came alive when he heard of Harrison Ford's marital troubles. The worldly scientist. At home, later in the day, looking him up on the Internet, I discovered he was a figure in the New York and East Hampton social worlds. He had been divorced a long time — over twenty years — and he was very much a man around town. He was friends with Martha Stewart and had dated her daughter; he had appeared in the tabloids as the escort of wealthy divorcées. He was negotiating to buy a huge estate in the Hamptons that had belonged to William Simon, the Secretary of the Treasury in the Reagan administration.

I found all this astonishing as the background of a scientist, and, in fancy, I sent him out there, conquering the world, sleeping with superb women, imagining his moves as if they were an extension of my desires. He escaped my body, like a character in an old avant-garde film from the silent period, and moved around in space. I had no desire to be friends with Martha Stewart or to date her daughter. But the scandalous bravado suggested by the dual relationship amused me a great deal. Was he a brazen sport who got away with everything, or just a creep? Sam pushed the envelope. Cancer was a perverted fount of energy — mutated cells that can't stop dividing. I relished the idea that it required not just science but an equal form of inexhaustibility to begin to tame the disease at last.

18

The Mountains of
the Past

THE postmarital man clung to his boys. Max had developed the
beginnings of a stubble on his chin and a dark shadow on his
upper lip. The young men in his school all seemed to be cultivating these debonair, Robin of West End Avenue beards. They
lifted tankards now and then—Max and his Merry Men. He
was definitely not a solitary youth like his father a long time ago.
He would be a handsome man, volatile maybe, and charismatic;
he grew beyond my height, beyond my temperament.

Max was away, on one of his summer trips. At the end of July,
on the twenty-eighth, I drove north to see the younger one,
Thomas, at his camp way up in the Adirondacks, near Lake
Champlain. It is a long drive. When you get to Albany, three
hours from the city, you are only halfway there, and I lengthened
the trip still more by pulling over now and then. I was trying to
buy a stock and was having an awful time doing it. The stock
was Corvis, one of the fiber-optic companies, a specialist in
ultra-long-haul networking, the company that David Huber was

head of. The previous Sunday, reading the *Times*, I had noticed that Corvis was going public on the same day as my drive upstate. I had to get in on it. Had to. I had missed all the big new issues in recent years, like Qualcomm, which famously went up by a factor of almost 26 in 1999, and Broadcom, the chip maker that made the electronics for set-top boxes in cable-modem rigs. I had bought Broadcom the previous March, at a frightening price of $233 a share. Looking for a breakout stock, I had just bought Mechanical Technologies, which makes fuel-cell batteries, but it wasn't going anywhere, at least not yet, and I was restless, looking for something else. All over again, the fever was in the blood.

I kept pulling off the road in upstate New York, amid dark green mountains. As I stood outside the car, holding my wife's cell phone, a crow or a hawk would appear in the distance, the birds coming down from the mountains, crossing the highway and heading east for Lake George. I had told myself I would never look at birds again. But these birds, flying alone, were heralds of the strange and singular melancholy of the Adirondacks. The mountains were vast and quiet, the area sparsely populated. At one point, after the Civil War (before the tourists began coming), the area had figured in the American imagination almost like Alaska—as heroic territory for pioneers in birchbark canoes. The pioneers were followed by tourists and factory workers, but the factories—furniture, paper, and leather—had long gone south in search of cheaper labor, and the New York and Albany gentry who had once taken the train upstate, or the steamer up the Hudson, began flying to Europe or driving to the Cape or the Hamptons. The big rambling inns along the lakes had lost many of their wealthy customers, and the towns were often shabby and poor. A meager church, a red-brick VFW post, seemingly always closed, maybe a convenience store, a hardware store . . . that was it. Whenever I drove up there, I felt that the place was grievously unappreciated, like a talented musician or actor who has lost his audience.

I took a deep breath as something flew overhead, and I called my broker, far away in Long Island. "Why Corvis?" the broker wanted to know. Answer: Of the three principal problems that had to be solved in order to get to Gilder's paradise of the all-optical network — broadband connections to the home, all-optical switches, and the necessary regenerators — Corvis had nothing to say about the home-access problem, but it offered to solve problems two and three. It claimed to have invented a switch that worked without the cumbersome transformations to electrons and then back again — an all-optical switch. And it claimed it could regenerate signals of much greater strength. I wanted in.

Oh, but it was hard. The initial public offering was not being handled by a retail broker. There were six underwriters — investment banks and brokerages with an investment-bank division — but my two brokerages (Paine Webber and the on-line version of DLJ) were not included among them. More than ever, I felt like an outsider. How do you crack this game if you're just a single, small-time investor? The opening price was first announced as between $12 and $14. Then at $36 I was beginning to understand how the game worked: The underwriters wanted to do a favor for certain clients and made shares available to them before the stock was publicly traded. Once the stock was actually traded, it could be "flipped," or dumped, even on the day of the offering, at enormous profit. As an outsider, you could get burned very badly if you bought the stock near the end of opening day.

Corvis finally opened to the public and shot up to a staggering $98. On the road through the Adirondacks, I called my broker, once, twice, three times, as the stock climbed and then fell back a bit. Each time I got out of the car, there were birds soaring overhead and not a sound except for the cars passing on the highway. I was en route to see my sweet boy with his pale skin and auburn hair, up here in the clean, empty mountains, and I couldn't stop calling a man sitting in a dour industrial park in Long Island. I didn't know what made me angrier — my own activity, the IPO racket, or Corvis's behavior. Lots of hot new technology companies had leaped up on their opening day of public trading. What was remarkable about Corvis's success, however, was that the company not only had no earnings, it had no revenues. Its famous optical switch hadn't hit the market yet, and David Huber had refused to answer any of the questions put to him about the company's technology. How did the switch work? He wouldn't say. He was keeping his hand to himself.

I drove north, past Lake George, got off the highway, and turned east toward Lake Champlain. Both lakes, glimmering in the sunlight, were filled with little sailboats and catamarans. Somewhere before I got to the shore of the lake, my broker and I agreed that Corvis's price was absurd, and not to buy the stock unless it fell to under 70. I gave up, and I was relieved. The air was clear and smelled of pine, and I remembered my days away from New York in April with R., when I had been transfixed by the dry, rotting wood of a bench and some buds growing nearby, and I was grateful for the fixed things of the world. In the Adirondacks, I realized there wasn't much *but* the fixed things of the world. Very little was manufactured in the forgotten mountains.

I checked into a bed-and-breakfast in Westport, New York. I would see Tommy in the morning at his camp by the side of a small lake near Champlain. Tired from the drive, I fell into a pleasant semi-trance, examining the curious corners and ornaments in the place. In the hall, there was an old brown radio from the thirties, the kind with a yellow dial, and in my room some dark volumes of Upton Sinclair and Somerset Maugham,

171

with flaking pages, sat on bookshelves topped with milk glasses — the glasses had a faded Popeye figure decaled onto the outer edges. The sad Adirondacks! Next to the bed, there were odd little crafts-shop lamps with red or green wooden switches. Maybe every bed-and-breakfast from Carmel to Cape Cod had such things, but I didn't care. I was immensely grateful for the crafts-shop lamps, made, perhaps, by campers like my son many years earlier. One must hold on to the things of this world. The Adirondacks were losers in the geographical competition for revenue; they were not part of high tech, not part of the future that I longed to be part of; they were stuck in a failed past, and they were unhappy. But they memorialized their own history, retaining photographs and prints and artifacts of the glory period. Nostalgia — which means, literally, a painful ache for return — was a form of sanity, because it was inevitably tied to pieces of wood and glass and paper and to a beloved, a body once loved, a wholeness once achieved.

Corvis closed at — at what? At 84.72, a gain of 135 percent for the day. The company had raised over a billion dollars for its unknown switches, the machines that would speed light pulses carrying vast amounts of information from New York to Sri Lanka. What gall — and what success! I would wait for the price to drop. Arriving at camp in the morning, I saw my boy. He was playing tennis when I came in, and he grinned and waved, even taller than I remembered, and his hair, bleached from the sun, had turned a lighter shade of red than usual. He threw his arms around my neck, a homesick child. Cathy arrived, too, and later, at lakeside, as the three of us stood looking at the far shore, a crow landed on the dock, nibbled at the corner of a canoe, and then took off again. There was a stillness on the lake as the bird flew across the water to the forest on the other side.

19

Envy

BACK at home, in August, I sat in the empty dining room one Sunday, listening to the sound of a jet taking off at Newark Airport, across the river. Now and then, a teenage girl, smoking and cursing ("Fucking . . . fuck . . . fuck" — some of them talked like London whores), would pass beneath the window with a friend, on her way to Riverside Park. And all the while, a melancholy silence within. I missed the chatter in the dining room. About five years earlier, we had stopped giving dinner parties, a sure sign of a marriage on the wane; and the many Sunday brunches had ceased, too. The ritual of brunch takes place all over the country, in a hundred forms, but I'm familiar only with the New York version — the two-hour meal outfitted with bagels and lox and fruit and cake, or perhaps something special, couscous with julienne vegetables, or potato pancakes, all of it slowly consumed with many cups of coffee as the children play in a bedroom or the adjacent living room, sitting on the floor with their books and toys or perhaps noodling at an instrument.

At table, the grown-ups carry on their endless conversation—it's one long conversation, really, stretching over years—about schools, real estate, vacations, and restaurants. Sometimes books and movies are discussed, too, or politics, but those are lesser preoccupations at these affairs at which successful couples, like medieval forts opening their doors and exchanging herbs from the garden, gather together in harmony and friendship. *Sunday brunch*. When Cathy and I were together, and the children were younger, we had a lot of them, and went to a lot, too.

Sitting in the dining room at a heavy-boarded English pine table—sturdy and cheap, the best kind of antique—I realized I missed the ease, the chatter, the Sunday-afternoon pause from work. But I also knew, looking back from my new vantage point, that brunch wasn't always so innocent an occasion. On the surface, these events were resplendent with the goodwill created precisely by the desire not to compete. This wasn't work, it wasn't business; everyone was on an equal footing. But, at times, underneath the friendship and care, silently, in the hollows of the talk, an unappeasable habit of matching and measuring went on. Who has the brighter children? Who has taken the more interesting vacation? Eaten at the better restaurant? And now and then, there were sudden moments of coldness, a dropping away of sympathy, only temporary perhaps, but as clear and startling as an icicle placed in your palm. A sudden silence across the table: One has blundered in some way, offering an unintentional, or at least unconscious, slight. Or perhaps one of the guests, a normally genial man, bursts out in a bitter tirade about a friend at his office known to everyone at the table. Like a character in Dostoyevsky, he can't stop himself; spitefulness pours haplessly out of his mouth as the others look on in appalled fascination.

What produced the dropping away of sympathy, the nasty tirade?

174

I had thrown aside Juliet Schor's *The Overspent American* in disgust, but I sensed then, and knew now, that my temper tantrum was caused by more than the pleasureless tone of her book. There was something wounding in her depiction of status competition. Back in March, going through the seven deadly sins, I singled out envy as the sin that meant the most to the modern temperament. No surprise there: Tocqueville had made it clear that envy was the vice of democratic societies; and Veblen and a modern disciple like Schor filled out the picture — they knew that a spiritual menace was lodged deep in the basic habits of our social existence. Yes, envy was the curse of the middle classes — particularly, I would add, the professional and intellectual sectors of the middle class, the Upper West Siders living in every city and suburb in the country. Envy was fully capable of destroying friendship. It existed most powerfully between equals, or near-equals — didn't it? We do not envy people much richer than ourselves. They have passed out of our league.

A couple of weeks earlier, I had gone to visit my friends the Carters (as I'll call them) at their country estate in Connecticut. The word "estate" falls uneasily on American ears. But what else could you call the place? The Carters had almost 400 acres in the countryside, in an area that someone in the great Preston Sturges comedy *The Lady Eve* called "the heart of the contract-bridge country." The Carters do not play bridge, but they have a big house, up on a hill, with a view south into New York. There's also a sizable "garage house" on the property, about fifty yards away from the main building, and two cottages. There are thick woods and open fields and a nursery and a pool-and-bathhouse combination. Behind the house, on the side that faces New York, a stone patio gives way to enormous elms and oaks and then to a hill that falls gently to a lake. I sat for a long time in the back, looking toward the woods on the other side of the lake, listening very closely for each distinct sound — a crow

175

cawing to its fellows in the tree, the faint dull clang of an oar hitting the side of an aluminum canoe.

Sam Carter had had a long career as a corporate attorney and then as a communications executive; he was retired now, and he and his wife, Josie, when they weren't in their New York apartment, were slowly redoing the big house and generally maintaining the property. The place was quiet, it was serene; it was also enormous, even sumptuous. But somehow it was not intimidating. That was the miracle. The Carters were easygoing people; they had put up posters of all sorts in the big house, and lots of books and magazines lay around in the den, which was outfitted with leather couches, a large TV, and a bar. Comfort, ease, amplitude, and a complete absence of designer ambition. The larder was full, there was plenty to drink, many things to read. It was the great good place.

They gave me the bedroom that had been Sam's as a boy, a green room on the third floor that ran from the front to the back of the house. It was the largest private bedroom outside of a palace that I had ever seen. It seemed the length of a bowling alley. From the window, through the elms, one looked across the lake into New York State. And I thought: This is it. This is true wealth — born to it, growing up in it, increasing it, and enjoying it. And, as far as I could see, not ruined by it. My friends were kind and witty, intelligent, generous — the ideal American wealthy couple, without the peremptory fashion consciousness of the Italians, the noise and dreadful hats of the Dallas rich, the sterile techno-hipsterism of the youthful Silicon Valley billionaires. Am I idealizing them? They didn't give charity balls, they couldn't care less about "society." They spoke in their own voices, not in the manner of some clan or social group.

In the green bedroom I felt the peculiar chagrin of the invited guest. The Carters' hospitality was casily and unceremoniously offered, but still, my comfort was tinged with the forlornness of something borrowed—this enormous bedroom with its adjoining bath would not be mine. Did I want it? The question shamed me, and I withdrew it, and then I let it float out again. No harm in facing these things. I certainly admired the bathroom. Only the rich have a bathroom like this. There were two sinks, yards of handsome old tile, and that view south toward New York. I admired everything on the property—the scale, the splendor, the comfort, the informality. But did I want it? Did I feel that the Carters didn't deserve it in some way? Did I envy them?

At the entrance to the Carters' property, one passed through open gates. A local policeman lived on the grounds in a small house near the gates, and when he was off duty, he kept an eye on things. As a guest, one never saw him. In the big house, there were no servants present—a gang came in, it seemed, once a week and cleaned everything in a day and left. In the country, the Carters shopped and cooked for themselves. The lead-up to dinner—the drinks in the den, the national news, the debate in the kitchen after the news as they cooked—was all part of their nightly ritual. In the bedroom, I climbed into a king-size bed, but I was unable to sleep. I had a bad hour or two. The Carters' property itself was a kind of paradise—a well-ordered harmony of the natural and the man-made, brought off with an amplitude of scale, an Edenic richness of woods, fields, and water. The Carters lived in the place from which the rest of us had been expelled.

They were gracious people, and my envy would wriggle through their good humor like a snake in the garden and, finding nothing vain to attack, would turn back and bite itself in bitterness. I coiled the emotion in and suppressed it. Anyway, I didn't want a large house, I seemed to want—still, still—a dowdy apartment on West End Avenue. What I liked, and wanted to continue, was my enjoyment of the Carters in their establishment; I liked the thought of them padding around among the posters and books and going to the bar in the den for a drink. I pulled the covers over my head with relief. I did not wish to expel the Carters from their house. I did not envy my hosts. They were too rich to envy.

Which did not mean that envy was not a genuine problem for me. Sitting in the dining room of many brunches, now reduced to echoes, I knew that my life, and the lives of my friends, were often suffused with competition and at times with unacknowledged spite.

I remembered my disbelief in 1967, when I first read Norman Podhoretz's *Making It,* a semi-autobiographical account of New York intellectual life in the fifties and sixties. Podhoretz insisted — and he was talking not only of intellectuals — that as Americans got older they tended to remain friends with people at the same income and social levels as themselves, while cutting off people at different levels, both higher and lower. Norman Mailer was the only celebrity Podhoretz could think of who would willingly undertake a conversation at a party with a non-celebrity. In general, peers stuck together. Once you had made it in Manhattan, you couldn't go back to the old working-class neighborhood in Brooklyn — it was just too embarrassing to reach across those status lines in middle age. So Podhoretz said. Only twenty-four at the time, I was gravely offended. Podhoretz's remarks seemed so defeated a way of thinking — a corruption of natural warmth and attraction. After all, this was *America.* Why couldn't anyone be friends with anyone? But I now thought that Podhoretz was right. Not right in every case, but often enough. His insight was a partial truth, and I extended it this way: Distinctions of income and status, except in those relationships in which the age difference was enormous, loused up friendships over and over.

178

I had a few unhappy memories. My best friend in high school, M., a brilliant and charismatic man headed for an academic career, was unable—the reason doesn't matter—to finish his doctoral dissertation and was forced to teach not in a college but in a New York private school. Hardly a terrible fate, of course—many of his students were very bright. His career problems don't stand high in the miseries of the world. But still, in his own eyes he had suffered a severe loss of honor and pride, so severe, apparently, that he cut off everyone who had revered him from high school and college days. It was not hard to understand why. No matter how necessary to students and parents, high-school teachers don't rank high in an American status system geared to wealth and publicity. As M. got older, the prospect of seeing his admiring old friends must have upset his equilibrium. We all took the rejection personally (how else could we take it?), but it was not, I think, aimed at us as individuals. In any case, my friendship with M. was over, and though I tried again and again to revive it—with jokes, with flattery, with appeals to his sympathy—I couldn't find anything that worked. He humored me each time and then cut me off again.

I grieved over the loss for years, carrying it around on the street with me, suddenly feeling it, like a shadow crossing the sun, at the oddest times—as I opened the paper in the morning and drank my coffee, as I put one of the boys to bed. I felt it as a physical presence. What, after all, had I done wrong? Was I being punished for a small amount of success? I felt deprived of M.'s company—and for what? I had not loved him any less when he began working as a teacher. Neither had any of his other friends: I knew this was true, because we would air our common bewilderment when we ran into one another. But he could no longer bear our love, which he must have interpreted as mockery. M. made friends with other teachers. In the jargon of sociology, he "reset" his expectations. I suppose he felt he had no choice.

Now, almost everyone has some sort of baffling and painful story like this one, and some of us, located on the other side of this tale, have suffered a fate similar to M.'s. So Podhoretz, sadly, was right. The drive for money and status in democratic capitalist societies could destroy friendships as you got older; it was easier to hang out with peers, as conventionally defined.

For what if someone close to you was simply better, what did you do then? Goethe is supposed to have said: "In the face of the great superiority of another person there is no means of safety but love." When I first heard this, I wondered what "safety" was doing in the sentence. But now I thought I knew: Goethe could see from his own experience, and perhaps from Beethoven's, that great achievement was just as likely to be hated or feared as loved. To avoid that danger, one must admire great merit unequivocally. ("I will never be an orphan on the earth so long as this man lives on it," said Maxim Gorky of Tolstoy. That was the kind of safety that Goethe required.) At some level, everyone agrees with Goethe's remark, and almost everyone disobeys, at one time or another, the stern injunction that it lays down. A friend, an acquaintance does well and we belittle her; she's a fake, she doesn't deserve it. I slighted my friend B., who developed considerable power and reputation as a critic; I told myself he was arrogant. Was that not a case of envy? I wasn't all that fond of him as a man, but I had no reason to avoid him. I might have learned a lot from him. Someone doesn't have to be flawless to remain your friend. I think now that I exaggerated his faults, protecting my own amour propre by ending the friendship.

The men and women I'm thinking of at brunch were never consciously malicious—they wouldn't have allowed themselves such vices—but they were often guarded and competitive. The funny thing about them is that, for all their intelligence, they didn't know themselves. Their guardedness and competiveness took a peculiar form: They were terrified of making a mistake — any mistake. They had the illusion, common in upper-middle-class New Yorkers of the professional class, that life's greatest dangers can be avoided, that everything will be okay, *if only one never makes a mistake*. Such people, otherwise sane and good-humored, became fanatics of the perfect path. They might have started out as free-spirited souls, devoted to art, music, and literature, and devoted to passionate love, too, but, by degrees, through some process they weren't aware of, they became more rigidly proper than nineteenth-century American Victorians — and far more conformist than middle-class Americans living in towns and suburbs all over the country. Their morale had been attacked by something more powerful than the normal hardening process of age. They couldn't see it; they couldn't see how much panic lay under decisions and tastes that seemed mere common sense to them. *One cannot make a mistake.* In an outbreak of narcissism which they would condemn in others, they forced their children to enact a platonic résumé that required the right schools, the right music lessons, the right friends, the right college, the right investment banking or Ivy League life. In upper-middle-class New York, children had become the unacknowledged flashpoint of status competition; they were forced to bear the burden of their parents' anxieties, and some of them hated it. Some of them became balky and stupid, refusing to read, refusing to accept the book-and-music culture of their parents, refusing to leave the car after their parents had driven them 300 miles to visit some college in Massachusetts or New Hampshire. Infuriating as all that behavior is, who could blame them? They had our number: They weren't going to listen, they were going to make mistakes. In the end, of course, if you were sane, you relinquished your dream of what they should be as vanity, sheer vanity — your vanity, not theirs — and you got out of the way so they could find their own ideal selves.

There was real success among the bourgeois intellectuals in New York, and at times generosity and even nobility, too, but the sense of security was about an inch deep, and fear produced some strange behavior. The no-mistake policy, which was intended to guard the family fort against rivals, was produced by money anxieties and powered by envy. If pressed, these very intelligent people would admit that no matter how smart you were, how shrewd and calculating, life played unexpected tricks — your company folded, your wife left you, things went wrong. But still they were devoted to their mad desire never to make a mistake. Having recently been dropped by some of the perfectionists, I knew that I, too, was now perceived as a mistake. I was one half of a failed marriage, a turbulent, self-dramatizing man marked by the "human stain," as Philip Roth called it. A failed marriage was a threat to other couples. The stain might spread to them, and I slipped from their attention.

In the dining room, I knew that Thorstein Veblen, and even the literal-minded and humorless Juliet Schor, had a point about behavior among peers that I couldn't escape: Envy and competition, the destroyers of friendship, were two of the weaknesses in capitalism's moral armor. My oldest friendships, the ones going back twenty-five, even thirty years, were preserved precisely by the habit of each party separately, and both together, giving up competition and enjoying the other's successes and commiserating over failures and losses. We might tease or shove back and forth — a certain amount of overt competitiveness could even preserve a long friendship — but we were *with* each other, as attentive as a barometer to the low and high pressure of the other's moods. At the least, one had to enjoy other people's success as well as one's own. That was the best way of earning a passing grade in bourgeois ethics. But that kind of parity and obvious common sense was more rare than many were willing to admit. All of which left me depressed as I sat in my dining room, not because I had behaved worse than anyone else (I hadn't), but because what was most valuable in life could be so carelessly damaged — the fine chatter of friendship, the tinkle of coffee cups silenced. There were elements in the pursuit of wealth that I had only been half aware of in the past. But I didn't think that, understanding these things now, I was likely to stop pursuing it.

20

The Mountains of
the Future

THEY get tall so suddenly. Tommy, only thirteen and ready to surpass me in height, his auburn hair tumbling down on his forehead and setting off his pale skin — Tommy was so elongated, fair, and thin that he seemed almost translucent, a translucent cornstalk emitting nut-brain teenage jokes. He was always laughing. When he had no joke, he would repeat what I said as if it were ineffably absurd, and then break up.

"What great adventure are we going to have today?"

"What *great adventure* are we going to have today? I don't know, Dad. What is your definition of a great adventure?"

In the beginning of September 2000, I was waiting for him in the breakfast room of the Ramada Inn in San Francisco, near Fisherman's Wharf. We were taking a little vacation together. As he showered in the morning, I would drink coffee and watch the Nasdaq run up on the big monitors overhead in the breakfast room. My heart was racing. The index went up to 4100; then, after another day, to 4200. The composite index had been

184

going up modestly and slowly all through August, a total of 11.7 percent for the month. The tech sector had recovered from the spring panic and then from the doldrums that had left me so bored. Corvis, the stock whose IPO I had failed to penetrate, still had not earned a penny of revenue, and its CEO, David Huber, had not yet made the technology of its all-optical switch known to the public. I was astounded by the company's arrogance, but it seemed to be working. By the second week of August, Corvis had attained a price of over $108 a share and a market capitalization of $37 billion; at one giddy moment, in the middle of the day, its market cap was briefly more than that of General Motors. No revenue, no product, and a cap greater than GM's. I still wanted to buy some, but I decided again to wait until the price was much lower.

"We will visit a vineyard," I said to Tommy when he came down.

"*Visit* a vineyard? Don't you mean drink at a vineyard?"

I had a second cup of coffee, and my heart beat faster. I was pumped. Through August there had been some talk of a possible general economic slowdown, talk of possible over-spending and over-capacity in the tech sector. Just a hint in the papers. Yet the Nasdaq composite index was 3.6 percent above where it had started the year, and our portfolio was alive, up a good 12 percent or so for the year. Obviously we could not get back to that incredible high of March 10, when Henry Blodget leaned across the table at the Judson Grill and the Nasdaq index, sometime after the fish course, hit 5048. For months I had known that we were not going to make that million — I'd kissed it good-bye with many vicious jokes in the late spring. But I was still hoping for a final-quarter surge that would bring the index up to 4500 or 4600 by year's end, a gain of about 12 percent and for us of maybe 20 percent. Yes, I would be happy with that. Could I hold on to my apartment without more capital? I didn't know.

185

It would be rough. I would have to raise a huge mortgage and also sell stock. Maybe I could do it. At breakfast, Tommy, blissfully unaware of all this, grinning at me across the table, told me everything that had happened to fat-ass Cartman in the previous night's cable rerun of *South Park*, which he was watching in our room while I tried to cope with George Gilder's telecosmic ecstasies.

We went to the vineyard, which was owned by a couple that had fled New Jersey and the mattress business. They sat on a hilltop in Napa Valley in a new and enormous house, an abode spotless, bookless, empty of children. They had wild pigs and an occasional mountain lion. They were wealthy people delivered into isolation and a stupendous boredom, and we drank the wine made from their grapes, which was very good, and I came back to the city free of envy of the rich and quite happy. It had been a nice adventure. To cap my mood, I read a recent issue of *Barron's,* easily the most hard-nosed of the investment rags. *Barron's* had put a pleasant drawing of an express train on its cover. The engine was decorated with stars and stripes along the sides and a dollar sign on its nose. "Can Anything Stop This Economy?" asked the cover line. The answer inside the paper was: *Nothing.* Despite an apparent consensus on Wall Street that a slowdown had begun, economics editor Gene Epstein was resolutely upbeat. The train was rushing down the tracks. No cow, no loose track, no stationmaster would slow its hurtling speed.

Hope or folly? My God, this was *Barron's,* not some preening Internet magazine swollen with ads for B2B software and images of grateful Third World peasants. Good to hear this reassurance from the tough guys, for certainly there was plenty of doubt from others. The *Journal* had published a skeptical article on September 3 titled "A Weary Bull?" And even Henry Blodget had finally lowered the ratings for his sector, which had continued plunging even as the rest of tech recovered. On August 7, he had marked down eleven of the twenty-nine Internet stocks he had been following as a Merrill Lynch analyst—stocks he had long been bullish about. He didn't recommend selling; he used such phrases as "weak hold." The re-evaluation produced a chorus of jeers in the press. After all, most of these stocks had already fallen a long way. Internet Capital Group, for instance, which I owned, had tumbled by 80 percent by August, eToys by 84 percent, Amazon by almost 56 percent, and so on. "Now he tells us," began the *Journal*'s report, and the *Times* commented: "The analyst, who once led the market up, now appears to be following it down."

Ouch. In an accompanying note to his downgrades, Blodget said that he was "resetting" the ratings, not making a new "call." But despite the delicacy of his language, the impression that he had lost faith in his darlings, and way too late, was unmistakable. In March, when I had heard him speak at the *Silicon Alley Reporter* conference, he did of course say that 75 percent of the Internet companies would fail, and even some of his most bullish pronouncements back then—on Amazon, for instance—were hedged with warnings of extreme risk. Still, he had stuck with "buy" ratings as these stocks, one by one, dropped off a cliff.

This business of analysts' ratings had become a bitter issue in the press. It turned out that fewer than one percent of *all* ratings were "sells." (You would think the market never went down.) Investors were forced to puzzle over Henry's "weak hold" for eToys, which, as it happens, had fallen from its fifty-two-week high by an unbelievable 95 percent. *Weak hold?* At what point does Henry Blodget actually recommend *selling* a stock? When it becomes worthless? Obviously, he never recommends selling. The word "sell" had become a literally unspeakable obscenity. "Weak hold" now means "sell," at least to the knowing—the large institutional investors whom Henry's ratings were aimed at. But how were ordinary investors to know that?

Reading of his downgrades in August, I had a furious moment. I had long suppressed my doubts about Henry, and I felt slightly used in some way, as if my trust had been borrowed and violated. Was he naive? Corrupt? He certainly wasn't stupid. I remembered his unpretentious directness, his friendliness, his seeming candor and straightforwardness, how intently he listened when you asked a question. I had wanted him to lead— oh yes, lead me, lead on into the future. It was beginning to seem a little silly, my infatuation. Even worse: I couldn't encounter his failure without facing the possibility of my own. As the press mocked him, there were moments when I wasn't sure whether I felt sorrier for him or for myself.

And there remained a rather large question: Could Henry actually find the companies with good businesses? Or was he good at picking winners solely in a market sent aloft by speculation? Among his picks, eBay was doing well, and Amazon might learn to make a profit yet. But most of the other Internet stocks looked shaky or dead. He avoided me in this period, fencing me off with e-mails, but I was sure he would see me again, sooner or later.

Let Henry take care of himself. I needed to find my winner among tech hardware stocks. Suspended between belief and doubt, with a pounding pulse allied to a skeptical mind, I took Tommy back East, got him going in school, and while Cathy stayed with him and Max, I headed back to California. It was time to confront the technological future.

"Yes, ahhh . . ."

It was St. George of the fibersphere himself, George Gilder, expounder and creator of wealth, kicking himself into gear at the beginning of his annual Telecosm Conference up in the Sierras at Squaw Valley. As the conference began on September 13, 2000, Gilder had assembled in the California mountains the entrepreneurs, inventors, and CEOs of the burgeoning optical industry — the leaders of the same companies that he recommended in his monthly reports. As I hobnobbed with the start-up billionaires and the ordinary wealthy investors — the Gilderites, who also attended the conference — I reveled in the open skies and craggy mountains around the valley. The Sierras! Such a pleasant setting for happy investment stories. As the mountains turned red in the declining light, the Gilderites held forth at the Bullwhacker's Pub Deck, the huge outdoor dining patio at the Squaw Creek Lodge. They had all made serious money from taking Gilder's recommendations — Qualcomm, with its appreciation by a factor of 26 in 1999, was on everyone's lips — and they were sure, these folks from Denver and Tucson and Los Angeles, that George's powers bordered on the miraculous. They were good-looking people — the men tanned, with steel-gray hair and muscular forearms; the women in great shape, even the women in their fifties, supple and slender with terrific high breasts. Happy and rich, they were more than willing to pay the $5,000 fee for the three-day conference in order to be near the great man and his favored companies.

"Ahh, yes, ahhh . . ." Once Gilder got going on the opening night of the conference, he sawed the air up and down with his arms, or thrust them outward from his body like the blades of a retractable forklift. Like Sam, he exuded physical enjoyment of enterprise; the abrupt hacking and thrusting of his limbs seemed to generate the dynamic process that he thought inevitable — the creation of an all-optical network in which the transmission speed of information would be so high that it would soon cease to be an issue at all. The name of the conference was "After the Flood: The End of Bits Per Second."

"I'm serious about bits per second being over," Gilder said to the participants, who did not object to hearing that their triumph was a fait accompli. Gilder, sixty, was tall and slender, with glasses and thinning straight hair and a fine straight nose, and he radiated a bounding authority and ardor. When he spoke, he had a thistle-dry New England twang and habits of fervent, spasmodic eloquence. "Wasting time is a degrading experience," he declared at the conference. "Using time efficiently is a moral experience." Listening to him, you might be in the presence of an erratically brilliant Calvinist minister from about 1790, although it was not hell that Gilder promised to his listeners but a vision of heaven on earth in which time would never be wasted.

It turned out that Gilder's certainty about fiber optics was based on a theory he had been nurturing for years. In each historical epoch, there were certain abundances and scarcities, and the relationship between the two transformed our reality. Nations in earlier ages capable of exploiting the cheap plenitude of earth, air, water, and labor had become the wealthy societies. The next great abundances were in power—steam, electric, and nuclear—and then in microelectronics. At the moment, we were living through an age of silicon abundance in which microchips were virtually free (they were being given away in cameras and toys and a variety of other disposable items). As the abundance became "free," the scarce assets turned into creators of vast revenue.

In the age of the telecosm, bandwidth would become so plentiful that it, too, would be virtually given away. According to Gilder, we were now entering a "new paradigm"—that is, the new dispensation in information technology in which light and the Internet would dominate, and silicon, microchips, and the computer would be relegated to roles as supporting players. And Gilder explained that the core of the network would soon be "dumb," or transparent, operating automatically, at light speeds, and the intelligence and interest would shift out to the edges—to the issue of how the material would be delivered to our homes and to content itself. At the moment, said Gilder, we

190

could watch an infinite amount of pornography on the Internet, but we couldn't watch something as central as *Casablanca*. As the Internet became capable of delivering *Casablanca* and everything we needed, such infuriating media as radio and television would quickly dissolve. We would never again shuffle through channels. We would choose only what we wanted—hundreds of episodes of *Law & Order* or of *Friends*, everything recently in the news about Guatemala, Patsy Cline's later recordings, the horror films of Tod Browning. At the same time, we would no longer fill out forms and stand on lines. The greatest scarcity of modern life is time, and soon we would cease to *wait*. We were ready for simultaneity. That's why men and women would become "bandwidth angels."

At the conference, the discussions were split into sessions representing the different parts of the network itself, including switching and ultra long haul and the last mile. It was Gilder's paradigm made flesh, a division of all creation into earth, air, and water. These companies were riding high on the Street, and one after another, like sultans showing off their prancing stallions, the CEOs boasted of their prowess before their peers. Leo Hindery, CEO of Global Crossing, was depositing cable along the ocean floors in order to link continents. Gilder saluted Global Crossing as "the most important infrastructure company for the global economy." Nick Tanzi of Metromedia Fiber Network brought "dedicated" lines of fiber right into the offices of certain major clients—the British government, or Chase Manhattan in New York—and sent data out over its own network, which stretched across the country. By contrast, Dan Hesse of Terabeam solved the last-mile problem by beaming the data stream right into corporate windows. "There's no digging, no trenching, no right of way," said Hesse, though he allowed that in San Francisco Terabeam had encountered a slight problem: It seems that fog sometimes shrouded the beams. I waited for a rustle of uneasiness around the room and detected none.

It was a brilliant gathering of serious men, though they were implacable boasters, all of them. Gilder created an atmosphere of market-cap exaltation in which boasting was accepted as common speech. Henry T. Nicholas III, Ph.D. (as he styled himself), the CEO of Broadcom, which made the chips for set-top boxes, promised that his boxes would allow games and point-to-point video conferencing, and would replace the PC for all functions except word processing. I owned some Broadcom, which *Barron's*, using an arcane measure of its own, had called the best company in the world, but still, I was astonished by Henry Nicholas's promises. He was a tall and muscular young man, bizarrely dressed for California in a three-piece black suit. He had a black goatee as well, and all in all, he looked like a fierce pirate in modern dress, or perhaps some surly knight defending the flower of his vanity. The market cap of Broadcom earlier in the summer had hit an astounding $47.1 billion. No one in the industrial world had ever attained great wealth and reputation much faster than Nicholas.

But there were oddities in the vaunting mountains of the future. Hesse's mention of fog was left hanging, and to me it seemed portentous. One couldn't help noticing an enormous contrast between Gilder's religio-plutocratic tintinnabulations and such realities as persistent moisture in the San Francisco climate, which screwed up Terabeam's signal. George Gilder, it seems, was a technological determinist: He believed that if something *can* be built, it *will* be built, almost as if there were no significant gap between the conceptions in his mind (how the parts of the system will work together) and the actuality in the field. The capital markets, Gilder was sure, would find a way to make all this happen. Simply by describing the paradigm, he took the invaluable first step in the process of filling it out — that was the myth we had gathered to celebrate. Of course, I knew that people all over the country were working on the fiber-optic network, and that the industry was driven not by George Gilder but by the hope for enormous profits. Still, Gilder's sparkling hype gave the future of communication a spiritual allure and an aura of inevitability. Fog interrupting beams just wasn't an issue for him. "Around here in the telecosm," said Gilder in his reedy voice, "we don't solve problems, we pursue opportunities."

The pallor of stained hotel carpets and wilted hopes that I had noticed in New York back in July were nowhere to be seen—not in California, where the mountain air, the pure oxygen of invention and risk made me giddy. The Telecosm Conference, whatever my doubts about some of the claims, had provided my most purely blissful moments as a rider into the future. I no longer felt like a spy; I was cast aloft in the thin air of wealth. Along with the CEOs and investors, I went for a hike in the Sierras; I was short of breath, gasping with pleasure. Later, I listened to the panel discussions and got slightly drunk on the Bullwhacker's Pub Deck. (What, by the way, is a bullwhacker? Perhaps we Easterners are better off not knowing such things.) Late in the evening, people gathered in excited little knots in the corridors of the hotel and exchanged figures and projections. Rollout would take so long; fresh capital could be raised in so many months. It was hard not to believe that greater fortunes might yet be made on still newer technologies—storage methods or ways of reaching the "last mile" which George would describe in his newsletters and future conferences.

The task of upgrading current networks and building new ones would cost corporations, as someone said in passing, a trillion or so dollars. That was the figure bandied about—"a trillion or so." Much of this figure, however, depended on the telephone carriers and networking companies continuing to purchase equipment at a high rate. But just before the conference started, at the end of the first week in September, the *Journal* had published a piece saying that the carriers were over-extended. They had mountains of debt, it turned out, and their revenue was growing more slowly than expected, mainly because of price-lowering competition for long-distance business, and therefore, they were simply not buying a great deal from such Internet equipment manufacturers as Cisco and Nortel and the rest—at least, not at the same rate as before. As for the little upstart local networkers, the so-called Competitive Local Exchanges (CLECs), they weren't receiving any more money from the capital markets, so they weren't buying as much as they once did, either. At the conference, no one in my hearing spoke of this article, and I have to admit that when I was up in the mountains, gasping with pleasure, I suppressed my memory of it. I didn't want to hear what it said—which was that the trillion or so was unlikely to be spent soon. After all, such optical-network stocks as Ciena or Juniper were holding on at high prices, and at the conference, Gilder said such mind-bending things as "Tech stocks are performing at a hundredth of their capacity."

On the last night of the conference, in a ski-lodge bedroom with a vaulted ceiling, I turned off the lights and sat in the dark looking out at the outlines of the distant mountains. The tingling in my body I had felt for the last three days was slowly fading. The reality of my situation was returning. Married, employed, a parent; in control, on top of things, and cruising along, I was happily settled in my life for years. Then most rudely unsettled. And I saw what many others have said, that our great system of democratic capitalism was just fine as long as things were going well for you. The security it provided, however, was thin, and when you fell through the crust, you were in danger of falling a long way. The sociologist Robert Lane has written that in a society like this one, which has so few communal instincts, the normal tragedies of life—losing a partner, losing a job—hurt much more than they should, much more than they do in other societies.

All right, then, where was I? I had pulled myself out of despair by taking on greater risk, an act of existential defiance that I did not regret. I was healthy and reasonably strong, but at the age of fifty-seven, I felt, now and then, the creak in the floorboards, and I heard the wind whistling through the slats in the outer walls—a little too much weight in the gut, an occasional kidney stone, a bout of diverticulitis, and, at the moment, the sexual desire of a nun. But I hadn't realized how much I feared age until I read and listened to Gilder—and then put his enthusiasms together with things that Sam Waksal had said to me back in the spring.

At the Telecosm Conference, I detected something curious playing under the claims and boasts—a ground bass of unease grinding away below the surface. At first glance, and at second, too, Gilder's conferees had swept everything before them. They had made fortunes, created new products, knitted the world together. As successful capitalist entrepreneurs, they had vanquished any alternate system of organizing an economy. Having licked the problem of wealth accumulation, they did not consider that the problem of wealth distribution—the rich and the poor—was any business of theirs. But there was one thing they could not lick. The one thing shadowing their triumph was aging and its scything climax, death. It was the final victory that capitalism, which had swept all before it, could not achieve—immortality, or at least a long, disease-free ascent into a happy and productive old age. And yet they were arrogant enough to *want* to lick death. And I believed it was that realization, as much as the drive for efficiency and wealth, that pushed the all-optical network forward.

Consider that George Gilder was obsessed with wasted time. He was a perfect nut about it. Communication might be infinite, but life on earth was not. Time was forever the ultimate scarcity. Therefore, we would, so to speak, steal from the end, nanosecond by nanosecond. We would postpone death by stealing time in little increments, withdrawing the "latency" — or wait periods — from all sorts of communication systems and then making new use of the time thus saved. For Gilder, that was the ultimate purpose of the all-optical network.

The notion linked up with certain echoes in my head. As I sat there in the dark, enjoying my own management of time — I was *thinking*, one of the most pleasurable of all activities — I remembered that at lunch Sam had been talking about biotechnology and health, and he was alarmed and merry at the same time. As always, his hands flopped and banged restlessly, his voice rose with laughter. He was amused as dire possibilities flashed before him.

"Our parents in their fifties were very different," he said. "We're in much better shape. But when the baby boomers start to age, half the population will have Alzheimer's and the other half will take care of them. Every man, if he lives long enough, will get prostate cancer."

He looked to be in superb health, but the threat of a sickened old age was haunting him. This specter, he thought, had to be vanquished — age postponed, vitality prolonged. Recalling this outburst, I thought that Sam's ambitions and George Gilder's were closer to each other than one might expect. The biotech revolution — was it driven only by the desire to lick cancer and Alzheimer's? By the desire to make a killing? That's quite a lot of desire, of course, but I think there was something else — the hope of men in their fifties like Sam Waksal that they would be able to think and to make love, to ski and to party as if they were still about forty. Sam Waksal did not want to get any older. Neither did Gilder, who wanted to steal time from the end. These men were not just fighting off thoughts of death, they literally

were not going to accept death, and that made them more ambitious than men of all other generations. At fifty-seven, lying in
the ski lodge, I suffered the common middle-aged emotion of
apprehension. I no longer had an infinitude of time. The past is
an abyss, the present is impossible to hold on to, and eventually
we run out of the future. At that moment, I wanted to hang on
to men like Gilder and Sam Waksal as they refused to die.

21

Crash

Quarterly Report, October 1, 2000
Cumulative Net Gain $85,000

DAZZLED by the hard-cut Sierras, red and gold at dusk, I returned home in mid-September to the leaf-softened streets of the Upper West Side. On my avenue, the dark summer green waved in the gentle breeze coming off the Hudson. I needed soothing, it turned out. Trouble lay ahead. After a few days, it became clear that the Nasdaq composite index, which was falling 60 and 70 points a day, was not undergoing one of its periodic cleansing dips but was taking a serious dive. There were occasional bounce-backs of as much as 125 points, but the day after one of these revivals, the plunge would simply resume, and as September passed into October and the slide continued, I fully understood for the first time what impossible odds I had taken up a year earlier.

Let's go over this again. I loaded up on tech-oriented Nasdaq funds in October 1999, and began buying individual stocks in

January 2000. The Nasdaq went up like a V2 rocket — a 48 percent rise in the last quarter of 1999 alone — and reached a high of 5048 on March 10, 2000. It crashed in April, recovered, and then plunged again in May, recovered in June, surged in August, reaching 4200 by the beginning of September, when I was in San Francisco with Tommy and was drinking too much coffee at the Ramada Inn.

So why the new slide? Wasn't corporate spending on technology still expected to grow at a rate of 25 percent a year? Yes, but it seemed that the market had priced stocks like JDSU as if spending were growing at 30 percent. Even though these companies were still profitable, *they were just not as profitable as investors had hoped.* A great company like Cisco, scrambling each quarter to push the rock as high or higher than the same quarter the previous year, was now engaged in a losing struggle with its own history. Cisco's stock price was rapidly falling and taking the whole tech sector down with it. Profit growth must continue at the same rate or better for prices to continue moving up — that was the inexorable logic of a long-running bull I hadn't quite understood a year earlier.

9/16/00

Only now do I begin seriously thinking that the index might fall in the year 2000. *Fall?* My getting up in the morning, my raising the children, my talking amiably with my departed wife, my seeing friends and dating women, my going to movies and fighting the movie industry while looking for winners was all a reality lived within the assumption that the market would keep rising. I *felt* it rising, dammit, felt it for years in my blood, the surging investment arm of the mighty American economy in one of its most stirring phases.

Corvis, the optical-equipment manufacturer whose initial public offering I lusted after in July, was around $63 dollars in early

October, way off its improbable midday high of 114 when it momentarily had a greater market capitalization than General Motors. It was low enough to buy. So, in an act of defiance — I would not give in to this sell-off — I bought some Corvis. This move came after selling Aastrom Bioscience, a stem-cell-research company I had bought in August and had hoped to ride up a few points. Aastrom sank instead, as did Mechanical Technology, purchased in July and sold in August, a fuel-cell-battery company and another of my ideas for a quick return. Restless, restless. It was too soon for these sectors to take off. Too soon. I had never done this quick buy-and-sell thing before, and I didn't like it, and wasn't having any success with it, but I was back in the game with Corvis.

Or so I told myself. But the Nasdaq kept falling, and as we moved into autumn, there was no escaping the gruesome logic of a long-running bull market. The logic swung its ax with a ferocity that overwhelmed me.

When Intel alerted investors on September 21 that its third-quarter sales would fall below expectations, the stock fell 22 percent the next day. Mighty Intel down by over a fifth in a single day! The company was still highly profitable, but the years of good news made any hint of trouble a devastation. All of a sudden the price looked insane to many people. The ax swung viciously. Eventually, the *Wall Street Journal* said, stocks like Intel will gain traction again, but not now. A downturn, then, a serious downturn. But lasting how long? The bears who had said "collapse" during the dips in the period 1995 through 1999 had been wrong every time and had missed out on enormous gains, hadn't they? Each of those dips had actually been the opportunity for the making of fresh fortunes.

10/08/00

I'm suffering the demi-anguish of purgatory here. Is this the moment to sell — to empty out all those funds with Nasdaq stocks in them? I just can't do it. What would I put the money in? I confess I don't know. It's not as if the rest of the market is booming. No, the Dow has been going sideways. And so, yet again, I hold. We're not in a crash, an actual *crash*, are we? I'm willing to ride out a downturn of a few months in the hope that the future — the golden promise Gilder and others held out — will rescue us, and tech will take off again.

Cathy was being good. More than good. We would meet or talk on the phone — fluent friends exchanging news of children, work, my life, her life. Mostly I kept my anxieties to myself, but when I said something about the slide, she would say, just as she had in the past, lowering her voice, "It will come back, it will come back," and I felt a flood of gratitude colored with misery. We would get a divorce someday, splitting everything down the middle, but for years the children would need maximum support. Max was now swinging through his senior year at school and eyeing colleges nervously, and Thomas was listening to more rap and less Dave Matthews. They knew little of the market, and in this period of decline, I was not going to tell them about it.

Gamely, I cheered the tenth anniversary of the bull, which came on October 10, 2000. Well, what a decade. The numbers were still amazing: The Dow had gone up by 347 percent, the S&P by 375 percent, and the Nasdaq by 931 percent. In that ten years, the total value of all U.S. stocks had gone from $3 trillion to over $13 trillion. Yet on October 10 the Nasdaq was down 17.5 percent for the year, which meant that in the short term the Nasdaq was not a bull at all but almost a bear. It was in free fall, in fact. What to do? My way of cheering the anniversary — and overcoming fear — was to buy still more Corvis, which was then priced at 60. You were supposed to buy when a market was falling, weren't you?

As I ordered the stock, I wondered, What does a fiber-optic

cable look like, anyway? I've never even seen one. And there was something else I wanted to see — a certain wayward Internet analyst now in semi-retreat.

It was quite an eye-opener, the World Financial Center. Not the World Trade Center, but its junior partner across West Street, the World *Financial* Center, with its flowing acres of marble, its stores named Monmartre, Georgiou, and Tahari — enough tang in the shopping to erase the onus of mere *mall* — and its high-vaulted Winter Garden, ten stories of unencumbered air, topped with glass, and filled with forty-foot palm trees from Arizona. All this splendor was lodged indoors, yet it opened up brilliantly to the sun. You stepped out of the Winter Garden into the piazza surrounding a marina, taking the wind in your face on a clear day, and the light was overpowering. The Statue of Liberty was out there in the bay, and the combination of distance and open sky — an open view was so rare in New York — was enormously stirring, for suddenly all of America with its extraordinary promise and bounty came rushing over you. It was the most Whitmanesque view in the city, even better than the Brooklyn Bridge seen at dusk.

I went down there in late October to see Henry Blodget, who worked in the North Tower of the center, where Merrill Lynch had its headquarters. The Nasdaq was falling and falling, coming close to 3000, recovering and then dropping again, but as I walked through the complex for the first time, scuffing the acres of marble, I thought of nothing but the wealth of the United States. It was a very plain notion, and I enjoyed the childish simplicity of it for a moment. We were enormously rich. You didn't always remember *how* rich until you got off at an airport somewhere and saw the huge industrial parks on the way into town, the skyscrapers in cities like Pittsburgh, Cleveland, or Cincinnati, the Denver airport, the modern polymer complex in dreary

Akron, the vast irrigated San Joaquin–Sacramento valley in California, where you could grow anything, the converted loft spaces and new hotels and conference centers south of Market Street in San Francisco. Or maybe you realized it when you drove out to the shrubbed suburbs, with their parks and playing fields and Volvos and expanses of upscale shopping. Juliet Schor might be too much of a prig to enjoy any of this, but there was no doubt that many people, and not just the top one percent, got pleasure from the overwhelming wealth — pleasure that was now hitting me so hard, flooding in with the light on the piazza behind the center, precisely when some of the wealth was drying up. The economy was turning down, hundreds of billions of value was vanishing from the Nasdaq, and Henry Blodget was in the doghouse as a false creator of value, a trumpet-blower for a paper army.

"Mr. Blodget's New Prescription" was the subhead on a *Journal* article on October 16 devoted to the myths of the tech boom. A sobering experience, that article, since I had believed most of the myths the previous winter — that technology companies would generate enormous sales for years to come; that they were immune from interest-rate shifts; that the Internet was growing at an exponential rate; that prospects or "market share" might be more important than immediate earnings, and so on. Henry was the principal exhibit for the last fallacy.

"I didn't expect the fall would be so brutal and so fast," he said. "I didn't realize how bullish I was perceived to be, how I had become a poster child of the Internet."

I hadn't seen him since March, and not since he had become a figure of fun in the press as a bullshitter, and we met now in a food court inside the Financial Center, where we ate salad and pasta, and tried to hear each other over the din. Why were public spaces in New York so noisy? Couldn't anyone figure out some way of dampening the clatter? But they didn't want to dampen the clatter — they wanted us to howl out the joy of wealth. Henry wore a tie and white shirt, but his sleeves were rolled up; he was ready for work, and he shouted at me in his friendly way, earnest and forward-pressing as always, though perhaps a little more urgent than I remembered him. He was on the defensive these days. I was angry at him myself.

"Everything I said in the past, I still believe," he said. "If you step back and take a look, $500 billion in wealth has been created out of thin air since 1995. We're in the same place now that TV was in 1950 and radio in 1925. It took years to figure out what radio and TV could do. The same is true of the Internet. We're five years into it, and there have been many disastrous mistakes, but also great companies like AOL, Amazon, and Yahoo!"

He made the case for Amazon that I had heard him make in the past, and he went on again about the press and CNBC. He was just beginning to learn that the media beast that seems to love you, that sends you way out ahead in the race of success, builds up resentment of its fleet-footed creation and suddenly pulls you back and takes a large bite out of your flank. It puzzled him; he wasn't bitter, but he was astonished by his public reputation, almost as if there were two persons in the world, *him*, doing his work and talking to me now, and then this other figure who appeared in the public as a genius and then as a fool, getting praised and then taking hits. It was the first person that he wanted to present to me. He wanted to see an ideal version of himself in my appreciative eyes. He offered me a privileged view, and I felt almost protective of him, and I wondered how he could have been so persistent in his ratings, since he clearly wasn't stupid. I had followed him into euphoria and I didn't want him to fail.

"Back in 1998," he suddenly bellowed, "we initiated coverage of Amazon at Merrill with thirty-five pages of analysis, and the only thing that got reported was the call that the price would go to $400. It's unfair, but since we were credited for too much on the way up, it's not surprising that we're being blamed on the way down."

"What happens now?"

"Oh, the equity analyst as media star is over. We will recede back into being geeks with spreadsheets."

But this was hooey. Being a geek with a spreadsheet was not going to be enough for him. It never *is* enough once you've had a taste of fame. Still, if he was angry, the anger was well hidden from outsiders — and now, as he shouted at me in the infernal food court, I felt the same rush of warmth for him that I had felt in the past, and I hoped that somehow he would escape the furies pursuing him across the investment landscape. Were they the same furies that were pursuing my portfolio? I couldn't quite let go of him without facing the possibility that all was lost. So I welcomed his stoicism. He greeted his own eclipse without overt regret. It was part of the game, he seemed to be saying.

"What do you think went wrong?"

"Wall Street handed everybody a prepaid credit card. 'Here's $50 million, see what you can do.' People with a company said, 'I'll get 75 more.' So they built an Internet business on that basis and burned through 125, and then the next 75 wasn't there for them anymore. Meanwhile, it was amazing to me how much incest was going on in the dot-com community. Maybe $5 million of the start-up money got recycled into Scient or some other professional-services firm, maybe $10 million went to Yahoo! or AOL, five to another software provider, a couple million to Dell and Sun Microsystems. Everyone was buying everyone else's services. So now, the first one fails, and revenues disappear from the second, and it fails, too. But look, the market is working the way it was supposed to. The big capital allocation to a new industry is a sawed-off shotgun, not a laser gun. It sends capital everywhere. And now it's a shakeout."

"You're still upbeat?"

"The industry has grown through the infancy, toddler, and childhood stages, and it's had its wild teenage years, and we're just now settling into adulthood. It's very much like the beginnings of the PC industry. Most of those companies disappeared."

Companies fail, but capitalism was still invincible. With a flashing nervous smile, he suddenly got up and rushed away, running back upstairs to Merrill, and I knew he had eluded me, or at least charmed me so much that I had not quite got an answer to the question of how he could have continued to issue "buy" ratings on Internet stocks as they fell by 50 or 60 percent or more. Amid all these testimonials to the beauty of the process, he had not said what responsibility he himself bore for the dot-com bubble and the loss of investors' money. He seemed to me vaguely in a state of denial, and maybe the true split in him was not between the public and private person but, as I was beginning to realize, between the analyst working for Merrill who attracted banking business to the company and the man whose realism had earlier impressed me. The two were at odds, contradicting each other, and the Merrill employee had won out. From his point of view, I was there to record his best self, but what I saw was a man telling his bosses what they wanted to hear.

I walked back through the Financial Center. Certainly no one looking at these Roman-temple corridors would think that anything was amiss. The buildings with all their munificence of marble and glass would continue to stand even if wealth were being drained out of them. By speaking of the shakeout as healthy—in his way, he was defiant—Henry may have wanted to remain a hero of wealth, even though the world was saying his magic was gone. I felt for him—at some level I still wanted to *be* him. But I couldn't, of course, do a damn thing *for* him. Nor could I do anything for myself as the market sank, except grasp wildly at the tools of the future.

★   ★   ★

A few blocks away, at the corner of Washington and Liberty Streets, just across from the southern tower of the World Trade Center, there was a manhole cover no different from thousands of others in the city. For all I know, I might have driven over it, hearing a dull *clank* as the rubber hit the steel cover, a sound made slightly more resonant by the hollow space below. That cover was lifted off in late October, a few days after I saw Henry, and I eagerly climbed down a small steel ladder and found myself in a dark and fetid cavern beneath the street. My partner, a man named Tony Gagliatti, an employee of the Metromedia Fiber Network (one of Gilder's champs), had installed some light and a narrow wooden catwalk about five feet below the roof of the tunnel, and together we stood in a space perhaps 30 feet long, 25 feet high, and 5 to 6 feet wide. Despite Tony's hospitality, I couldn't quite stand upright — though my knees were bent, the top of my hard hat still scraped the cement above. To the immediate left and right of the catwalk there was open space and a scary drop to water below — not to sewage, but to the lordly Hudson, some of whose splendid flow had leaked into the rocky substrate of Manhattan (we were only a couple of blocks from the river). "Not many rats but lots of waterbugs," said Tony, rating the accommodations.

When I showed up at Liberty and Washington, Tony made me remove the jacket of the Italian suit I was wearing, and he gave me one of those orange going-down-the-manhole plastic vests that workmen wear in New York. The suit pants got blackened anyway, with earth, or rot, or whatever it is that collects underground. What, exactly, was I looking for down there? I was sick of George Gilder's metaphysical speculations about the bandwidth revolution. For weeks, I had been thinking that I needed to see the *stuff*, something I could touch and bend, a nugget in my hand and not just a promise.

This particular cavern had neither power nor gas lines but

only communication wire. On both of the long walls, and extending all the way down to the water, lay cable after cable, black, orange, yellow, red, perhaps eighty cables on each side, and as I staggered on the catwalk and held on to the cables themselves for support, I looked straight into the geological strata of New York communication going back perhaps a hundred years. Ancient telephone wire lay tangled among fairly recent coaxial cable. And something else was there, many strands of it gathered in thick cords, something very new, which would supplant all the other wire, past and present. That is what I had come to see. A bit of the network, the network to end all networks.

After about twenty minutes below, Tony and I climbed up the ladder, and he led me into Metromedia's truck, right next to the manhole, and laid some individual strands of optical fiber in my hand. Well, this was it at last. As a physical object, a single strand of optical fiber is flabbergasting—so thin that you may, for a second, have trouble seeing it at all. The strand is pure glass and colorless, flexible but sharp-pointed at the end (you don't want it stuck in your skin—you might not be able to pull it out). To get a decent look, you have to strip off a bit of the opaque plastic sheath that covers it and place the fiber against a dark surface. What you see then is no more than the width of a human hair—about 125 micrometers, or .005 inches, across the diameter. But thin as it is, the entire strand of glass is much larger than the actual working part of the fiber, a tubular core within the strand that is a mere *eight* micrometers in diameter. That's where the real action takes place (what surrounds the core is a cladding of thicker glass that serves as a mirror containing and reflecting the light).

Tony told me what happens inside the core. A laser generates a pulse of light (on-off; on-off), and the light waves, trapped by the core and the surrounding cladding, race down the strand like a bullet train, though one has to add that the waves come a good deal faster than a train and faster than Superman, too, so therefore much faster than a speeding bullet — fast enough, and with enough capacity, to carry anything that we might conceivably speak, write, draw, compose, design, count, photograph, film, videotape, or play, and all in the impatient snapping of a finger. Philip Roth's complete works zipped to Turkestan almost as fast as Portnoy could think a dirty thought! Yes, this was what we wanted, this was what we would achieve! The vision couldn't be killed by a Nasdaq downturn.

"Let me give you a real piece," Tony said, and unraveled a generous length of cable from a spool, and I put it in my briefcase and carried it around with me, for the moment a happy man. I had in my possession something material, sheathed in yellow plastic, that was perhaps as capable as any invention in human history, my arterial line to the future of commerce and culture. With that strand in the briefcase, I saw myself as a traveler along the network. The market might have been in retreat, but I was moving forward. It was pretty obvious what the next stop should be.

When Corvis's price jumped from an offering of 36 in July 2000 to a momentary high of 114 a couple of weeks later, investors were giving a vote of confidence to one man, Dr. David Huber, CEO and founder of the company. Huber, who holds forty-one patents in the optical field, had invented wavelength-division multiplexing — the technology that so remarkably increased the carrying power of fiber — at the optical equipment manufacturer Ciena, in the early nineties. After a dispute with Ciena's board, Huber left with $300 million in stock. He founded his new company in 1997, not far from Ciena, establishing a "campus" in Columbia, Maryland, in the kind of posh corporate scientific and technological community in which low-rise offices and manufacturing plants lie hidden behind trees and sculpted shrubbery. A blander setting for revolution could not possibly be imagined.

From the beginning, Huber had announced ambitious plans for an all-optical suite of switches, routers, amplifiers, and re-generators—a one-stop solution for carriers trying to upgrade their ultra-long-haul networks or build superior new ones. The only thing known in July, before Corvis's initial public offering, was that a couple of carriers, Broadwing and Williams, had suc-cessfully tested the entire suite, and that Corvis's equipment had sent signals 3,200 kilometers through Williams's network with-out electrical regeneration—about six times farther than any-one had been able to do up to that point. I was disturbed by Huber's habits of secrecy, but the news leaking out was encour-aging enough for me to buy the stock, and I thought of him as another example of the enterpreneur I had been looking for. He was just as much a gambler as Sam Waksal, but unlike Sam, he had a proven track record.

Encountered in his Maryland industrial park, Huber, forty-nine, was tall, with a long face and thinning light brown hair. He was educated at Oregon State and Brigham Young University, and when I went to see him, he met me in a beigy-brown CEO's office so plainly furnished—technical journals, a globe in a brass holder—that it seemed like a set for a public-televi-sion show from about 1962. He seemed less a pioneer than a sci-ence teacher who had won a regional award for using advanced plastic models in his tenth-grade class. A straight arrow, then, though arrogant to the point of imperviousness. When he talked about Corvis's technology, a boyish smile broke out on his face. I asked him about the company's valuation approaching that of General Motors, and he grinned at me and said, "Look, we've increased the capacity of fiber by 16,000 in four-and-a-half years, which has produced an enormous decrease in networking cost. If you look back at what General Motors has done in that time, it's probably not much—their cars are only marginally better and sell at pretty much the same price. At our rate of declining cost, the Corvette would cost about ten dollars."

Yeah, well . . . That was a semi-meaningless analogy, since the car at any price was sufficient to get you around town, whereas Huber's optical suite, to be of any use at all, had to fit into a matrix of buyers and users—a clearly defined atmosphere of demand. Huber wouldn't reveal to me the technology of the switch, which would soon hit the market. But I asked to see the damned thing and was taken to the doors of a locked and secured facility. Led at last into this sanctum sanctorum, I was astonished. Silent men and women in blue lab coats worked rapidly amid the roar of an amazingly powerful air-conditioning system. No public-TV-set blandness here. I was suddenly immersed in a bristling sci-fi atmosphere—an industrial melodrama, an optical hot zone. What were they chilling and hiding in there? The switch itself, including the equipment necessary to get traffic in and out of it, filled four standard telecommunications racks—yellow plastic racks seven feet high and about three feet deep. People buzzed around it, as in a corny B-movie from 1956. So the switch was large, much larger than some rival switches I had heard about. But it had greater capacity, too, with six ports, each channel handling as many as 160 multiplexed wavelengths at once.

In ultra long haul, a potentially multibillion-dollar market, Corvis was possibly the asteroid that crushes all the other companies. Yet no one could really be sure. Corvis got there first, but it had numerous competitors who were threatening to release equipment in the coming years that could handle even higher transmission rates. "There's a big advantage in being first, but the technology is changing very rapidly," said Huber, sighing, and I realized with a shock that even this blandly imposing industrial-scientific whiz was not assured of success. Was his blandness a mask of panic? Why wouldn't he reveal his technology? Since I owned the stock, I wasn't too happy about his remark, and I was astonished that a company which had recently attained a market capitalization in the tens of billions might actually be just as much a projection of hope as a dot-com selling monogrammed toilet paper or patent-leather cheerleader's shoes.

Back in New York, and on the job as critic, I wanted to get happy again. But as I traveled about that fall, carrying my talismanic strand of fiber-optic cable in my briefcase, the conglomerate waves, flowing in and out, catching critics in their tidal flows and dumping them in the surf, was offering nothing of special value. The great hope in the fall of 2000 was Cameron Crowe's *Almost Famous,* an autobiographical account of Crowe's teenage years in the 1970s as a reporter for *Rolling Stone.* As a fifteen-year-old, Crowe had hung out with a mediocre road band and partied with groupies, and though the picture was made with great affection, it was too mild by half. Where were the balls out there in H'wood? The thrillers might have been viciously exciting, the spectaculars full of explosions, but the real-life movies were usually soft as lambskins. As always, I was looking for the artistic success that also made contact with a large audience. But I couldn't be a player on *Pay It Forward,* either, which offered, by way of consolation in this period of collapsing markets, a sentimental myth of benevolence — a smart little boy who devises a scheme of altruism in which a given person helps another for no reason at all and then insists that that person help three *other* people. Soon the drug addicts and alcoholics are turning into saints. It's a provocative theme, and a morally curious writer or director might have done something with it. If people are generally out for themselves, altruism becomes a kind of spontaneous ethic — random grace in a dog-eat-dog world. But *Pay It Forward* was a bad movie — it

212

sentimentalized its own naïveté. Anyway, this was a rich society and, at times, a generous one, but it was not benevolent. No, as sociologist Robert Lane and others said, When you fell, you *fell.* Precariousness was our daily bread.

Illusions curdled in the autumn air. The market was declining rapidly, and one by one the beliefs that investors had lived by were disappearing. Abby Joseph Cohen, of Goldman Sachs, herald of the bull for five years, whose confident words had sent the market up on many occasions, was quoted as saying the S&P 500 was 15 percent undervalued, only to have the index in subsequent days drop 5 percent more. Cohen and the others waved their wands, and nothing happened. As the weeks went by, and October turned into November, it became clear that investors had become convinced that companies were simply not going to deliver on the level of profitability that they had once promised. In this period, forty-six Internet companies alone issued warnings of slowing revenue, and such first-tier tech outfits as Intel, Microsoft, Lucent, Amazon, and Yahoo! slipped way down from their highs. The ax swung again. Doubts that had been growing since the previous April gathered together and tumbled into outright skepticism. Corporations had overinvested in technology and were cutting back. And many people now reasoned as follows: Of what use was a dot-com's dominant "share" of a given market if that market was minuscule? Share of *what?* The questions that had been postponed, scorned, or deemed irrelevant in the winter were now pressed harder and harder.

I went to the office, went to screenings, wrote my reviews, took care of the boys, and refused to sit glued to the set. And as I moved around, I noticed again what I had experienced back in April, when I went away with R during the first big slide — a curiously dead feeling inside, a numbness as the market fell through empty space like a body dropping down an elevator shaft. Of course it was *my* body that was dropping. But what I felt was no more than a distant grief, an ache of helplessness. At some level, I was still hoping that the slide would stop. I refused to believe that what I feared was happening really was happening.

Now and then, there were flickers of life, and through it all we never suffered a catastrophic day like October 28, 1929, when the Dow fell 23 percent and the margin buyers were slaughtered and some 4,000 banks ran out of cash and defaulted on their savings accounts. No, nor anything as awful as October 19, 1987, when the Dow fell 22.6 percent and some stocks couldn't find buyers and liquidity disappeared. Still, by late November, the results after many days of selling were just as devastating. On November 22, 2000, the Nasdaq landed at 2755, down 1500 points since early September, the drop worsened by the lingering uncertainty about the outcome of the presidential election, which was up for grabs amid chads and chumps in Florida. Everything, it seemed, was bringing the market down. Greenspan was bringing it down with his rate increases. Projections of slower growth in tech stocks were bringing it down. The mess in Florida was bringing it down. The market was crashing.

As it crashed, irony took bloody revenge on memory.

We were sure a year earlier that advertising on the 'Net would be a goldmine. *No, it was a bust, taking Yahoo! and AOL–Time Warner down with it.* The gauchos in Argentina, as my friend Rothstein and I believed, were dying for cell phones. *Maybe, but the infrastructure to build wireless was too expensive for the amount of demand.* Okay, but why aren't hyped new inventions generating mass purchases — handheld devices, for instance? *Well, they're selling, but only for a few hundred dollars.* For more than a decade, over a hundred million PC units a year were sold at $1,000 or more. These new consumer products were too inexpensive to provide the same bonanza. And so on, the ax swinging with a slight whistling in the air.

As for the network to end all networks: Just as the *Journal* had warned before the Telecosm Conference, the telephone carriers who had to pay for much of it had rung up billions of dollars of debt while building capacity and were now desperate to make adequate returns on their huge investments. They were buying much less. Catch-22: As bandwidth abundance increased rapidly, competition drove the cost of it to buyers down to about one-tenth of the price four years earlier. It was just as Gilder had said — bandwidth would eventually be almost free. But why didn't the guru of technological redemption realize that if bandwidth was "free," some of the manufacturers he was lauding would rapidly begin to lose revenue? Unacknowledged by Gilder, a lamentable "glut" of fiber sat in the ground, millions of miles, and much of it was "unlit" (i.e., unused). Meanwhile, the last-mile problem went largely unsolved, with only a fraction of Americans bothering to sign up for broadband connections at home. The access to home was still largely clogged — and the promised delivery of movies and opera and whole libraries of data and technical information still postponed to an indefinite future.

At last, at Thanksgiving, I put up my hand and stopped the shaft of the swinging ax, waving it out of consciousness.

We were placed in a semi-enclosed chamber at one side of the main dining room, a room of our own away from the general clatter — "The Library," it was called, a book-lined haven in the Andover Inn in Massachusetts. The walls were filled with the kind of forgotten tomes one finds only in the old places — novels by the once-famous, now as grievously ignored as the gods of vanished civilizations, J. P. Marquand and Joseph Hergesheimer and William Saroyan, and also the kind of book that you couldn't imagine anyone actually reading at any time. There was a study of the rural economy of China published in

1936; a book about the curious efflorescence of bitternut hickory and red pine trees on Massachusetts mountains. Most books slid into the past slowly but inexorably, like abandoned stations on a disused railroad line.

It was a time to celebrate one's own survival—Thanksgiving 2000. They were all there, Cathy and the boys, and also my mother-in-law, still beautiful at seventy-two, with red hair and a big smile, and her grouchy, intelligent second husband, and her sister, and her sister's children, and Cathy's brother and his wife and *their* children, all dressed up and talking at once, while my two boys grew tipsy from the weak sparkling rosé they sipped between disapproving appearances by the waiters. Finally the manager arrived. He curtly informed us that we were in violation of the laws of the Commonwealth. If the young gentlemen drank any more wine, we would all be thrown out. The boys turned their sipping into a game to see how much they could swallow without being spotted.

It was not an ideal Thanksgiving banquet. No, it was a routine, mass-produced Mass-inn banquet: sweet apple cider; pumpkin soup with a cream base followed by lettuce-and-tomato salad; sliced turkey with a flour gravy and stuffing and cranberry sauce; whipped and sweet potatoes and pearl onions and butternut squash and little side orders of those knobby big peas they serve in New England inns, all of it delivered with baskets of cornbread and muffins and topped off with multiple desserts—sherbet or ice cream with raspberry sauce, Indian pudding, and either pumpkin pie or apple pie à la mode. Outside "The Library," in the main dining room, an ancient pianist hunched over his Steinway played fifties pop standards. The men, many of them solemn old boys with creased faces, wore green plaid, the women wore white or flowered dresses with heavy jewelry at their throats and wrists. It was a traditional event, square even, a refuge from the tormenting present. Both

216

Bushes, *père et fils*, had gone to school right there, at Phillips Academy — or Andover, as everyone called it.

Yet it was the ideal banquet anyway. Let us say the routine sublime of Thanksgiving. Because here it was: I looked around the table, and the children were healthy, we had good jobs, and the country was not at war. The moment lasted, and I savored it a great deal more than the knobby peas. The economy, despite an obvious slowdown, was not in recession and might pick up again. The banquet itself, however lumpish as food, was an example of the extraordinary American plenitude. I looked around, and I knew that my wife's mother, brother, and aunt wanted me to remain part of the family forever.

In a market crash, one returned to the basics. We were all okay; we had work to do; the market could not destroy my life. As the gathering broke up, everyone a little bloated from the gravy and corn bread, I pulled some of the old books off their shelves and gazed in wonder at the faded irrelevant pages, produced by an effort no less feverish than our own, an effort long obliterated by the rushing ticker of the current moment, and the next moment, and the next. Unless reputations radically changed, these books could no longer be saved, but our own books might be preserved before they slid into oblivion. Market slowdown or not, technology, which in its onward rush hustled and pressured the present, was now the only likely way of saving what became the past, and I would not let go of it.

22

Poof!

THE year 2000 ended with a taste of real happiness amid the general disintegration. Steven Soderbergh had come through again — twice in one year. In the full tide of the Christmas season, as half a billion dollars of imagery and publicity washed ashore, knocking critics and audiences off their feet, the wonderful movie *Traffic* opened to general acclaim. It was a more intricate and daring picture than *Erin Brockovich*. I wrote that it offered "an astoundingly vivid and wide-spanning view of the drug war — high and low, dealer and user, Mexican and American — and the ambiguity of its many encounters is a good part of its meaning. In the drug world, no one is quite what he seems: greed and hunger change human character as acid changes virgin soil." Well, now, that last phrase didn't pop out of the ether — my preoccupations had linked up with a powerful strain in a good movie. When I saw *Traffic*, however, I laid aside, at least for a while, my ambition and anxiety. Here was Soderbergh expressing himself fluently, as an artist, in a complicated and rather pessimistic thriller made for a sizable audience. Occasionally the artists would win, which meant the critics won, too, and the crazy big-money operation of movies made sense — at least for a time. From a distance, I sent Soderbergh a blessing, tasting his victory for as long as I could. *Someone* had to crash through.

As opposed to just crashing. On and on it went. But with teasing interludes. Early in December, on the fourth, Alan Greenspan had hinted, merely hinted, that the Fed might consider an interest-rate cut in the coming months, and on the same day, the Florida circuit court seemed to resolve the presidential election. And so, like a dying man who tears off his bandages and leaps from his bed in one final effort to assert himself, the Nasdaq composite index, on the following day, jumped an astonishing 274 points, or 10.5 percent. Obviously there were still some hardy folk around who (unlike me) had fresh money to put in the tech sector. It was by far the largest one-day point and percentage gain in the history of the exchange. Just as in the old days, I stayed at home, watching CNBC pump the thing up.

The boys and girls of financial reporting had lost their shine and part of their audience; they were no longer pop culture darlings. Many people now believed that they were part of the lurching irrationality of the market. When the market went up, they were accused of hype and of indulging CEOs in shameless optimism. When it went down, they were accused of overzealousness for a clear-cut story and of pushing the negatives too hard. That is, they were so eager for the story that they became part of the story, depressing the market further. Everyone was using them quite unfairly as scapegoats, including me, and in recent months, as the market slid, I had wanted to strangle them, one at a time, starting with Joe Kernen, whose sardonic tone I was finding more and more enraging, and ending with the all-too-incisive Liz Claman, who had a cold clear intelligence that drove the nail home. But on December 5, 2000, as the Nasdaq jumped, I was in no mood to criticize, and they all seemed like princes of wit, and every now and then, taking deep, satisfying breaths, I would walk away from my media companions, plump myself down on the living-room couch, and think, At last! At last! For surely the resurrection was at hand.

Blasphemy, because nothing was at hand. The very next day, the index slid 90 points, and I realized, with a little prodding from the *Journal*, that dying markets always produced these sudden one-day eruptions. But only one day each time. Investors were not buying on dips, as they had done in the past, but were selling on rises, trying to recoup some of their losses. In the vile jargon of the Street, the one-day spike and subsequent collapse was a "dead-cat bounce." *Ho! Humor!* The dead cat, you see, lands a second time, and it bounceth no more. A bull market, by contrast, doesn't bounce; it goes up slowly and steadily.

About two weeks later, I left the office and walked up Fifth Avenue and stopped at Rockefeller Center, close to the spot where, eight months earlier, I had been struck dumb with amazement by the summer-night-blue handsomeness of an Audi A6. The usual enormous Christmas tree loomed over the ice-skating rink, a Norway spruce 90 feet tall and lit with 30,000 bulbs. The tree was heralded, in the narrow plaza leading toward Fifth Avenue, by rows of glass angels blowing their long-stemmed golden trumpets: Christ had appeared on earth. More to the immediate point, shoppers had appeared in New York. I was a sucker for this traditional Manhattan pomp. I remembered my parents taking me to see it, a little boy in a cap, fifty years earlier, and now I joined the shoppers who were pressed together and shouted and laughed with that peculiar dazed jubilation of New York at winter holiday time. As I looked at the tree, I got jostled by families, banged in the knees by shopping bags. I was a little out of it. A camera on a leather strap swung into my middle; a drunken dad, lurching my way, clipped me on the elbow.

POOF! read an enormous headline in the *Journal* of December 18. And the subhead said: " 'Smart' Investment Ideas Go Up in Smoke, as Market Tumbles." *Poof!* It was a brilliant headline, but the merry sound of it was like a knife in the side. I had lost money—*their* money, the money belonging to the family that would gather in the apartment on Christmas Day. I had not killed my wife, or tried to. But I had wasted her assets (as well as my own), just as the would-be murderer John Nyquist had wasted Kate's money.

12/22/00

I have slipped, by degrees, into a minicatastrophe. And what hurts most of all is that I *knew*—I knew about the delusions, the *tulpen-woerde*, the South Sea disaster. I knew, and was convinced that this time it was different and that Kindleberger's paradigm of folly was not our story. For this was the era of *new wealth!* Hope and greed are such commanding emotions that I filtered, censored, and abolished what I didn't want to hear, and when the boom collapsed, I hoped that tech would right itself. There was never any single moment when the direction was clear and I listened again to those I wanted to listen to. After all, many strategists at the beginning of the year predicted solid gains, and continued to do so all year long, right until the conflagration in the fall.

Chagrin lifted at Christmas. We all gathered at the apartment, where our own big fir, scraping the nine-foot ceiling, was mounted in its metal base. We threw aspirin into the water so the green would stay green, and the boys, driven on by the *Nut-cracker Suite*—their sparkling annual promise of good times—

stood on a ladder and trimmed the tree. By Christmas morning, it was covered up to its skirts with Gap jeans, a Nintendo Gamecube, Polo shirts, L. L. Bean fleeces, books, Dave Matthews CDs, ties, slacks, shaving kits—the usual heaping American mound. On that day, as on all others, no fighting took place between separated husband and wife. No one asked the boys to choose sides. There were some things you didn't stoop to, no, not even when you were losing a fortune. Especially when you were losing a fortune.

The last trading day of the year was December 29, and at the close, the Dow was down 6.18 percent for the year (not so bad), the S&P 500 index was down 10.14 percent, and the Nasdaq . . . the Nasdaq was down 39.29 percent. It closed at 2470, a total of 1598 points down, the worst performance since the new exchange was created in 1971, and the worst for any major index since 1931. It had dropped almost 33 percent just from the beginning of October, 45 percent since the beginning of September, wiping out $3 trillion in value.

It turned out that such Old Economy sectors as health care had done okay in 2000. In fact, many sectors of the market were okay—this was no general rout. It was tech that collapsed, *my* sector, and the terrible news was pouring in from all sides. Encouraged by possibilities for vast new markets, companies had fallen into bad habits that Wall Street encouraged, such as valuing sales growth over profitability, adding employees and building factories in expectation of limitless demand. In the *Times*, the young market reporter Alex Berenson pointed out that technology and telecommunications companies had raised $330 billion from American investors and venture capitalists in 2000, about $1,200 for every American. Corporations had then invested far too much in software, storage, Internet infrastructure; they didn't *need* all that stuff. They had been suckered by the same illusions that I had been suckered by. A lot of the capital investment would prove to be uneconomic—yielding little in the way of profits. So fresh orders were drying up, and the stocks of the manufacturing companies were now paying for excessive optimism.

The ax had swung, and heads lay all over the ground. For once, I could not claim that irrationality or Alan Greenspan was the villain. Tech had been driving the boom for the last ten years, and now a slowdown, maybe even a recession, was at hand.

Among my own stocks, JDSU, which I bought at 128 3/4, was down to 41; Broadcom, purchased at 233, was down to 84; Corvis, bought at 63 and 60, was down to 23; Internet Capital Group, the Internet incubator, had fallen from 120 to $3.28 a share. And funds, too: Fidelity OTC was off almost 27 percent, Alger Capital Appreciation 28.3 percent, Van Kampen Emerging Growth by 14.1 percent, and so on. ImClone had fallen from a high of 88 to 44, but we were still in the black and I had high hopes for it.

God grant peace to our vanities; 2000 was the year in which I was going to make a million. I had not quite done so. From the high in early March, we had lost, on paper, about $400,000. For the entire year, we had lost around $155,000. I couldn't see how I was going to buy out Cathy's share of the apartment. But I still hoped, as I cleared away the needled and tinseled remains of the Christmas tree from the living room, that somehow, some way, the whole thing would come back to life in 2001.

PART II

THE YEARS 2001 AND 2002 — LOSING MONEY

23

Pants on Fire

Quarterly Report, January 1, 2001
Cumulative Net Loss $155,000

ARTHUR Levitt was right: A prolonged downturn kills your interest. You can't open those magazines. Never, never again this amazed attention to Maria Bartiromo assailed by traders as she held the floor of the Exchange like Horatio at the bridge. I hoped that the stock market would come back, but I could not follow it closely, could not go there anymore. I was not pulling out of the market, but I was pulling myself out of obsession. But what, then, was my goal? Tech slowdown or not, I was still charging into the future, an eager student led by Sam Waksal and David Huber and by the halfway-discredited Henry Blodget and George Gilder. Disappointed as I was with the last two, I wanted them to remount their steeds and keep going.

Not yet unhoused, I could still play for time. I could hold on to the apartment for now. I resisted Cathy's request that we sell and split up the money. What was the hurry? A common bank account was an easier way of taking care of the boys. The real-estate market was high, maybe going higher, why rush the sale?—and I told myself that maybe, just maybe, I could still buy her out. She was willing to wait—guilty, perhaps, for the hurt she had caused and not wanting to make it worse. In any case, I would not sell, and I clung to the olive-drab couches as if they were the ancestral turf itself. There was nothing out there, no place to live, no future, beyond my house.

Though there was a woman, at last.

My new friend had two young children, and she held to them with a tigress's strength, but she was also stranded in a marriage that had gone sour. We had to skulk about, and I wasn't crazy about it. No home wrecker by temperament or inclination, I was nevertheless desperate for company—her company. We greeted each other like long-lost friends who were astonished by their good luck in finding each other after so many missing years. Where have you been all this time? It was if we had known each other in the past, in some earlier existence—a notion which has, I know, a mystical and synthetic sound, but that's the way it felt. The relief from loneliness was one of the most ardent elements of the affair—my relief, certainly, for she was warm-spirited, she was plugged in to everything in the world, in the arts, in her family and the lives of her friends. A real dynamo, she would bound out of bed early in the morning, bake cakes, make a half-dozen phone calls, work for hours, invite people over and feed them, do stuff with the kids, and start all over again the next day. A hardworking, loving, virtuous person. I had entered the affair reluctantly, though in the end I became the eager one, hoping for a lifelong connection, even a new marriage. I needed her, and I plunged ahead, though I knew at some level that it was screwed up, it was wrong—a mistake even if one says to oneself that the two of you deserve happiness and can make a new union better than the old ones.

In adultery, everything one tells oneself has the taint of self-justification. The motto of Dreiser's hero Frank Cowperwood, "I satisfy myself," may be a stirring creed, but it was hard to maintain in upper-bourgeois New York, where not only the walls but the doormen and mailmen have ears, and skulking about was less a thrill than a constant risk of exposure. The paths in the enormous city were shockingly narrow for people of like-minded temperament and habits. You couldn't go to the movies together without being spotted on Broadway by some friend passing in a taxi. There was right and wrong to consider, families to consider. And there was getting caught to consider, too, and all the messes and unhappiness that would follow in the wake of it.

Was I pulling myself together, or falling apart still more? At times I wasn't sure. The relationship began at the end of 2000 and blossomed in early 2001, and it was picking up speed, on Thursday, January 3, when the Fed delivered an emergency cut of one-half percent in the federal funds rate. The move occurred between official meetings—three weeks before the next scheduled rate-setting confab—and the markets were cattle-prodded into life by the cut, which was announced at 1:13 P.M. By closing time, the Dow was up by 2.8 percent, the S&P 500 by 5 percent, and the Nasdaq, really taking off, climbed 14.2 percent, or 325 points, a much larger jump than the previous one-day record, which had been set only a month earlier on December 5, 2000. Was this surge an illicit pleasure—a relief from pain—or the beginning of something sustained?

The Fed move was widely seen as an admission that it had overreacted in 2000 to the possibility of an overheating economy, and in particular as an admission that the final rate increase, by half a percent in May 2000, was a serious mistake. "They tried too hard to bring down asset values, too," I said to myself, still

229

sore over Greenspan's odd speech and odd reasoning almost a year earlier. So this was Greenspan's mea culpa, and his gift to the market. I rushed home from the office and, despite my resolve never to watch CNBC, enjoyed the jump on television. But I was wised up about one-day spikes: *I won't fall for that one again.* And sure enough, despite some pleasant sessions, the market was nervous. The implications of Greenspan's emergency move were obvious. Mea culpa or not, what really concerned him was not the market but the fear that the economy was slipping into a recession. If tech spending had fueled the boom all through the nineties, a drop in tech spending could put us into a tailspin.

1/08/01

If I could only get back to where I was a year ago! Only to get back! But that's 2600 points higher in the Nasdaq, and it's gone, gone, and may take years to return. To sell, then? To sell now? Technology is explosive, and an enormous amount of money is waiting on the sidelines. To sell would be to lock in losses and cut out the chance of gain as that money went back in. Investments, once liquidated, are rarely made again, until too late. You never really know when to get back in, do you?

Had I been weak, crazy? I accepted the doctrines of the nineties: Buy and hold for the long run. Robert Shiller was right: The armature of delusion is virtue.

Chagrin was followed by disillusion, and disillusion by anger, snapping at disillusion's heels. What had we swallowed, what had we believed in? The Internet, it was now clear, was less a revolution than a superb tool. Advertisers hadn't any idea how to use it. Magazine ads were often sensuously beautiful, and TV ads were funny, but most people considered on-line advertising an annoyance and a distraction. Internet users were balky and spoiled. Requests for subscription fees were annihilated by the early sixties idealism of free content—with a few exceptions, people won't pay. And many *like* store shopping, they enjoy the elaborate flirtation and seduction built into the activity—handling goods, putting them back, taking them up again, caressing, examining, rejecting, accepting. The young entrepreneurs had assumed everyone was as impatient as they were. But for many people, shopping was a form of desire. And satisfying one's desire took time.

In February, my friend's husband took the children away for a long weekend, and I stayed in the family apartment for three days. The two of us were tempting fate, and fate, often lazy and inattentive, on this occasion roused itself and demonstrated a considerable gift for comedy. I brought a suit with me to the apartment, a fine gray pinstripe from Barneys, and wore it on Saturday morning to a bar mitzvah. My wife was there—I hadn't seen her in weeks, though we still talked all the time—and many close friends, too, and at the reception after the service, surrounded by happy families, I felt a little uneasy. The suit seemed not to fit very well that day. Whatever else it is, a bar mitzvah becomes the community's way of celebrating the success of a family. The thirteen-year-old boy performs, and everyone basks in his moment, glorying in the sense of well-being provided by family love. Arriving back at my friend's house, I took off the suit—my formal acknowledgment of membership in the celebration—and hung it up in the front-hall closet. And there it stayed. When I left for home on Monday, carrying my laptop, a bag of clothes, and a gym bag, I forgot all about the gray pinstripe. All week long it sat in the closet, unnoticed by my friend, until it was discovered by her husband the following weekend.

How could I have forgotten the suit all week? And how could

my friend not have noticed it? Was this some sort of new, Jewish form of adultery in which the participants acted in such a way as to be caught? Had the bar mitzvah, a celebration of family well-being, clothed the suit in invisibility until just that moment at which my friend's husband, the head of a family, was ready to notice it? Adultery, which is said to be an intermittent element in the majority of American marriages, was a furtive, lying way of life at best, but to be caught in so idiotic a manner was to turn a serious love affair into a scene in an inferior French farce. *Le pantalon dans l'armoire*, by Jean-Jacques Haut-Fatigué. After the discovery of the garment, there had been many words between husband and wife. And many words between wife and boyfriend. By the end of winter, the love affair was sinking fast. Skulking about was an art, or at least a craft, and if you couldn't master it, you were better off listening to the conventional morality that Cowperwood scorned. Had I become cynical? What about love? When families and children are involved, love is enmeshed in a web of relations and loyalties and money and real estate. The only way it can be "free" is if you leave guilt and shame behind in a closet rather than a Barneys suit. Again, I was clearly not in the same league as the super-financier Frank Cowperwood, and maybe that was not so bad. My friend was not going to end her marriage; she did not want to hurt her children, and although I fought to keep the affair going, even fought quite hard, part of me was also sure that she should not hurt the children. I eventually got my suit back, but the affair faded. The connection was vital, but we were both too burdened to ride it out to the end.

It turned out that I was not the only one leaving a suit in a closet. All over town, telltale pairs of pants were suddenly hanging in full view. The bubble having burst, the market was scraping bottom—the Nasdaq down to 2053 on March 9, having

232

fallen 60 percent from the high a year earlier—and examples of hanky-panky were surfacing all over the place. Ever since the end of 2000, the press had been exposing the impostures of the tech entrepreneurs and the financial community, and the exposure was taking the market down even faster. Gretchen Morgenson of the *Times,* rampaging through the business section of the paper in 2001, made a catalog of swindles and outrages. Morgenson accused the stock analysts of salesmanship; she implied they were little more than shills for the banking section of the great brokerage houses. After all, Merrill Lynch and Morgan Stanley made serious money issuing bonds and underwriting stock offerings. And the serious money for an analyst, it turned out, came in the year-end bonus that reflected the analyst's success not in making accurate predictions on stock prices and assisting brokers but in attracting banking to the firm. How could these men and women offer objective advice? They couldn't recommend *selling* a company that might do business with the house—not if they wanted to hold on to their jobs, they couldn't. Anyway, no one was about to pay them $10 million or more a year (which is what the best ones got) for mere analysis. The Internet and tech analysts, Morgenson implied, had been inventing spurious new criteria for valuing stocks, criteria that had no basis in reality but that served as justification for the continued buy ratings, whose real purpose was to keep the bankers at the house happy.

For some time, I had been fighting off Morgenson's reporting—I didn't want to know this stuff—but I couldn't do it anymore. Analysts like Henry Blodget issued ratings; the companies in question tapped the equity and debt markets; the officers of those companies received options and sold their shares at enormous profit. And, at the end of 2000, as stock prices collapsed, the analysts cleaned up on their bonuses, and the ordinary investors who had taken their ratings literally got dropped into a void. It suddenly appeared to be a racket, a fixed game, and Henry, along with Mary Meeker of Morgan Stanley and Jack Grubman of Salomon Smith Barney, were among the prime players.

More pants in the closet. In March, John Cassidy, the congenital bear at *The New Yorker,* the man who, a year earlier, had hissed at me, "You will lose your money," now dropped by my little windowless office. With great amiability, Cassidy said, "I don't mean to be flip. I realize you've lost a lot." He went on to say that one of the reasons for the bubble of the previous few years was something called vendor financing. "Let's say Lucent invests in some of the little companies that are potential customers," Cassidy said, standing sideways and talking at an angle, as he always did. "Or maybe it even gives some of its product to its customers as loans, writing it on the books as cash sales. But they aren't cash sales. They are propping up these new companies. Within the Internet, there were a lot of people buying from one another, a lot of money sloshing around within the bubble."

He didn't have to fill in the rest: When the little companies went bust, Lucent was unlikely to recover its assets — the investment had to be written off. Bubble, bubble, boil, and trouble! Companies offered stock options instead of wages and refused to consider the options as expenses. Blow it up, blow it up! It was all coming out in 2001. A company like Cisco would use the inflated price of its own shares to buy a new company. When Cisco's shares went down, both companies were in trouble. On and on it went, the behavior that I had ignored, that I had not wanted to hear about a year earlier. Good God, suppliers financing their *customers* — this was analogous to the directors of the South Sea Company loaning money to investors, who would then put up a fraction of it to buy more shares in the company. The same garbage had been happening all over again. And most of us hadn't noticed.

* ★ ★ ★

"The perennial conflict between banking and research," Henry Blodget said, as if reciting from a dreary old text, a mere playbook of clichés. "Journalists always seize on this. Yes, it *exists*. Okay? It's *true*, the banking people put enormous pressure on the analysts."

Again, I had wanted to see how Henry would respond to the relentless attacks on him. I was full of doubts myself, and at times very angry—and then each time I swallowed the anger. "Leave off, he got caught up like everyone else, he's young, he made mistakes. . . . How can you reject him without rejecting yourself?" It was hard, as I noticed in the past, very hard to get truly angry at this man. Such a fine, quick smile. But now I wondered, Is he a scoundrel, after all?

In April 2001, we met again in the food court of the World Financial Center, sitting off to one side of the dinning inferno. The noise wasn't quite so clangorous, and Henry, sleeves rolled up again, talked in long, violent rushes, almost in spasms. The stock analyst, he insisted, was pulled one way and then the other. It was the nature of the job. If he downgraded his call on a failing stock, his own brokers razzed him: "Why didn't you call it earlier?" At the same time, a big institutional client who was long on the stock—a mutual fund, say—would call and say, "Stop trying to be a hero! It's a long-term investment. It's a buy." He shaped the analysis and the calls for these institutional investors, who understood risk, not for individual investors, who were astounded, he said, when the market actually went down. He expected the institutional investors to know that the ratings were offered in a kind of code.

He was explaining himself, justifying himself, and at times a deep disappointment and gloom welled up and came bursting through his good cheer. And at other times, frowning, and as angry as he ever got, he lashed out, and I let him go on, with few interruptions, since he clearly wanted to make it all come together as a coherent defense.

"Honestly, going into last summer, I thought we'd have a shakeout in the Internet sector," he said. "I thought big stocks would fall 50 to 60 percent, the dogs 80 percent. I was *not* expecting the dogs to fall 95 percent, the big stocks 70 to 80. And I'm surprised by how widespread the devastation is. I thought Scient in consulting, Exodus in storage—at least these companies and a few others would come through. But the devastation is complete. And now the implication of the criticism seems to be that there was an in-the-know crowd of Wall Street snakes who profited from the collapse. Yes, a few shorted on the way down. But look, even the smartest institutional investors got burned. Janus got burned, and Soros, too. They got *hosed*. A lot of us were stupid."

But he was not stupid, and I said to myself that the admission of stupidity was easier and more convenient for him than an admission that he had acted cynically. Anyway, he quickly retracted the self-accusation of stupidity.

"We made *mistakes*. But now, everyone is saying that we were wrong because we had 'conflicts.' But the reason everyone was wrong was that for five years at the end of the nineties you had a rising market, and strategists and analysts who got out of it early were shamed, and the people who resisted and got on late didn't make much money. And we had an unprecedented economic situation, too: low inflation, increased productivity, world peace, globalization, and world markets. Every year, the market set new records. If you were recommending 'hold' instead of 'buy,' you were wrong, so everyone put his foot on the throttle. Even in hindsight, you do yourself a disservice if you say the collapse was obvious."

In other words—that is, putting it negatively—he got caught up, and he lost his judgment. But he reminded me, looking at me sharply, that a year ago, at the peak, he was telling everyone not to put more than 5 or 10 percent of their portfolio in so risky a sector as the Internet, and that was true, I had heard him say as much at the Infotech conference in early 2000. He had never suggested anyone do what I had done with the tech sector, and I couldn't hold him responsible for my disasters.

"All the warnings were ignored," he burst out. "We are described as cowboys shooting off six-guns. But in January 2000, at the height of the boom, we said at Merrill, 'It's time to take some money off the table.' I'm sorry now that I didn't say, 'Sell the whole Internet group, take it all off the table, and come back in two years!' But I didn't. Still, just saying that much, throwing a little cold water on the scene . . . it was amazing how much shit we took. I got death threats every night, e-mails threatening to kill me.

"People have now lost a lot of money. They can say, 'I made a mistake, I lost a lot,' or they can say, 'Somebody fucked me.' It's so much easier to say the latter. In two years, the revisionist view will be that nothing bad would have happened if the system weren't broken. But nothing would be further from the case. It was a *bubble*. This is just the way that markets behave and the way that people behave."

He spoke with patches of objectivity, but as I listened, trying to keep up with the flood of claims, I heard much that was sheer self-justification. After all, despite his warnings, he was generally bullish in 2000, and he could have altered that perception if he thought it was wrong. He could also have refused to go on television and talk about his calls. No one becomes a star in the media—and later a whipping boy in the media—unless they want to. You can always say no when they call.

Before he left, we exchanged good wishes and hopes for future luck—he winced when I told him that, on paper, I had lost a lot—and then I wandered into the Roman riches of the

World Financial Center and walked through the Winter Garden, where, a few months earlier, I had had such soothing thoughts of American wealth. But now I was furiously upset. What stuck in everyone's craw was that Henry kept promoting the damn Internet companies. If you assumed he was honest, he was just as guilty as investors of refusing to admit that markets could collapse. So what right did he have now to get sore at investors for taking his words literally? He said his words were intended for the institutional traders, but was everyone else supposed to know that and assume that the ratings were offered in code — that the reports and ratings merely winked at reality for the convenience of institutions with enormous holdings? If the institutions understood that the true evaluations were about two grades lower than the ones stated, why not simply throw away the code and use the true evaluations? No, it didn't make sense — there had to be a remaining, unacknowledged intention to deceive part of the audience with phony ratings. And that audience was the common investor — people like me. And were we now supposed to be so sophisticated as to know that he was lying and excuse it? And also enjoy his making big money —$5 million or more a year — by attracting banking business to Merrill while we lost our shirts?

Henry's explanations were more and more desperate and contradictory. He had been discredited, and there was no easy way out for him. He was in a lose-lose situation: Either he had been blind or he had been disingenuous. As I went to bed that night, in a foul mood, I wondered, What the hell did he want from me, anyway? He knew he was a figure in a book I was writing, and I suppose he wanted to come off well. He wanted to live up to my admiration of him as a man of the future, a seer with money-making ability and all the rest of that; and by not challenging him directly — after all, he could cut me off at any time — I had allowed him to think my admiration was intact. So I was being

238

slightly disingenuous, too. But that's not why I was depressed. I was sad because I had to let go of him. Despite his considerable candor, the view of him that he wanted me to hold was less accurate than the cynical idea of him in the press as a guy who mainly wanted to maximize his compensation. And though I found it hard, almost impossible, to come round to seeing him that way, I no longer had any other choice in the matter, and it hurt like hell.

24

The Cancer Show

Quarterly Report, April 1, 2001
Cumulative Net Loss $395,000

THE Brain Tumor Society was there, and so were a variety of blond convention girls, oh-so-friendly, with that dear *welcoming* smile, holding up drugs in their hands — they gave me some literature on stomach cancer. Eli Lilly, the giant drug company, was there, too, and offered ice cream at its booth, and of course, many thousands of cancer doctors had shown up, 22,000 of them, from all corners of the globe, serious, stolid-looking men in wire-frame glasses. In May 2001, hot on the trail of Sam Waksal and his cancer therapy, I was back in San Francisco, this time attending the annual three-day meeting of the American Society of Clinical Oncology. Sam's company, along with independent researchers they had employed to conduct trials, were going to make a number of crucial presentations.

Whatever my difficulties, I had jumped and landed. The future, at last, was all around me. It was on display in sessions spread out through rooms in the gigantic Moscone Center and in such nearby hotels as the Hilton, the Palace, and the Marriott. As well as the clinical sessions, there were panels and lectures and the rest of the hive-like intellectual activity of oncology. It was a branch of medicine that had become ready, in recent years, to leave its condition of semi-impotence and take off into genuine effectiveness. Outright cure of the worst forms of cancer was still remote, but many researchers spoke of patients living with cancer in the future as a manageable disease — living with it not for years but for decades, the way people live with diabetes or hypertension. There were many signs of clinical success. Yet the circus aspects of the cancer trade . . . well, it was amazing. Below-ground, in the giant exhibition halls of the Moscone Center, some 250 companies had set up display booths, complete with slides, computer games, elaborate translucent plastic panels, and all the rest of the exuberant commercial paraphernalia of an American consumer event. *Selling* cancer? In America, it seemed, there was the Automobile Show and the Boat Show, and now there was the Cancer Show. Some of the companies offered videos of patients talking calmly of their treatment. These folks smiled a lot, too. The presentations verged on black humor.

I called Cathy from the convention hall. "It's a goddamn trade show — the Cancer Show."

"Get some free samples," she said.

Sitting down in front of Lilly's ice-cream machine, I took a deep breath. Better get used to it, I thought. Only a few decades ago, the word "cancer" was whispered in tones of awe and terror. Frightening metaphors had emerged from its paradoxical nature: the form of immortality that produced death. But now the disease had been robbed of its metaphysical and satanic properties, its aura of annihilation. Cancer had become a commercial culture, its treatment packaged and sold just like anything

241

else, its terrors enmeshed in the daily traffic of capitalism. It was a ready source of cash not just for pharmaceutical companies but for graduate students, clinics, hospitals, research institutes. Gleevec, a successful biotech drug for certain strains of leukemia, had just obtained FDA approval, to universal fanfare, and Novartis, the Swiss company that manufactured the drug, was hawking it all over the exhibition floor.

I was disgusted, but also unsure of my disgust. Was the crass salesmanship necessarily a bad thing? Perhaps the very banality of the trade-show hype was a hopeful sign; maybe it was the most hopeful sign on earth. Universities and research institutes still performed the theoretical and early clinical work, but the development of the actual drugs was driven forward, as I've said, by the capital markets. The booths, the illuminated panels, the patients selling their treatment with a smile all proclaimed that the newly commodified disease would be tamed by commerce as well as by science. Cancer therapy was now pulled forward by the zipper.

Yet the process was still expensive and arduous, requiring years of trials and anywhere between $100 and $500 million in cash outlay. If a company was new and had no revenue stream to speak of, the officers of the companies—not just Sam Waksal, but most of the CEOs—had to tell their stories to investors again and again. They were like tent-show evangelists, or like Burt Lancaster in *The Rainmaker*, holding his arms up in supplication: It will happen *if only you believe it will happen*. Yet constant selling created disbelief as well as belief. Biotech drug discovery was a shaft hurled into the future, and everyone knew that some of the shafts would land on the ground with a clatter.

At the conference, ImClone was presenting the data for its colorectal cancer therapy, Erbitux, a month before the company's official submission of the material to the FDA in June 2001. The company was going to ask for "fast-track" consideration. Why "fast-track"? Because the trial sample consisted entirely of *advanced* colorectal patients — people for whom all other treatment had failed, including irinotecan, the reigning chemotherapy for the disease. These were awfully sick people — in many cases, they were dying — and the FDA was willing to speed up consideration of potential therapy. Successful treatment in ImClone's way, with Erbitux and irinotecan taken in tandem, would not cure them (it was too late for that), but it would increase the length of their survival — by six months, or perhaps longer. By presenting its results to the oncological community in San Francisco in advance of FDA submission, ImClone was reaching the customers — the medical press and investment professionals, and the doctors and researchers who would order the drug, once it was approved, for their hospitals, clinics, and private practices. These 22,000 oncologists also *bought stock,* as Sam had not failed to point out to me back in New York.

Since the company had gone public in 1991, ImClone had spent more than $200 million on Erbitux without much return. In New York, before the conference, Sam had told me in his office that ImClone had first tried the drug, in the early nineties, on animals, and had then applied to the FDA for the right to do human trials in January 1994. In January 1995, the company injected the serum for the first time into human beings. They began testing slowly, for safety, and as they proceeded, they tested each study in combination with a separate chemotherapy agent and with a gradual increase in dosage. This caused the company to use more patients than they needed. So Sam said. According to his account, ImClone had moved forward very cautiously and in collaboration with the FDA. "You don't go off half-cocked, you check with the FDA at every point," he insisted, and he gave every assurance that the drug would be approved.

In that meeting before the conference, Sam had held forth for over an hour on the workings of Erbitux, drawing diagrams, expounding the science to me with great fervor, and in as much detail as I could understand. He held forth on all the risks of failure, too, scorning companies that had floated irresponsible "stories," in which the science had made no sense, companies whose applications had ended in dismissal. Then he mentioned the trials, which had recently been concluded, and told me the results, which would be released at the oncology conference. "The best colorectal results in the history of research," he said.

"If the drug is approved," I asked, "what would be the likely revenue from it?" That is, for advanced colorectal patients alone.

"There are around 60,000 Americans each year in this situation—new patients with advanced colorectal cancer. They have failed other treatment, including chemotherapy. We'll get the sickest patients."

The treatments would go on for twenty-six biweekly periods, and the price of the injections (Erbitux was a serum) would be $1,000. I then wrote in my steno pad the following: "60,000 x 26 x 1,000," and Sam suddenly reached across the table with his long arms, grabbed the notebook, and did the multiplication. The total was $1,560,000,000. That's nearly $1.6 billion in potential gross revenue for one drug, treating one strain of cancer in its advanced stage, in only one year. Was this Sam's fantasy or an actual potential? Either way, I was flabbergasted. I had no idea that the total could reach anything like that amount. Sam smiled and laughed. This was just the beginning. Erbitux could be used on other cancers as well (ImClone was running trials on pancreatic cancer and head and neck carcinomas), and the company had several other, quite different, cancer therapies in the pipeline. So Erbitux was not its only shot. But it was surely the main shot. "We *own* colorectal cancer," Sam had said in New York. "We will be a leader in pancreatic cancer. And we will be a player in lung cancer."

★   ★   ★

He was so busy at the conference that I barely saw him — or rather, I saw his fleeing body as he rushed off to a meeting with investors or medical journalists. He raced through corridors like Groucho Marx chasing a blonde in satin, his torso sweeping low to the ground for extra speed. He entered and exited conversations quickly, seeming to come at groups of people from underneath, smiling and laughing as he rose and laid his hands on shoulders and arms. I enjoyed his scurrying entrepreneurial panache, and though I spoke to him very little, I never felt closer to him than during those hectic three days.

Over the last year or so, I had continued to visit his house, a more and more eager attendee at his evening parties. Waiters glided among the guests, pouring white and red burgundy. Rack of lamb and grilled skate came next, with arugula-and-endive salad, followed by little tarts with whipped cream and strong black coffee. In a brutally competitive city, Sam's evenings were as close to gracious and luxurious ease as social life ever got. There were fresh flowers everywhere, and, as the speaker of the evening began talking, the candles at the windows and on the tables were still burning. It was Sam's dream palace of the intellect; he had brought it off, joining together people with power and people who made art or at least journalism. I had never met anyone who so enjoyed the ritual of introduction. The proffered names were always accompanied by the most lavish praise — "the greatest paleontologist in the world, the smartest biotech analyst, the best movie critic I've ever read."

All through 2000 and 2001, as the trials went forward and rumors of good results were pushing up ImClone's stock, the glow of Sam's coming triumph attracted people to his house — not just investors, but powers in the city, celebrities, good-looking women, and literary and academic people alike. The actress Lorraine Bracco, who plays the shrink in *The Sopranos*, was a Friend of Sam. So was the Irish novelist Colm Tóibín. Martha

Stewart, large and blond, imposing in heels, and strikingly pretty at almost sixty, loomed over me at one of the parties and offered her hand and a level stare. Carl Icahn, the investor and corporate raider, was there a couple of times, and Peter Peterson, who was both the Commerce Secretary under Richard Nixon and former CEO of Lehman Brothers — those two were present when Sam gathered the wealthy investors for a power dinner with Ehud Barak. I sat at the edge of the policy conversations, an eager journalist all agog, and was bear-hugged by the former Prime Minister of Israel, who told me in his vigorous, thick-accented English to throw my notes away, this was a private affair.

Movie stars in the flesh had never done a thing for me. They wanted to talk about oil slicks. They wanted to save the whales, save the Native Americans or the Dalai Lama. They wanted to save *something*. Except for Jack Nicholson and Warren Beatty, who were too intelligent for this stuff, they were dreadfully earnest and often dull; Elie Wiesel talking about the death camps couldn't possibly have been half as serious as a Hollywood star in redemption mode. But this was different. *A private affair.* These people were not show-offs; they talked seriously because they exercised power every day. Floating out of one of Sam's evenings, warmed and satisfied, I knew I had been flattered, my head turned. As I understood from the very first time, the candles and the stage-set loft with its white and gold colors allowed people to be seen as they ideally wanted to be seen, as smart or witty or strong. The gathering of Sam's friends was a splendid hall of mirrors, and I had seen an image of myself that I liked. But what, I wondered, was I being seduced *into?* I couldn't do Sam any good — he had Carl Icahn, a major investor in the company, for serious help. I told him that I would make him a figure in a book — this book — but the claim might have sounded vague and even illusory. So many promised books never get written. What in the world did he want from me, from anyone? Belief, perhaps, and the admiration of the discriminating, each of whom must be conquered, one at a time, and then held in place.

At a Christmas party back in December 2000, Sam's overflowing sociability got a little out of hand. Downstairs, in front of the elevator on Thompson Street, no one was on duty to check invitations, and a stream of New York types, not just Sam's friends but strangers, showed up at the loft. The room seemed to be pulsing with light and noise, and with arrogant flesh, too, and I stood off to one side, a little awed by the tall men with barrel chests and abundant white hair. They stood talking to beautiful Amazonian women with golden flesh and boots rising nearly to their hips. Some of the more majestic call girls in New York, getting wind of the party, had arrived looking for dates. I believe they found a few. His eyes dancing in mock alarm, Sam seemed surprised. But it was what he wanted — wasn't it? Things almost going out of control? A slight touch of scandal? Mention in the tabloids?

He was the technology entrepreneur who would help rescue my failing portfolio. But more than that, he was a man who would do some actual good, and he would do it, startlingly, as entertainment, pulling others into the spectacle of success. I knew, of course, that he was more important to me than I was to him, for I was just one of many, many people in his enormous entourage. But there was a bond between us nonetheless. He was my hyperactive doppelgänger, the laughing mover with long arms gathering in information and cash. He had the quality essential to the most potent nectar of charm, the ability to make you think, as he talked to you, that you were the most important person in the world. And should you speak of your own projects and hopes, he would nod vigorously, completing your sentences, anticipating the brilliance of your work as it burst upon the scene. He wanted to include everyone in his triumph.

★　　★　　★

In San Francisco, the man who served as principal investigator for ImClone's Phase II trial, Dr. Leonard Saltz, of the Memorial Sloan-Kettering Cancer Center in New York, took the floor in the Moscone Center to explain the results. Saltz was short, dry, intense; he was completely matter-of-fact. To get into his trial, Saltz said, the patients needed to show "measurable metastatic colorectal cancer" and have documented evidence of failure with irinotecan, the reigning chemotherapy. He addressed us in tones of studied neutrality, without hesitation but without emphasis or heightening, either. The facts had to speak for themselves, that was the way of medical research. And I heard again the results Sam had mentioned back in New York: The patients took Erbitux and irinotecan in tandem, 120 of them, and the results were that 27 of the 120 had shown a "partial response," which means a reduction in tumor size by 50 percent or more. That's an efficacy rate of 22.5 percent. In other words, 27 of the 120 would live some months more. It wasn't a cure (none had been promised), but it was the first serious blow against a disease in its final, murderous phase. Nothing like it had ever been achieved before with advanced colorectal cancer. And the implication of the trial results was that patients treated at a much *earlier* stage of their disease would show a much better rate of response (though this possibility had to be separately tested for the FDA). Saltz answered a few questions, and there was a buzz in the hall, a definite buzz. Such, I thought, is the sound of cannon fired in a medical revolution.

Outside the hall, Sam ran past me in his Groucho low-to-the ground scamper, moving from one group of doctors to another, answering questions, laying on hands, laughing and gossiping. "The press loved it, and the oncologists are going crazy," he said. "ImClone is the talk of the convention." He was right: The *Times* and the *Journal* ran pieces the following Monday hailing the Erbitux results as a potential breakthrough in cancer therapy.

On Sunday, late in the day, ImClone threw an enormous party, at which the Doobie Brothers played, but I skipped the event. Instead, I drifted back to the exhibit hall in the basement of Moscone.

Genentech, one of the best-established biotech companies, had set up a video game in which you pointed a gun and shot at the best treatment for such things as breast cancer and non-Hodgkin's lymphoma. *Bang!* You picked the right drug for breast cancer! *Zinged it, fellow!* Capitalism vulgarized almost everything it touched, but it had produced Genentech's successful drugs, Herceptin and Rituxan. Greed, in itself (I returned to my old reflections), was neither good nor bad; it drove research, and it drove the painfully silly displays in Moscone, too. Ten years after going public, ImClone had no revenue to speak of, no drug yet approved, but it had 66 million shares outstanding and a market capitalization of about $2.6 billion. The entire enterprise was a gamble by investors that the company might be worth tens of billions someday. At that moment, in May 2001, all this capital was risked in support of a trial in which one quarter of the patients had had their lives prolonged for a few months before dying. The system seemed to work, but the precariousness of it stunned me.

Before leaving San Francisco, I drove with Sam and other ImClone officials from his hotel to an analysts' meeting near the Moscone Center, and someone in the car remarked that the entire weekend, with its crucial presentations of data and meetings with investors and press, had been a nerve-racking experience.

"It's supposed to be that way," Sam said. "That's the way to live."

"Maybe you get off on its being nerve-racking," I said, but he just laughed.

25

September 11, 2001

Quarterly Report, July 1, 2001
Cumulative Net Loss $251,000

AN ordinary morning, that's all it was, and while making coffee in the kitchen around nine-thirty, some ninety minutes after Tommy had been shipped off to school, I turned on the boom box that always sat on the windowsill. A little Stravinsky early in the day on WQXR, that's what I wanted. Something mordant and spiky to clear out the morning cobwebs. So why, I wondered, was the announcer talking about the 1993 bombing of the World Trade Center? Was this some sort of radio docudrama? What was it doing on a classical music station? Puzzled, I turned on the little TV in the kitchen. There was no need for coffee. My heart was pounding, and I moved to the bedroom, where I sat in front of the TV until four the next morning.

Like millions of New Yorkers, I wanted to *be* there, to be *down* there, but I didn't have a cell phone, so I stayed where I was and waited for Tommy to call from school. This was no time for theatrics: Stay available to your younger son. The older one was home, asleep. Max was supposed to leave town that week for a pre-college job in New Zealand, but now he was stuck. Horrified by the pictures on TV, he groaned and pulled the covers over his head. Late in the morning, Cathy came over and watched with me for a while, and we embraced, releasing a little of our fear into each other's arms, and after checking in with Max, she returned to her apartment.

I sat stunned in front of the set for a long time, though I had none of the sense of unreality—*this can't be happening*—that some people experienced. Nor did I feel the "clever" response that emerged in some statements later, the notion that the falling buildings were just an image in some way, just an extension of the media, an aesthetic event, a demonic "work of art"—all those peacock-feathered profundities delivered by intellectuals who had read (or written) too much French literary and sociological theory. Images were my job, and I could see that, except for a few educated show-offs, people had not lost their ability to respond to the suffering behind the pictures. They had seen hundreds of decorative explosions in movies, but still, they responded. They had not become insensible.

9/12/01

Sitting at the set for eighteen hours straight was a case of duration, all right, and that's what I wanted more than anything, wasn't it? But this is no time for irony. Let's look at it straight: The world will stop moving for a few days. The markets are closed, the ticker is still, the movies have ceased to exist. Time is filled with acts of rescue, grief, and consolation, a formal articulation of time rather than the usual head-over-heels rush. For now, at least for now, ritual counts as much as movement, sensibility matters as much as will, community transforms and transfigures the isolated man and woman. The strangers falling into each other's arms on the street are saying that the usual competitive relation among citizens must cease for an hour, a day, a week. The dead remain uncounted. Some of those still alive, the ones covered with ash, look like ghosts.

9/14/01

The American fortress has been breached, and we will never be absolutely safe again. My children are at risk in this city. When JFK reopened this afternoon, Max left for New Zealand, and Cathy and I felt an enormous sense of relief. At least one of the boys has left this charnel house. Who knows if there will be another attack? Late in the afternoon, at the office, I stood in the TV room, the one looking east, where I had enjoyed the Nasdaq highs, and watched as a thin dark layer of smoke, floating up from the financial district miles away, slowly wrapped itself around the building.

9/15/01

Back in 1985, when Claude Lanzmann brought out *Shoah*, his great documentary about the Holocaust, there were some bizarre confusions in the press. Several writers described the movie as a warning that such an event might happen again. But that was not what *Shoah* was about. *Shoah* was about the physical improbability of the destruction of the Jews happening *once*. Not: How could God allow it? But: How could reality allow it? Lanzmann paced off the terrain. Where did the trains to Auschwitz stop—where, exactly? How far from the entrance to the subsidiary camp, Birkenau? Who ran the trains into Poland, and who among the Polish peasants saw them pass into the camps? And the same thing this time: A great desire to know how, exactly, the Al Qaeda operatives had captured the planes, overwhelmed the crews, steered the planes into buildings, fooled all the intelligence services. In such films as *The Matrix* and *X-Men*, digital invention had altered the rules of time and space, but these events had taken place *within* time and space. How? What routes, what speed, what resistance, what weapons, what means? We needed to understand what was possible in actuality, not in the dimension-shattering poetic reality of the cinema. On September 11, the sky was so much more heartbreakingly blue than in any movie.

9/16/01

The aim was to kill Wall Street, to throw the system into chaos and crash the market. Certainly the market will fall, the economy will be hurt. Our portfolio will fall further than it already has. Fall, fall, let it fall. Bigger things have fallen, and my little financial problem has been overwhelmed by the general sorrow, the vast fear, which Americans have never experienced before, not even in the worst days of the Cold War. Let the smart guys switch to Treasury bonds, or whatever it is they will do to protect their money. To sell stock now would be unpatriotic. Hang in there and ride it out, wherever it goes. This is not the time to withdraw money from an economy that needs to stay liquid, stay loose, repair itself.

That little communication tunnel on Liberty Street that I had so innocently visited a few months earlier in search of fiber-optic cable, the fetid cavern in which I had been so happy as I dirtied my Italian suit while waterbugs ran up and down the walls from the leaked bit of Hudson running below — that place had been obliterated by the falling southern tower. It was just one little sewer, and as far as I knew, no one was working in it when the towers fell, but it had been crushed, and the sophisticated advanced technology embedded in it had been crushed along with it, just like the parking garages and subway tunnels and everything else below the colossi. The future had been stopped, at least for a while, by a few unimpressive men wielding box cutters — death-loving fanatics snarling the West's infinitely subtle inventions. I felt a shudder, a small one compared to what others experienced, but I sensed that my tracks had been hounded by destruction. Among other things, in the last two years I had lived in the ignorant bliss of making and losing money in a city in which I thought my children were safe.

After an enormous amount of work, the exchanges opened again, on Monday, September 17, six days after the attack. It was still an utter mess down there. The entire neighborhood was shrouded in gray plaster and cement dust, an industrial snowflake combined with the acrid smell of burning plaster and burning flesh. The dust coated the walls and fouled the computers, yet somehow the exchanges functioned with considerable smoothness. Show the flag, I say. Get the zipper moving again — the market opening after only a few days' break was an act of defiance.

No courage was exhibited by big-time investors, however. Despite exhortation from the President, the Vice President, Warren Buffett, Jack Welch, and Robert Rubin, the Dow fell by 684 points, or 7.13 percent; the Nasdaq by 115 points, or 6.83 percent; the S&P 500 by 53 points, or 4.92 percent. Expecting war and the diminution of domestic travel, the mutual funds and the hedge funds bought defense stocks and sold airline stocks; they sold Disney and American Express and anything else that was travel-related. The buildings fell, the ground swallowed up the dead, and the big-time players pursued their narrow self-interest as if nothing had happened but a normal shift in market forces. God, the coldness required to make those calculations! And with their colleagues lying dead in the rubble!

For the first time in a year and three-quarters, I was truly angry. When Cathy left, I grieved and hid in caves and threw money at the market and dismissed anger as destructive of myself and my family. Anger, I thought, was for losers, and I had repeatedly mastered and swallowed irritation over Henry Blodget's evasions and double-thinking. I took out my disappointment over the falling market on institutional investors, on Alan Greenspan, and on myself. But now, like millions of my countrymen, I was delivered into full-sighted rage. We had been slaughtered by calculating madmen, and I wanted to hit back. I wanted to do something, to contribute in some way. Walter Bagehot, the nineteenth-century English journalist and analyst of political economy, said that Americans were protected in part by their habit of pursuing their own private and selfish interests — what Bagehot called, with some irony, "stupidity." Applying Bagehot's insight, we might say that America was immune, in the twentieth century, to such totalizing philosophies as communism and fascism, the kind of apocalyptic and disastrous notions of struggle and redemption that had laid waste to Europe but had never seriously taken hold here. Good, safe, banal, consumption-mad America! Stupidity saved us! But now we were under direct attack by another such philosophy — Islamic fundamentalism — and the pursuit of selfish and private interests, such as the work of those hedge-fund managers selling airline stocks, was not enough of a response. Stupidity could no longer protect us. As for myself, anger was better than paralysis, but what on earth to do with anger? In Afghanistan, where American forces quickly began operations, a film critic and misguided investor would be of less use than a lesson book teaching Farsi to little girls.

There was no end to my frustration, and the only thing I could think of doing was to attack stupidity — literal stupidity, not Bagehot's metaphorical kind. The world of narrow, selfish private interests could itself be flushed clean of idiocy. In my life as an investor, anger had been building all year long; I just didn't know it, or didn't have access to it, until the buildings fell. I was stunned, like one of those cows half electrocuted into a stupor before the saw hits the neck. For me (well, not just for me — for millions of Americans), the buildings falling down brought many things into focus. One of these things was that it was a joke, a great joke, this Nasdaq bear market arriving at the dawn of a new reality in technology. If only I hadn't been the butt of the joke, I might have enjoyed it. Getting the joke now, I was appalled.

At the beginning of 2001, most economists thought the economy was turning down. But perhaps this downturn, even if it became a recession, would be shorter and sharper than such declines in the past. So the speculation went. It would be a "smart" recession. The new information technology would give managers immediate knowledge of smaller orders coming in, or alert them to dangerously large inventories, allowing companies to cut purchases or reduce personnel quickly and then, presumably, reorder and rehire more quickly, too. Greenspan even said as much. But if this tech information was so capable, why, I wondered, had so many large companies blundered in the first place, building up the overcapacity and excess inventories in 1998 and 1999 and 2000 that eventually had to be threshed out? The New Economy claim that the business cycle had been licked was obviously nonsense.

It seemed that something bizarre and unprecedented had happened in a fair number of corporate offices. The neat little companies, the Internet start-ups, the e-commerce and software and storage and fiber-optic companies, had literally shaken the big corporations to their roots. In the New Economy magazines, the general line about the Old Economy was "You just don't get it, old guy, do you?" The contempt for experience was stunning, the self-confidence of youth amazing. "Swim with the Sharks or Sleep with the Fishes. It's Your Call," an ad said in the May 2000 *Industry Standard*. Wasn't that charming? "You're toast," as another ad put it. Oh yes, it was time to break up hierarchies, smash old ways of managing, because technological youth was inspired, youth was issuing edicts, turning on the toaster. The youth mania became a jeering revolution from within capitalism. And some of the big corporations, afraid of being left out of the future, improbably allowed themselves to be bullied from below and arranged to buy tons of equipment that they might not have needed, or only half needed, setting up e-commerce divisions, plugging into fiber-optic networks, buying management software, storage, and so on, and they had invested in the little companies as well.

The big dopes! But I was hardly in the best positon to fault them, since I, too, had wanted to believe what *Red Herring, The Industry Standard, Fast Company,* and *The Gilder Report* were selling. But all this overbuying and the new underordering caused a few companies in 2001 to write off excess inventory—a staggering $2.5 billion inventory write-off of unusable parts by Cisco in mid-April, the largest in corporate history. To a non-business mind, a miscalculation on this scale seemed inconceivable, even laughable. And this happened not just to any company but to *Cisco,* allegedly the best-run outfit in the New Economy. Clearly the supply-chain management software was not fully in place. At the same time, the decline of a giant like Nortel caused *its* suppliers, Corning, JDSU, and Avanex, to decline, too. By 2001, the big companies were selling their investments in the hip little companies, and laying off their own workers by the thousand. "I've never seen a sector in which earnings have deteriorated so rapidly," said Wharton professor Jeremy Siegel on CNBC in April, speaking of the telecom sector, which was dragging down the entire market. Siegel was now the only guru I considered worth listening to.

Irony turned to rage—that was the emotional rhythm of 2001. People weren't buying on the dips as they had in the past, because they assumed prices would go lower. So they waited to buy at a lower price. According to market pundits, only when there's widespread belief that we have hit bottom will everyone start buying again. Yes, but how will we know when we have hit bottom? *By the market rising—that is, by people buying.* Was I crazy, or was this sort of tautological reasoning insane? Or was I insane for having got caught up in it? The Nasdaq slid 50 or 60 points a day, and at every point you thought it couldn't go any lower, and then it did. Each support level vanished. The market drifted down, just as Robert Shiller said it would—Shiller, who had infuriated me, because he seemed to welcome a long, dreary period as a necessary form of punishment after the joyous pop-cult investment atmosphere of the nineties. But he was right, the market was grinding us down—there was a dead feeling in my soul, a void, dreary, limitless, and gray.

Some of the key assumptions of the previous decade were falling to pieces. After all, what we now call, with almost biblical reverence, *investing* is a relatively recent invention, at least in its modern form. In the nineteenth century, and even in the last century, at least in the period around the 1929 Crash, playing the market was considered a dangerous activity. Scoundrelism in the market—speculators forming pools and shorting stocks and so on—was even celebrated in some quarters as a wildly exciting blood sport in which men destroyed their enemies and gouged their friends. Dreiser's Frank Cowperwood was a master of that arena. "Investing" in the contemporary sense really begins after the Crash, particularly in the watershed years of 1933 and 1934, in which the major regulatory agencies and safeguards were set up. These things never go in a straight line, of course, but after the insider-trading scandals of the eighties, the remaining aura of chicanery and roguery had been largely vanquished, and by the late nineties, many of us were convinced that risk itself had been eliminated. The Dow climbed 1,409 percent from the beginning of the bull in 1982 to the high in March 2000; the Nasdaq climbed 3,072 percent over the same period. That's an increase by a factor of thirty for the entire index. As I made all those little shifts in our portfolio in the nineties, I never seriously considered loss as a possibility. By 2001, in the midst of a bear market, the arrogance of it seemed incredible to me, but for all those years, I thought only of how to maximize gain.

In 2001, illusion ended for Americans. The illusion of endless gain, the illusion of safety, the illusion of limitless electric power and water. In the spring of 2001, I met with my friend James Stevens, and we talked about illusion. Stevens was the fellow who had, in the late nineties, quintupled his portfolio, from $200,000 to $1 million, by betting on just a few tech stocks. We met in the café that Fairway had built over its seething store — the café a flourishing new neighborhood spot ladling out leeks and couscous, also quiche that was far too rich for anyone's blood. Stevens, however, was lean (a runner). "Why own anything but technology?" he said, recapping his racing strategy of the late nineties, when he had done so well. But, like me, he had suffered through 2000, the previous year, and he had responded by moving stuff around, unloading part of his Microsoft holdings in favor of Juniper, a networking stock, and still, he had watched his pile diminish to $800,000 ("I was sure that was the bottom") and then to $600,000 ("I said to myself, 'You've now blighted your future'"). His brother's brother-in-law, a money manager out in the Midwest, had told him he was crazy and had offered to manage the remaining money, but Jim had refused.

We agreed that the illusion that was dying in the spring of 2001 was the future. In 2001, big companies like Cisco and Intel were saying that they didn't have "visibility," by which they meant they couldn't say what their revenues would be for the next few quarters. The all-optical future was stalled, and Gilder's determinism — the notion that if something is possible and useful, the capital markets will find a way to make it happen — turned out to be daft. The disintegration of the telecom market exposed St. George as a dreamer and a shill. At the Telecosm Conference in the late summer of 2000, I had perceived that the only thing the triumphalists couldn't lick was aging and death.

Oh, they were very grand, these men—crazy, perhaps, but noble and defiant. In 2001, however, they had been vanquished not by death but by the commonplace workings of the market—by equipment glut and lack of demand.

The all-optical network was stalled by the most banal kind of problem. For the providers of "content"—music and movie companies, publishers, libraries, museums, photo archives, corporations, government agencies—the task of digitizing vast amounts of material did not make economic sense if there was not a sufficient audience for it. No, not if there was not an enormous number of people with broadband access at home. And for the home user, there was no reason to spend an extra $40 a month for cable modem or DSL if large amounts of program material were not available. The music file-sharing site Napster was the "killer application" for which people were willing to cough up the extra cash, but after a lot of back-and-forth with the courts, Napster was ruled illegal by July 2001, and a fair number of subscribers canceled their broadband service. They didn't think they needed it. So broadband was rolling out, but much more slowly than people had anticipated. The result: The "content providers" were waiting for an audience, and the audience was waiting for content. Alphonse and Gaston, an absurd dilemma!

Gilder, in the midst of his religio-plutocratic tintinnabulations, and his abstruse technical considerations, had overlooked this commonplace of Alphonse and Gaston. He announced in his newsletter and in an article in the *Journal* that the all-optical network was being stalled by excessive regulation of the telephone companies—by government interference with the market rather than by the simple workings of the market. So there was another joke, if you were looking for one. One of the premier celebrants of capitalism in the country had been done in by the normal workings of capitalism and couldn't admit it.

Stevens and I chewed it over as we ate Fairway's leeks. Enthusiasm had trumped the most elementary common sense. Again and again, entrepreneurs had misunderstood their own markets. In 1998 and 1999, when everyone was buying fiber-optic networking equipment, David Huber of Corvis might not have known that his bulky all-optical switch, secreted in the thrilling sci-fi atmosphere of his chilly Maryland lab, would have very few customers in the future. For it turned out that Corvis's optical switch technology, which Gilder and others considered superb, was simply too expensive for most of the newly impoverished telecom companies. Williams was a customer, and Broadwing, but that was about it. Of course, no one warned me of this possibility in the summer of 2000, when I was chasing the IPO through the empty, bird-haunted Adirondacks, and I wasn't shrewd enough to figure it out myself. But now, talking to Stevens, I had a nasty thought. Maybe Huber *did* know, even on that day when I visited him in Maryland in the fall of 2000. Maybe the lack of potential customers was the extraordinary secret that he was hiding in the months before the IPO and the cause of his unease when I was there. If *that* was his secret, he was very clever—the stock price jumped up in those few weeks after going public. But Huber overplayed his hand, and investors were now taking their revenge. Not only did Corvis have very few customers, it was providing the solution to something — long-haul travel of data — that was far less of a problem than unclogging the metropolitan networks and getting data through the last mile into homes and businesses. By April 2001, less than a year after I bought the stock at 60 and 63, it was heading down into single digits. I had been suckered by an illusion, and possibly by a lie.

When it came to investing, intellectuals, it turned out, were no smarter than anyone else. They fell in love with technological concepts and theories of the market and ignored the actualities.

They were too much in love with their abstract ideas to change them. His eyes opening still wider, Stevens said, "I'd sit there at the computer, fill in 'Sell,' but I couldn't do it." His father had lost 60–70 percent of *his* money by being impulsive and selling at the bottom of the market, and he was determined not to do the same. But now, in the spring of 2001, Stevens felt something like horror at the absurdity of his position. His pile had gradually diminished to around $300,000, which was not much more than the amount he had started with a few years earlier. Unable to sell myself, I was as nonplussed as he was. First the two of us were paralyzed by illusion, then by the loss of illusion. In truth, we didn't know what to do. "I've been walking around thinking I'll never be able to retire," said Stevens at the Fairway café.

But others knew. They just swallowed hard and got out. Edward Rothstein, the friend with whom I had placed cell phones by the millions into the hands of eager gauchos, had sold out after serious losses. "Every day is ground zero," he said to me early in 2001, well before "ground zero" began to signify something else. Rothstein meant that the past history of your investments didn't matter, you had to plant your feet in the present and do the right thing for that day and the future. And Jackie, the day trader, had got out, too. Jackie had closed up his pseudo-business, the telephone-answering service Bells Are Ringing, where bells did not ring, and had relinquished his real business, the daily routine in front of the two computers set up at work and in the two houses in Florida. I saw him walking on Broadway, a big guy with a broad grin on his face. "Aww, it wasn't fun anymore, and I had enough money," he said, and waltzed away, a happy man. Now he was truly retired, not bullmarket retired. He had ceased carrying his cave around with him; he was free. But James Stevens and I were not free; we were fully conscious players in Kindleberger's accursed paradigm of euphoria and disaster, and it was now too late to pull ourselves out of it.

Rage expanded and fed on itself and overwhelmed irony. All through 2001, I had increasing doubts about my high-flying friends. By consulting Yahoo! Finance, I discovered that Sam Waksal had, in recent years, repeatedly received warrants and purchased options from ImClone for company shares, and so had his brother, Harlan, and other company officers. Sam had cashed in options worth tens of millions of dollars. Of course, they were all doing it, the CEOs. The salaries were good, but the real payload was the options. What Sam did wasn't criminal, but it struck me as vaguely unethical, and I felt a small contraction in my chest, the darkening of a mood. It was one thing to get rich from a public offering of ImClone stock — that was a reward for years of risk — but another to get the company's board to vote options so you could buy another property in the Hamptons or mount paintings by Mark Rothko and Cy Twombly on your walls.

I didn't say anything to Sam about my dismay. I buried my doubts, in part, I think, because I also enjoyed the Rothkos and the Twomblys, and if I had looked too closely into how he paid for them, I might not have enjoyed them anymore. After the triumphant oncology conference in May, I went to Sam's loft, met him a few times for lunch, read about him in the papers; and his obvious greed, and the high living that demanded big money and fueled the hunger for more, looked more and more manic to me. I figured he was revved all the time from the coming FDA approval of Erbitux. Yet he was disturbingly vague, even absent, in certain ways. When I talked to him at length in his office in April 2001, I had noticed something dismaying that I then suppressed a month later at the oncology conference: When Sam had multiplied with such dexterity the yearly gross revenue for Erbitux as a treatment for advanced colorectal cancer, he had said not a word about the good the drug would do in the world. He did not talk of patients, except as necessary participants in the FDA trials. Was his money talk an instance of refreshing honesty? Or was he insensitive and indifferent? I had never wanted him to be a stiff research personage, solemn in a white coat. I liked his worldly game and his curiosity about everything. But how serious was he about medicine? During the summer of 2001, he was off in East Hampton, trolling among his properties, and the rest of the time he was working on a rumored deal in which he would sell a share of ImClone to some big company in return for the rights to distribute and take part of the profits from Erbitux.

And by summer's end, Henry Blodget's reputation, frayed a year earlier, was in ruins. Back in March, a private investor named Debases Kanjilal, a forty-six-year-old physician in New York, had filed for arbitration with the New York Stock Exchange over one of Henry's bullish ratings. It seems that a year earlier, in March 2000, Kanjilal had made a heavy investment in the Web service company InfoSpace and had then lost $500,000 as the stock tanked. In 2001, Kanjilal maintained that Henry's "buy" rating for InfoSpace the year before was biased: At the time, Merrill had been retained as a financial adviser for another Internet company, Go2Net, which InfoSpace subsequently purchased in July 2000 for $4 billion. Because of this pending deal, Kanjilal claimed, Henry would not have said anything that could hurt InfoSpace's stock price.

When Kanjilal's lawyer filed the arbitration claim, Henry and Merrill Lynch dismissed it as absurd (Henry described the suit as "ridiculous" to me on the telephone). Both analyst and company insisted that Henry Blodget had no advance knowledge in 2000 of the upcoming deal with InfoSpace. And yet, to everyone's amazement, in July 2001 Merrill settled the claim, agreeing to pay the indignant investor $400,000. "To avoid the expense and distraction of protracted litigation," said a company spokesman. Really? You pay off $400,000 to settle what you've been describing as a baseless claim? And what does that do to your analyst? The payoff seemed to confirm the usual charge that stock analysts hyped certain firms so that the house could collect enormous fees from banking deals. Would Merrill have settled if they were not afraid that an investigation would cough up evidence proving Kanjilal right?

I had a sick feeling in my stomach. How deeply mired in compromise and confusion was Henry Blodget? When I tried to get some response out of him by e-mail, he said he couldn't talk about it—that was his agreement with Merrill—but to my eyes, and to everyone else's, the settlement was a shocking blow to his standing at the company. He was now a diminished man. Merrill was beginning to view their star analyst as a liability.

Those were some of the doubts and furies that were accumulating before September 11—the chagrins large and small suddenly brought into focus by the catastrophe. For weeks after the attack, I drifted in fear. My children were not safe. "Stupidity" could get us killed. The American forces were in the field, but what could I do? Immersion in a crumbling market suddenly seemed a trivial waste of time.

I had done something small a long time ago. In the dear, safe, touchingly straightforward days of the Cold War, I made two minor excursions overseas as a propagandist for the Free World, showing movies and describing American institutions to elites in Burma, Thailand, Singapore, and Malaysia in the early seventies, and then, later in the decade, taking *All the President's Men* to media workers and students in the Communist capitals of Eastern Europe—in Warsaw, Prague, Romania, and Budapest, where the official line was pro-Nixon and most of my audience had only the vaguest information about the activities of two young journalists in Washington during the Watergate affair. I was young and eager to travel, and the United States Information Agency (known overseas as the United States Information Service) sponsored the trips. In those days, they sponsored everyone willing to make the American case — poets, professors, dancers, musicians, basket weavers, storytellers, theater people, even young and obscure cultural journalists. The audiences in Eastern Europe, mostly university students, were rapt, the questions searching, and I was extraordinarily happy in my role of enlightened propagandist as I celebrated a key American value, embedded in the Constitution and going back, at least as a theory, to John Locke — the right of a free people to cashier an oppressive leader.

Could we do it again? Could we win the war of ideas in the Islamic world as we had won it in the Communist world? In late 2001, as young men in immaculate white cloaks and handsome black beards rioted all over that world in an ecstasy of loathing for the United States, the notion of arguing with Islamic fundamentalism seemed crazy. What did I know of these people? They were very different from Czechs and Poles. In the movie version of *The War of the Worlds* (directed by George Pal; 1951) a minister, disgusted with the endless violence, advances on the Martians holding a Bible. "We've got to *reason* with them," he cries, and promptly gets reduced to a hill of powder about an inch high. Well, the Islamic world might say that the Americans were the Martians in the current encounter, but you get the idea: Your likelihood of success when reasoning with people from an old and complex culture who hated you was not very high. And yet, disgusted with my immersion in the market, I wanted to get out there and make the case for secularism, for free speech, for transparency, for the writ of habeas corpus. I wanted to expound the Constitution and tell them who John

Locke was and why his insistence that a religion freely chosen by individuals rather than imposed by the state was the single most important idea in the modern world.

Who better than me? Muslims would say that we Americans have lost the spiritual element of life; we are possessed with getting and spending, we are materialists, we are "stupid." Yes, well, on the surface, this is true. So far, however, none of our public officials had found the words to explain how limited a truth it was. Our president and our secretaries of state and defense were too mute to say that an exuberant civil society was itself an amazing spiritual achievement. Not just a material and legal achievement, but a spiritual achievement. Someone immersed in money who nevertheless prized civil society might be the kind of person who could meet Muslim objections to the West. I had written a book about Western classics and Western values, and now it was time to get out there and talk about our secular scrolls and great writers and all the rest of the spiritual achievement of the West.

Foolish? Vainglorious? A dodge, an evasion, a displacement of anguish? Maybe, but a little preening felt good after the battering I had taken, and I proposed the propaganda war in an article and gave some talks at universities suggesting that educated people should get off their butts and get out into the Islamic world. Of course, I didn't *go*. Not then, not when the bullets were flying. I couldn't. No one would have sponsored me. But my obsessions had shifted yet again. Gently reasoning with people who hated us would be a good thing to try, no matter how vain (in both senses of the word); a good thing even to fail at. I would do it sooner or later.

In late 2000, when the market was beginning to fall, I had skated through the marble hallways of the World Financial Center, and I had had that soothing fantasia of American wealth, the brilliant commercial pomp of the center itself a reminder of

267

the office buildings, hotels, industrial parks, and factories all over the country. Well, the buildings had fallen — the *buildings,* as well as the market. The Financial Center had not been hit directly like its twin cousins across West Street, but it was badly mauled. The windows were blown out of the huge complex in which Henry Blodget of Merrill Lynch worked, and the Winter Garden, with its trees and glass roof and its marvelous opening to the Hudson and the Whitmanesque view of the bay and the Statue of Liberty, had been completely destroyed. As we fought the war in Afghanistan, we had to rebuild the Winter Garden, reclaim the Whitmanesque view, and tell ourselves and other people what it meant. Balled up still, and terribly frustrated, a warrior without a battlefield, I knew I couldn't be quite as passive as I was before September 11.

26

The End of Investing?

Quarterly Report, January 1, 2002
Cumulative Net Loss $800,000

EARLY in the winter of 2002, I removed the strand of yellow-sheathed fiber-optic cable from my briefcase and threw it into the trash.

The future was stalled — Alphonse-and-Gastoned — and I had to let it go, at least for now. And as the market kept falling, and we lost more and more, I had to let go of something else, too. I had been fighting off the realization for months, but now it was inescapable: I couldn't buy Cathy out, and it just didn't make sense to hold on to a seven-room apartment in Manhattan. The marriage was over, for godsake, and we had already spent too much money renting apartments on the side. I had given up my little place in October 2001 and moved full-time into the big apartment; and Cathy had given up her studio with the view of the Hudson and had taken a five-room place at a preposterous rental, but now it was time to sell, split up the winnings, and buy smaller places, as Cathy always had wanted to. I had resisted the idea that money would shape my behavior—as if I had any choice! Money shaped everyone's behavior, but I hated losing the freedom to be irrational. For two years, I couldn't account for the revulsion I felt at the idea of moving.

We fell into the usual practice of parents who are splitting up, sending Thomas back and forth between us. Max, now a handsome, intense young man, was out in Colorado, at college, arriving there after a fall spent in New Zealand working on an enormous sheep ranch. What he had done in the paradisal southern island became important to me in ways that I hadn't anticipated. Max had spent his days on the ranch shoveling, penning, chasing, digging. When a ewe died, he went out and retrieved one of its lambs, carrying it back to the pen in his arms. Dirt, wool, feed, and shit. My boy had his hands on something solid—actual materials in an economy increasingly obsessed with methods of transmission, with conduits and connections. Empty conduits, often enough. By early 2002, the fabulous New Economy was beginning to look like an endless unlit fiber-optic cable. I would gladly have strangled a roomful of tech gurus and then myself with the miles of dead wire.

Give it up, give it up. The yards of books in the apartment would have to be divided, no small matter for two writers who nurtured an intimate relation to each novel by Trollope or Dickens or Muriel Spark or Saul Bellow. Again and again, I walked around the place tracing my hands along the books—way stations, each one of them, on a journey that had been good until it ceased being good. I brushed against other things, including memories of the children that I had passed over for years—old pictures of the boys that Cathy had put in frames and set up on a table or stuck into a bookcase, the two of them with thin white shoulders and mops of hair, lying side by side in bed in a

Caribbean resort or standing in a hole they had dug in a scraggly beach on Long Island Sound. And in the dining room, I noticed my mother's old teacups in an antique cupboard, very old cups with a pattern of pink roses surrounded by leaves and branches. "Tuscan Fine English Bone China," it said on the bottom. The bone china and the heavy silver laid away in a drawer somewhere were all that remained in the house of my mother's enormous drive and ambition. The cups were the same ones that years ago sat in the faux-antique green cabinet in the unvisited parlor in Sutton Place. We hardly used them ourselves, but we kept them displayed, a trophy of the old rising middle class, which worked long, solid days, making and selling things in the burgeoning manufacturing economy after World War II.

Americans, always on the move, a rootless, immigrant-derived people, cling to memories and mementos not only because we are cut off from the past but because we are cut off from continuity and coherence in the present. Action in our movies is chopped into fragments, the divorce rate is a killer, many of us don't quite know where our grandparents came from, the stock market annihilates time, everything annihilates time, people move from job to job. Corporate downsizing and the slashing of workforces have been managerial religion since the early eighties. In recent years, the old hierarchies within many companies had been broken up, and employees now jumped in and out of "projects," rarely developing loyalties to colleagues and bosses. For me, the break was coming in my life at home.

By the winter of 2002, I was beginning to understand at last why I had hated the idea of moving so much. All along, I couldn't see anything beyond the apartment but a blank wall, and that blankness, I now knew, was the end of my emotional life in middle age, a kind of death; and so I reached for the future, not just to get rich, but to make the most of my time and avoid the sentence of nullity hanging over me. I hoped that Sam

271

Waksal and Henry Blodget and rhapsodical George Gilder, too, would all lead me to that place in which we would steal time from the end and not get any older. All this I knew in the apartment as I examined my mother's veined teacups and looked at pictures of the boys when they were skinny little children with mops of hair falling over their ears.

After the plunge in the wake of 9/11, the market wasn't doing anything in particular, it was stuck in a long trough in the winter of 2002, moving up and down, rallying and then falling, and my emotions weren't engaged in it. We were definitely in the downside of a business cycle, even enduring a mild recession at the end of 2001 — a profits recession, as everyone said, in which the detritus of the popped bubble lay about everywhere in the form of too much equipment, too many new factory wings, too much debt, and overcapacity in general. The Federal Reserve had cut rates again and again, eleven times in 2001, all the way down to 1.75 percent by the end of the year, but with little effect. My hero was now impotent, his magic gone. Tech spending was way off, and no new revolutionary technology or killer application appeared on the horizon. For me, the obsession was over.

I was beached, and at last, after so many postponements and refusals, I lightened up a little, finally draining some of the tech funds out, putting the money in a low-price stock fund. I felt a mixture of relief and despair; we had lost on paper over $800,000 from the high less than two years earlier. Our high-yield bonds issued by Globalstar, a favorite of George Gilder's, had defaulted and were almost worthless. My shares of Corvis, another Gilder favorite, so ardently pursued in the melancholy Adirondacks, had almost completely lost their value, and Gilder's premier networking company, Global Crossing, in which he personally had invested a fortune — I had a few shares myself — had gone belly up, filing for bankruptcy protection at the end of January. Nokia and Broadcom were way down; Fidelity Biotech, after peaking in 2000, had lost half its value over the next two years.

Yet even as I lightened up on my blasted sector, I remained fully invested. I wouldn't "capitulate," though capitulation was what the market hard-noses wanted. Their theory went this way: If those of us with depressed stock held on, when the market rose at last, we would sell when we reached a personal marking point — when the Nasdaq, say, went back up by 30 or 40 percent and losses were minimized — and these defensive sales would stop the new bull in its tracks. It would be better for the future bull if we sold our semi-worthless stock *now*. Yet I couldn't do it; I was afraid, as always, of missing the recovery, of simply being stuck on the sidelines when it began, and I reasoned that a true profits recovery — which was what we really needed — would lead to waves of buying that would overcome the many morose sellers determined to minimize their losses. Having contributed to the bubble, I was now, after the bubble had burst, apparently part of the reason that it was so hard to get out of a bear market. Well, tough.

What was so special about teacups, anyway? I held one up. It was fine but brittle, invaded by spidery signs of age, just like a human face. When a teacup cracks, one thinks of death — the fabric of life torn after a long period of stability. As I moved around my apartment in the winter of 2002, turning over in my hands the floral-patterned fruits of manufacturing and selling, I heard the sound of discord and fury in the distance — not the usual drone of an airplane taking off at Newark airport or the comforting sound of F-18s patrolling at night (a regular feature of New York life since September 11), but something sharp and angry. That the seventh-largest corporation in the country was nothing but an enormous shell, a raided hulk with rat holes of hidden debt and cargo pits plundered by its own crew — a pirate vessel stripped and then abandoned by the captain and his officers — was a fact so astonishing that, at first, people were mainly amused and regarded it more as spectacle to be enjoyed than as an economic disaster. Quickly enough, however, amusement over Enron gave way to the conviction that something enormously significant had happened. The age had found its name, its face, its metaphor — so much more powerful than a crapped-out Web site — and rage over the scandal burned its way into one's senses like a magnifying glass concentrating light onto a page.

In time, journalists and scholars will trace the origins of the disease — the hardening of attitude and softening of morals that produced the disaster, the inner rot of a business culture gone mad. But the immediate cause was obvious enough. Originally a pipeline and natural-gas company, in the nineties Enron began to sell contracts known as derivatives on future supplies, and then wound up trading everything — newsprint, TV advertising time, insurance risk, bandwidth. Some of the deals were so complicated that no one could follow them, not even the banks that had loaned Enron money. The company, in other words, had freed itself from the sordid ancient process of *manufacture*. It had ascended to the empyrean heights of finance. Investing all over the place, Enron admitted in October 2001 that it had made bad bets on plants in India and Brazil. But what quickly became clear as the scandal broke was that Enron had hid debt from hundreds of other deals in partnerships known as "special entities." As the investments failed, money was siphoned out of the dummy companies into the hands of a few Enron executives. So the dematerialization of American industry was thus complete, and I thought, Good old Max, putting his hands on a shovel, moving the feed and shit on a ranch in New Zealand. By the time it fell, Enron had few hard assets left, almost nothing to offer as collateral, nothing to hold on to as a reconstitution of the firm. It had became a publicly traded investment bank run by thugs in suits.

Roguery ran wild. The executives cashed in options while urging employees to hold more company stock in their 401(k) plans. The firm made deals with itself, moving assets around from one "entity" to another, and then booked the transfers as gain. Enron's auditor, Arthur Andersen, bought off with fees as a "consultant," colluded in the phony accounting for years, then destroyed part of its audit records as the company came unwound in 2001. The enormity of the imposture, the extensiveness and depth of it, the cynicism and cruelty with which it was executed, the sheer nutty absurdity in financial terms, the hiding, the cowardice, the bland lies, the refusal to admit error or even to apologize . . . Enron hadn't paid a dime in federal income tax in four out of the five previous years. They were teasing us, teasing the government and investors, and we, in turn, were corrupted by collusion or a simple desire to look the other way. Collusion and looking the other way were key elements in the South Sea Bubble, too. We knew, we knew, and we fell for the same pack of scoundrels all over again.

As I moved around the house, looking at pictures and sifting through the children's old games and toys, the teacups trembled from the agitation and anger gathering outside. All over the country, investors were livid. Despite my new indifference to the market, I heard the agitation; I heard it on the streets and in heated conversations at coffee-shop counters on the Upper West Side, and from *Kudlow & Cramer* every night on CNBC, where the new regulars of financial journalism, the hysterical but intelligent James J. Cramer and the smooth, cuff-linked Reaganite supply-sider Lawrence Kudlow, of gravid voice and Barbasoled demeanor—Kudlow looked like the kind of sport who tipped the pretty little blond manicurist well—held forth with increasing virulence on the great betrayal. I watched the two men with pleasure. In a time of dereliction and disgrace, they weren't required to be polite. The suave Kudlow quivered

275

in his beautiful shirts and Cramer lowered his head, blew steam out of his ears, and shrieked with rage. I joined my anger to theirs and let it out. Rage was my pleasure, my knowledge, my life. Enron was hardly alone. It seems that no fewer than 723 companies had been forced to restate their earnings between 1997 and January 2002. In February 2002, Moody's, the bond-rating service, requested additional information from 4,000 more companies. The hanky-panky was covering corporate America with shame.

The desire to believe in heroes dies hard, and scorn comes slowly. But when it comes at last, overwhelming all resistance, it is molten hot. The behavior of some of the CEOs, not just at Enron but at many companies, was so astoundingly vicious as to be demonic. I was shocked, and personally, I needed to understand these men, I needed to see what connection their greed had to my own.

It became clear in the winter and spring of 2002 that a year earlier, even two years earlier, as the economy stumbled, and individual companies fell into serious trouble, certain CEOs and other top managers had found a legal way of plundering their own firms. They took the money, in many cases, just before the stock price disintegrated, when they must have known profits were about to fall. There was, for instance, the case of the formidable Henry T. Nicholas III, Ph.D., whom I had heard at Gilder's conference in the mountains in September 2000 — Nicholas, the piratical-looking fellow with the black three-piece suit and black beard, who boasted at the conference of the enormous gains to be made in the market for broadband. Nicholas sold options all through the boom — a staggering total of $799 million worth before he finally stopped because "the price just got too low." I bought Broadcom myself in 2000 at $233 a share, and I was foolishly still holding it in the spring of 2002, when it was under $30. In his later remarks to the press regarding the boom period, Nicholas expressed a gee-whiz befuddlement. This from *Fortune* in 2002: "I would sit and talk to people, and I would ask, 'How do we rationalize any of these valuations?' There seemed to be a disconnect. I was sitting there going, 'Wow! Look at these valuations.' But I was also sitting there thinking, 'Maybe this is a new economy.'"

"How?" "Seemed." "Wow!" "I was thinking." "Maybe." The weak language was itself a giveaway of deceit. *How,* indeed. This sort of hapless mock-naïveté, after the fact, would be funny if it wasn't so contemptible. Nicholas was hardly paralyzed with wonder at the time—he sold $799 million worth of options. I walked around the apartment that I had lost mainly because of my own foolishness—but also because of the lies of these men—and I was sure the teacups would crack from the reverberations felt from outside. How could they stand the shock? Nicholas and many of the others who cashed in were not necessarily being rewarded for the continued high performance of their companies. No, many of their companies were suffering severe profit reductions in 2000 and 2001, or even losses. But were they abashed by this? Ashamed of it? Or perhaps a little chastened and therefore restrained in their behavior? There were those, like Gerald Levin of Time Warner, who did not cash in. Michael Dell, though certainly well compensated, was not a faker. But many others . . . they were making annually three hundred, four hundred, even one thousand times what the average employee made, yet no matter how much they got, they wanted more. The closer the company came to serious trouble, the more predatory, voracious, and insensitive their behavior became. A few made sham deals at the end of fiscal quarters in order to temporarily inflate profits, or concocted absurd business plans, hiding the first from analysts, selling the second to investors. Some managers borrowed money from companies to buy options and then won a forgiveness of the loans from the company boards, in effect using corporations as a peculiar private bank — a bank that gave away money. And how could the shareholders know what was going on? They couldn't know that a CEO might be lying about the company's prospects in order to kick up prices short-term so he could quickly cash in his options. Or that he might be hiding company debt. The cups shook and rattled.

Lying, scheming lowlifes. Smug, self-entitling, other-annihilating, boasting, thieving lowlifes. The righteousness, the assurances, the ruses and scams, the fatuous denials! "History had created something new in the USA," Saul Bellow wrote in 1975 (in *Humboldt's Gift*), "namely crookedness with self-respect or duplicity with honor. America had always been very upright and moral, a model to the entire world, so it had put to death the very idea of hypocrisy and was forcing itself to live with this new imperative of sincerity, and it was doing an impressive job." That was the corporate style; they insisted on their own rectitude, an insistence which they somehow imagined absolved them of actual rectitude. Once you were *in,* you didn't have to tell the truth or behave well, you had only to maintain a certain manner. And they had nothing but contempt for the outsiders, the nonplayers, the schnooks who didn't get it. And what was it that we didn't get? *We didn't understand that for them, compensation was not linked to performance the way it was for the rest of the world. Gaining position to take big money was the only reality.*

2/25/02

In a way, they were right. We were naive, we didn't want to believe — because it sounded resentful and lame, mere Marxist melodrama, didn't it? — we didn't want to believe that the rich lacked all honor and fellow feeling and would simply gouge everybody in sight if they had the chance. Vaguely, we hoped they had our interests at heart.

Wasn't that one reason there was so little resentment of the rich, so little class solidarity among the poor in America? Admiration for the big guys. Belief in them. We were all Americans, weren't we? We were all in the same boat. So why should they cheat us? Thinking this way, Americans of every generation got taken. But the robber barons at least built industries. These guys built the stock price, then made themselves much wealthier as the companies fell on hard times.

We outsiders understood what made the corporate managers want to be rich, because we wanted to be rich ourselves. What we didn't understand, however, was what made them think they could have *all* the money. If they wanted to screw each other, that was fine with me — that's the way the big boys play. It was their habit of screwing those less powerful that I found extraordinarily unpleasant. In my disgust, I knew I had to look at this greed thing again. I had underestimated the ferocious and insatiable side of it, for in the winter of 2002, it was just beginning to hit me (and many others) exactly what had happened in America over the previous four or five years. Small investors, overcoming seventy years of mistrust, had invested in the market for new companies, in effect serving as venture capitalists, allowing the new companies to develop products, to build capacity, to buy other companies, to try out experimental business models. All very well, but the more cynical insiders talked up hope, took advantage of the money flowing in from the IPO onward, and then cashed out. At the end of the bubble period, an enormous transfer of wealth had taken place, from us to them, from me to Henry T. Nicholas III, Ph.D.

We had been blinded by our own desire and by the dazzling lies. Chumps! Suckers! Some of the insiders stole from us — from ordinary shareholders, and in some cases from employees, too. They stole from *me*.

★   ★   ★

The cups rolled around in their saucers and turned on their sides and came close to breaking from the noise outside the walls. But what about inside the walls? What about my own friendships, the two men I had taken into my affections? I went to see my two big shots in the winter of 2002. They were now both in disgrace, the role models I had so assiduously studied for signs of how an ideal, entrepreneurial version of myself would grasp the future and the art of making money. My desires, taken to their ends, had turned to criminal behavior. But this time I didn't laugh, as I did (asking for God's forgiveness) a few days after hearing of Nyquist's crimes. I was closer to these men.

Back on September 19, 2001, the deal with Bristol-Myers Squibb that Sam Waksal had been working on all summer was finally signed. The big pharmaceutical company agreed to buy 19.9 percent of ImClone's stock for $1.2 billion; it also gained the right to market Erbitux and take 39 percent of the profits. And Bristol agreed to pay ImClone another $800 million outright after FDA approval. A magnificent deal: No arrangement of this size had ever been made before with a small biotech company, and Sam was exultant — more dashing and generous than ever as he adroitly led his intellectually distinguished soirees, which I faithfully attended. All that remained to complete his triumph was the inevitable FDA approval of Erbitux, and then a quick display of marketing prowess by Bristol-Myers and ImClone combined.

In July 2001, ImClone had been on the cover of *Business Week,* and inside the magazine Sam and Harlan were photographed with jackets slung over their shoulders, like a couple of tough, big-city homicide detectives. They were on the case, these two. Colorectal cancer would be booked and fingerprinted and put in the slammer. By October 31, all the data had been submitted to the FDA, and five weeks later, on the day of Sam's annual Christmas party, December 6, the stock reached a high of

$75.45. Sam had assembled a classier crowd than the year before—no hookers with great leather boots this time, but many bankers, investors, fine-looking executive women, powers of one sort or another. The New York movers had gathered to celebrate Sam's ascendancy. He was now an unprecedented combination of entrepreneurial genius and Great Jewish Healer (Jonas Salk, move over), and Sam performed his usual, head-swelling introductions. "The greatest art dealer . . . investment banker . . . in New York . . ." Sam's big parties exhausted me, so I left early, missing the appearance later in the evening of Mick Jagger, the greatest rock star in the world.

In the second half of December, the stock mysteriously began to tumble. There were rumors of trouble with the FDA, and the price fell into the 50s. What was going on? No one told me, and I couldn't find out on my own. Then, on the night of December 26, 2001, Sam, on vacation in the Caribbean, received notice from his brother that a fax had arrived from Washington. The unimaginable had happened: The FDA had notified ImClone that it would not review the data for Erbitux. They were not actually turning down the application—*they were refusing to review it*. It was the kind of devastating "binary event" that biotech analyst Matt Geller had spoken of. The trials, the FDA said, were flawed, badly designed; more trial work was needed. The fax arrived at ImClone after the market closed for the weekend. In a conference call with major investors on Monday, December 31, Sam insisted that the FDA's problems with Erbitux mostly concerned the documentation for the patients in the trial sample—the X-rays of tumor size and the materials proving that they had failed all other treatment—and he said the problem would be cleared up in six to ten weeks. It was a question of reconstructing evidence. In February, sitting me down in a corner of the room as guests swirled all around, he smiled and laughed and waved away the problem. "We got the right sums," he said. "Now we have to show our homework."

This kind of evasive remark after his earlier account of the care they had taken — oh yes, the infinite care — with all the clinical procedures! And what about his scorn for all the companies that had merely spun "stories"! I was astonished by Sam and astonished by the FDA's refusal, and I didn't know what to believe. On January 7, a Web site called "The Cancer Letter" had printed excerpts from the FDA's refusal letter, which someone (the FDA itself?) had leaked to the site, and the excerpts suggested the problems were far more serious than sloppy documentation. "In order for your application to be complete, you were informed during the meeting of August 11, 2000, in our letter of January 19, 2001, and during the telephone conference call of January 26, 2001, that the application must provide evidence that the addition of a toxic agent (irinotecan CPT-11) is necessary to achieve the clinical effect." In other words, the FDA wasn't sure that Erbitux wouldn't have worked *by itself.* At the last minute, in 2001, the company *had* performed a single-agent trial (Erbitux alone) and had got results about half as good as it did when it administered Erbitux in combination with irinotecan. This was precisely what ImClone had always said would happen. But the patient sample — only fifty-seven people — wasn't large enough to satisfy the FDA, which considered the results inconclusive.

What kind of man was this? A dreamer, a screw-up, a crook? I had been uneasy ever since I noticed in Yahoo! Finance that Sam had repeatedly purchased options on ImClone stock. In the summer of 2001, he purchased a great many more, and with money borrowed from the company, too. With $18.2 million from ImClone, he bought shares at an option price of $8 at a time when the market price was $45. In October, Bristol announced that it would pay $70 in its tender offer for ImClone stock, and Sam exercised the options and made $57 million. I quickly add that I sold some ImClone myself. In fact, I wanted to sell all of our 1,600 shares (the stock had earlier split two for one), but the tender offer was oversubscribed and my broker managed to sell only a small amount — 129 shares. At the time, I shrugged off my disappointment. Erbitux, as far as I knew, was cruising toward approval, and the stock was moving north of $70. I would sell the rest sometime in the future. But later, I thought, *One difference between me and my friend is that the son of a bitch sold shares purchased at an enormous discount with borrowed money. And the other difference is that back in the summer he knew very well he would make a killing, because he was negotiating the deal with Bristol.* He had a stupendous advantage over a common investor. I felt a slight pain in my side, something like a withdrawal symptom from a powerful drug. Sam did nothing illegal with the options — his behavior was just opportunism flecked with greed. But one began to tire of the phrase "nothing illegal."

And once the FDA refusal came down at the end of December, all hell broke loose. Did Sam know in the summer that the agency would turn down the drug? If he did know, had he snookered Bristol-Myers into the fantastic deal? In January 2002, dozens of class-action lawsuits were filed against him by shareholders on the ground that he had given "false and misleading" information about the drug's prospects. In mid-January, Christopher Byron, the financial reporter of the *New York Post,* went on the attack: "Sam has been loitering at the fringes of the New York society crowd for two decades, leaving an oil slick behind him that has been colorful to say the least." What I had always found charming — the avid attention flowing everywhere — was now rendered with a tabloid snarl. A playboy, a scam artist, a liar.

Through all this, ImClone's stock was falling rapidly: From the 50s in late December to the 30s in early January after the

FDA refusal. Exasperated, I sold my remaining shares on January 22, 2002, for $19.25. Between this sale and the previous one in September at the time of the Bristol tender offer, I made $37,000, a profit of $16,000 over a period of ten years. Okay, we didn't lose money, but I would have gotten $120,000 for my shares if I had sold at the early-December peak. ImClone was our one winner among the tech disasters, and we lost most of the winnings. Sam's mishandling of the trials had cost me a lot of money. I was not about to join a class-action suit, but I was beginning to be very, very sore.

As it turned out, the declining share price threw Sam himself into personal trouble. Earlier, he had pledged many of his remaining shares (the options purchased in the summer were only part of his stash) as collateral for loans from Bank of America and UBS Paine Webber. When ImClone's stock tanked in January 2002, margin calls were set off and the ImClone shares were sold automatically — a good percentage of Sam's remaining holdings went to cover the loan. I was thunderstruck. What was he doing borrowing money from brokerage houses, anyway? Why was a wealthy man buying stocks on margin? What kind of reckless gambler was this? Was he on the brink of ruin? He darted around his apartment at the soirees and said everything was fine.

But then the rest of the roof fell in. In February, the Securities and Exchange Commission released a document alleging that Sam's younger daughter, Aliza, twenty-eight, an actress, had sold 40,000 shares of ImClone, worth $2.5 million, on December 27, the day before the FDA refusal was made public, and later we learned his father had sold on that day, too, and Sam himself had tried to sell. His order had been refused by his brokers at Merrill Lynch and Bank America. *Insider trading,* that was the implication of the SEC disclosure. Dear God, was he nuts? A crime, an actual crime, committed by a man who had everything?

I went to see Sam in his office on March 11, 2002. The SEC, the House Committee on Energy and Commerce, and the Department of Justice were all on his tail, but he talked obsessively that day about Jack, his risk-taking father. The daring of the man, the sheer heroism, Jack swimming across a river and breathing through a reed at the end of the war to escape the Nazis! These feats were part of a movie, I realized, that Sam played in his head, a movie in which there was always a way of escaping disaster. Bristol was acting tough with ImClone, threatening to take over the company, but Sam said he and his brother were not going to cave in. They were not going to resign or sell out or lose control. "I grew up in a home where if you were right about something, you fought for it. You didn't cave, you didn't even blink." He said this as if courage and the ability to fight were the only issues at stake. Was that the way he had resolved the disaster with the FDA in his mind? It was a matter of fighting?

He was ebullient as ever, giving long, detailed answers filled with jokes, anecdotes, and asides. He defended the results of the Saltz trials, and insisted again that the FDA mainly wanted more information on the patients—the size of tumor reduction after treatment, and so on. ImClone's German affiliate, Merck (not to be confused with American Merck), would do a new study with 225 patients, testing both irinotecan and Erbitux alone and then in combination—that was what the FDA wanted, a big double-blind trial. The drug would pass early in 2003. He was sure of it. He brushed off the competition, laughed at the financial community—people in Wall Street were jealous, he said, because the Bristol deal was such a winner, and they wanted to bring him down. The media had frightened the shareholders. Everyone was to blame but him.

I left ImClone's office wondering not only about him but about myself. In the past, was there any end to my credulity, my desire to believe? I had always loved the way Sam threw himself into his many activities and interests, and I had scorned the prigs who wanted him chained to a lab bench. But now it did seem clear enough—even I had to admit it—that he had become inattentive to everything but his own net worth, and maybe inattentive to that, too, given how much debt he had piled up. Every day revealed business failures in the past that I hadn't known about—a restaurant called Sam's; the downtown magazine, *Nylon;* a dot-com venture called ibeauty.com, which sold beauty products and went bust. All failures. Former associates were suddenly coming out of the woodwork to sue him for "distress" or "illegal and unethical conduct." There was talk of swindles large and small, of friends cheated and then charmed out of pressing charges. It was open season, and I wasn't sure that he didn't deserve it.

Yet the FDA's refusal remained puzzling, since ImClone from the beginning had insisted that Erbitux worked best in tandem with irinotecan. They hadn't *proved* their contention, however. There was even some question whether irinotecan alone was reducing the tumors. After all, some patients might not respond to chemotherapy for a while and then suddenly begin to respond. To be sure of an agent's effectiveness or failure, you needed to observe its workings for a long period. From information later developed by a congressional hearing into ImClone's problems, it became clear that, originally, in 1999, ImClone had promised the FDA it would give the drugs in tandem only after patients had failed two cycles of irinotecan alone. But later that year Im-Clone had amended that protocol and allowed combination therapy *as soon as the patients had taken any irinotecan at all*. Im-Clone, however, didn't explain this shift to the FDA. In other words, rushing to get the drug approved, the company tried to pull a fast one, and the agency, which may not have spotted the change early on, had now caught up and was taking its revenge.

So there it was, and it broke your heart even as it astonished you with its idiocy. Sam, O Sam, you can't hustle the FDA!

For the second time, I felt sick. A kind of dread, a pit-of the-stomach dismay. Sam was either a faker or he was fantastically careless, a dreamer who let the details slip through his fingers as he envisioned, not very far in the distance—why not partake of it now?—glory, glory, glory.

In exile from Wall Street, Henry Blodget, in the warm winter of 2002, had taken up residence during the day at Rafaella, a quiet café in Greenwich Village outfitted with well-worn upholstered seats, antique tables, and demure lights. The place had a down-at-the-heels but companionable air: a good café for reading and writing; a place to pass the time, to molder or hide in. Henry had got married, and he and his wife had a new baby, a little girl; he lived a few blocks away, in the West Village town house he had purchased. The previous December, about five months after Merrill's settlement with the investor who claimed that Henry had misled him, Henry had taken a buyout from the company. He was unemployed and, in the Village, unknown. For several years a familiar face on CNBC or in the *Wall Street Journal* and the *Times*, he was now a disgraced prince among indifferent commoners—N.Y.U. graduate students with their philosophy and history texts and a variety of time wasters sipping their way through a long day. Henry wore slacks and a sweater over a white T-shirt. He sat at one of the antique tables typing on a lap-top. He was working on a book about his time on the Street.

As we started to talk, he seemed rueful, saying again that he was sorry he had not downgraded the entire Internet sector on January 2000. He abruptly took off his sweater—the winter warmth had crept into Rafaella—and I felt the melancholy ab-surdity of his situation, just as I had felt it the last time we talked. He was forced to choose between two unappetizing possibilities. Either he admitted that Gretchen Morgenson and everyone else ridiculing him was right—that he had behaved in an unethical way, touting lousy stocks in order to bring in banking business—or he had to say that he blew it and simply got the Internet sector wrong. He chose the latter defense, but I wondered to myself, Was he really sorry he had not downgraded the sector in early 2000? Or was this a mere fantasy of rectitude? As he knew better than I, if he had downgraded the entire sector, he would not have made a huge pile from bringing in banking business over the next two years. His magic as a predictor of shareholder value had faded by the summer of 2000, and yet he was still paid a staggering $12 million for his work at Merrill in the year 2001. The enormous compensation after failing at his nominal job was the giveaway. He was pleasing his bosses and maximizing his pay.

He put his sweater back on. What *about* the conflict charges? I pressed him harder than I had in the past, and he sighed.

"Sure, the possibility of conflict is enormous. There's a tremendous amount of pressure on an analyst. But it comes in this order: The most powerful pressure comes from the investors, particularly the institutional investors. They don't want you to downgrade a stock that they own. Second, the pressure comes from the company itself. And only third does it comes from the banking division of your own house. You can't believe the unpopularity of a 'sell'—everyone wants to rip you to pieces. If you issue a sell rating and you are right, you get honor and praise maybe one year later. But if you are *wrong*, the amount of damage to you is enormous. You have no further relationship with the company that you've told people to sell. They will not do banking with your house—forget it. The risk-reward factor is against saying 'sell.'"

Damned if he didn't take his sweater off again, and as he pulled the garment over his head, I said to myself, "Well, that's as close to the truth, as close to a confession, as you are going to get. No analyst has been more candid. *There's no gain in ever saying 'Sell this stock.'*" But now he was screwed. Wealthy, maybe, but screwed. And maybe not wealthy forever. Eliot Spitzer, the Attorney General of New York State, was looking into Merrill's operations. There was talk in the air of punishment.

What, I wondered, was Henry going to put in his book? Was he going to emphasize all the ways he had misunderstood the Internet in 2000? Explain again and again why he had not seen that this company was in trouble or that that company had a ridiculous business model? Would anyone believe that he had simply not seen? My guess was that after his initial enthusiasm, born out by the rising prices in 1998, 1999, and early 2000, he had seen all too well, and had played the game to his own and Merrill's benefit for as long as he could. He said in the café that he still loved the life, that he wanted to get back into Wall Street—he would work for a hedge fund, perhaps. But was he still employable?

We left together, shook hands, and wished each other well. I walked up Seventh Avenue in the warm winter air with a stone in my heart. He was trying to be straight, and not quite making it. He couldn't be straight without admitting that his ratings were a fraud. He kept taking that sweater on and off because he no longer knew who he was—a young employee following orders and therefore an aggrieved fellow, unfairly scapegoated for others' sins; an opportunist making a quick fortune; or a trapped man preparing a legal defense. He was trying on identities—that unfinished portion of his face that I had noticed two years earlier was still a blank. As for me, I couldn't be straight without admitting that I thought he was lying to himself and to me. I got into the subway and went home with a depression that took days to wear off.

*   *   *

In March, as winter ended, I escaped the scandals and my own disappointments and took Tommy to Japan. Not quite fifteen, he was six feet tall, a longitudinal joker who had unaccountably developed a serious interest in Japanese culture and all things Eastern. He read enormous samurai narratives like Eiji Yoshikawa's *Musashi* and reveled in the sanity of the Eastern religions. I didn't have the time for the trip, I couldn't afford it, but as a self-appointed, unofficial celebrant of the West and its Great Books, I told myself that ignorance alone required that I go — I knew nothing of Japan and Eastern religions. Tommy happily led me into Shinto and Buddhist shrines in Tokyo, Osaka, Nara, and Kyoto, and I was blank a lot of the time — in Japan, one thinks of nothing but Japan.

Blank until one night in Kyoto, when I lay flat on a tatami mat in a country-style inn. In recent months, the New York apartment had become a painful place to be. The sharp noises outside had entered my house. There was scandal among my friends, and the scandals affected me. What was in me that had made me blind for so long — blind to what was obviously wrong with these guys? I was attracted to the vaunting ambition, mesmerized by the reckless desire for fame and wealth and an obvious disdain for rules, proofs, cautions. And I liked their style, obviously, the intellectual panache of these brilliant men. The critic had been fooled, and now, lying on the mat, I wondered, as everyone else did, Did Sam know? Did he know in the summer of 2001 that the FDA would turn down the drug? Because if he did, he was an abominable scoundrel and I would have to think of my own relation to him over the previous two years with nothing but shame.

I lay there quite a while as Tommy slept on the mat beside me. And I decided: Despite my new skepticism about Sam, I didn't believe that he knew. What would be the point of making a killing only to run into disgrace when the drug failed? He would make much more money if the drug were a success. The truth, I thought, was that he believed it *was* a success. He had never taken the FDA's problems seriously. He wanted the money so badly; he wanted the high-rolling friends, the parties, the gossip, the Hamptons, SoHo, the writers, the art, the candles burning brightly and turning his loft into a theater of intellect; he wanted it all so badly that he couldn't get himself to believe that they would turn down the trials. After all, there was nothing else out there for patients with advanced colorectal cancer — the patients, I realized as I lay there, who would now continue dying without hope. At least not until German Merck completed its trials and the drug was resubmitted to the FDA. Many people in biotech believed that Erbitux was still a usable drug and a financial winner. That was the lacerating irony embedded in Sam's many troubles.

As for Henry, he was a young man who had been faced with enormous temptations and pressures and had acted unethically, and eventually had been expelled and ridiculed, and was now lost in delusional self-justification. Along with Sam, he was a player in the massive transfer of money from shareholders to managers and to people like himself. Of course, we went along willingly, we investors. I couldn't blame the bubble on Henry Blodget and Sam Waksal. Neither of them had asked me to invest in anything. Nor had their actions ever been aimed at me personally. But the effects of their actions had hurt me and other people, and I said to myself, lying on my back and aware of the absurdity of the thought occurring at that moment — in Japan, in a country-style inn, lying on the floor — that what we really needed was ethics. We needed ethics selfishly, for our own survival. We couldn't go on this way in America. We needed to pass some sort of standard on to our children — to Max shoveling the solid stuff and to Tommy reading samurai narratives.

In one way or another, I had finally come around to the anger

I had forbidden myself to feel against my wife. September 11 brought me around, and then the scandals, and now my wayward friends. That two men had betrayed my faith was of course no more than a single strand of bitterness in the maelstrom of fraud, job loss, and equity loss. The larger wound was that Sam Waksal and Henry Blodget were part of the general discrediting of the market, the breaking down of trust that had taken over sixty years to build up. Millions of disgusted people were pulling out. And this departure posed a real threat to the future. Even if profits recovered, the market would not climb back if few people trusted it enough to invest in it.

I was lucky that Tommy's new interest had led me out of the apartment and over to Japan. In my own house, the teacups had cracked and fallen into pieces.

27

The End of Capitalism?

Quarterly Report, July 1, 2002
Cumulative Net Loss $720,000

YOU could see the changes easily enough. At the newsstands on Broadway, the 500-page Internet magazines had vanished, and the vendors, chatting on cell phones, half in English, half in Urdu, omitted any mention of Ariba or Vitesse (my Urdu, of course, is flawless). Jackie, the retired day trader, just waved at me and smiled when I passed him on Broadway. At lunch counters, the muscular young men talked about the Yankees. No one shouted tips near the subway entrance at 72nd; people shouted rap lyrics or complained about the weather, and in the No. 1 train, going downtown, only the Wall Street types read the *Journal* or *Barron's*. Robert Shiller and Arthur Levitt had got it right two years earlier — when the market stayed down, the air slowly oozed out of the obsession, the gleeful smile vanished from ordinary conversation, the culture returned to its normal preoccupations of sex, politics, and sports.

Times Square, however, seethed more violently than ever. It was bursting with events, the police were all over the place. At times, banging against teenagers, cops, Iowans, Italians, and Brits, I literally had to fight my way to the office. Perhaps Jennifer Lopez was shooting a video at the corner of 44th Street and Seventh Avenue. Or maybe the NFL was kicking off its season with a rock concert right in front of the northern side of the zipper. Again and again, the kids on the street who served as background material for MTV stood waving their arms in unison like dim Corybants in some hapless and obscure religion. Choking and impassable as it was, Times Square, in the last two years, had only increased its centrality as the site of news, entertainment, and finance for the entire world. Reuters, the British colossus, had built an enormous office tower on Seventh Avenue and 43rd, and now its electronic billboard joined the other neon wonders dumping redundant and depressing stock results into the agitated air.

Standing in *The New Yorker*'s office late one day in September 2002, I could see, from the west side of the building, the glow of the fleeting zipper way below me. But the views of the Hudson River and New Jersey, so lovely when the magazine moved into the building in 1999, had completely disappeared. The Reuters tower blocked one good swatch of water, and from the southern side of the building, a second new office tower blocked another glimpse of the river. For a year or so, we had been watching that forty-nine-story building going up to the south with the words ARTHUR ANDERSEN running along the side of its steel frame. In the summer of 2002, it no longer said ARTHUR ANDERSEN. It no longer said anything. Andersen, the giant accounting and consulting firm whose name had turned up as auditor not only for Enron but for many another wayward corporation, had been indicted by the Justice Department, crushed, and reduced to a shell.

294

A threat hung over the tumultuous neighborhood. The zipper itself, for instance, ran around another shell. One Times Square was now empty, inhabited by a surly guard sitting in the lobby behind closed doors. The money for the redevelopment of Times Square — the huge hotels opening on 42nd and 43rd, the amusement and movie-theater complexes stuck in everywhere — had been committed before September 11 and way before the Enron and accounting scandals. But those disasters had further weakened the economy and had sunk the stock market, and now one wondered if the new buildings in the square would actually find tenants. Andersen had planned to fill *its* new building all by itself, but now the structure, 7 Times Square, was slated to be a commercial space available to anyone. As we now knew, buildings could fall down. They could also turn into the kind of uninhabited "see-through real estate" that dotted Jakarta and other Third World capitals. A wave of doubt, ripening into panic, went through the American republic of capitalism in the summer of 2002 — in its intensity, the fear was perhaps unlike anything felt since the Great Depression.

After fading for a while, the issue of corporate malfeasance had sprung back to life on June 25, 2002, when WorldCom Inc., the second-largest telecommunications company in the world, announced that its audit committee had turned up an accounting error of $3.8 billion. The company had billed as capital expenditures what were really expenses. Expanding its network early in 2001, WorldCom treated the costs as an asset that could be written down over time. The transfer helped boost cash flow, which is what analysts and investors look at. For a while, the scam worked. But by 2001, when it became clear that Internet traffic was not, as people had insisted earlier, doubling every ninety days, and that, further, long-distance telephone rates in WorldCom's vast service had seriously fallen, the bottom fell out. When the company filed for bankruptcy protection on July

21, it claimed serious assets of $107 billion. It was still a powerful entity, but it was a company run by hustlers and sold to the Street by a liar, telecom analyst Jack Grubman of Salomon, who had been adviser to CEO Bernard Ebbers, coaching the rudely formed Ebbers on what to say in public meetings. Meanwhile, Grubman had bribed other telecom CEOs with offers of IPO shares on the first day of trading for new little companies. My IPO hunt in the Adirondacks looked more ridiculous every day.

On CNBC, Kudlow quivered and shook his cuff links, and Cramer lowered his taurine head and bellowed. Who could trust the accounting numbers? Companies used whatever accounting standard was most favorable to their situation: pro forma, EBITDA, "operating earnings," "core earnings." Some of the results were kosher, and others, which hid debt and write-offs and artificially improved cash flow, were sheer humbug approved by lazy or corrupt outside auditors.

Corporate management, the golden trophy of national virtue for the last decade, was within months degraded and tabloidized and, fairly or not, reborn in the public mind as a squalid mess of profligacy and corruption in which yachts, ranches, and ski chalets were purloined from shareholder equity. The examples of bad behavior were legion. My favorite: Dennis Kozlowski of Tyco trying to avoid New York State taxes on his new art collection by pretending to ship the art to New Hampshire. Like many scoundrels, Dennis Kozlowski had conservative taste in art. He liked flowers gathered in shy, innocent bowers or handsomely arranged in vases — Caillebotte and Monet and also John La Farge's *Hollyhocks*. Irony of ironies: *There* were the material things that I had trouble locating in the New Economy — there, in the Hamptons estates, the golf courses built with company money, the Renoir paintings. In the spoils stolen from investor value.

In response to the scandals, the market tumbled again in late

July, the Dow fell over 600 points in one week, the indexes hit five-year lows, with all the billowing gains of the late nineties wiped out. Gone, all gone! People were getting out, and the market was going way, way down, *burrowing* into the depths; it was one of the worst markets of the century, and it made a mockery of investment itself. Money salted away in 401(k) plans was routinely halved or cut by two-thirds in value; millions of people in their late fifties shelved their plans to retire; 500,000 people had been thrown out of work in the telecommunications sector alone — the wreckage was awful to behold. My own disasters had been overtaken by the common disaster.

And I let it crash. What could I do? It was down way too far to sell any more now. Just wait until it came back, however long that took.

Standing at the western end of the building, above the zipper, I had to laugh. For if WorldCom was the tipping point that caused millions of people to pull out, then the illusions of the telecosm that had enveloped me had helped bring down the entire market. Many of the prancing steeds of the telecosm present at George Gilder's conference in 2000 were in deep trouble or had gone bust, and Gilder himself was reportedly broke, the victim of his own nonsense. His ecstatic praise of companies heading for bankruptcy was a fatuity worthy of the tulip-mad poets of seventeenth-century Holland, who compared the carmine-tinted *Tulipa clusiana* to the "faint blush on the cheek" of some darling virgin or other. A rising market buys bad poetry as well as lying analysis. By mid-2001, Gilder's conference racket had fallen way off, the newsletter subscriptions were down by half, and his recommended stocks, over the previous year and a half, had lost 75 percent of their value. Yet he continued writing of an all-optical paradise in his proudly incomprehensible jargon. The technology was there, he insisted, and the financing would come back someday. I prayed that Gilder was right, if only be-

297

cause I was sure that minority tastes in culture—old feature films and documentaries, foreign films, blues, jazz, and classical music recordings—would not survive without the transparent network delivering them to our homes. Certainly the commercial marketplaces as now constituted—the Blockbusters and Towers—wouldn't support those tastes with yards of space forever and ever.

As I stood there, I realized that in the morning, when I had walked through Times Square, fighting my way to the office, the zipper was moving, but I hadn't seen it. The words just flitted by, meaningless, weightless. Time passed, but time no longer commanded attention from second to second, pulling me along with it head over heels, my arms grasping wildly for it as it rushed away from me. "The cradle rocks above an abyss, and common sense tells us that our existence is but a brief crack of light between two eternities of darkness." So Vladimir Nabokov wrote in his autobiography, *Speak, Memory*. "Although the two are identical twins," Nabokov pleasantly goes on, "man, as a rule, views the pre-natal abyss with more calm than the one he is heading for (at some forty-five hundred heartbeats an hour)." Yes, and fear of the second eternity, and anxiety in general, makes one's heart go even faster. I was beginning to wonder if my dread of not catching up with information—of falling behind the zipper—was not, in disguised form, a simple apprehension that time was running out. We don't live *in* time, Heidegger said, refining his definitions. Our *being* is time, the only existence we know.

Whatever the cause, time was losing its rushing linear quality. My heartbeat was returning to normal—my pulling away from the market had restored time to its neutral state. Like everyone else, I worried about other things—the security of my city, my country, my children. It had been a bad time, but at least I had kept the vows made two years earlier — the vows made on the knees of my ambition after reading of Nyquist's attack on his wife's assets and her life. I had not killed my wife, I had not shorted the market, dabbled in exotic investments, invested borrowed money. I had lied only once — failing to tell Cathy, out of shame, that our junk bonds in Globalstar had become almost worthless. The sudden evaporation of nearly $30,000 was too awful to describe out loud.

I left the western end of the building and went back to my windowless office. Dead Internet magazines and piles of the *Wall Street Journal* lay all over the place, some of the publications stacked neatly in promising piles, waiting to be consulted, others viciously scattered and trampled on the floor. What a period this has been. *What a period.* I pulled shut the door, so the rest of the staff couldn't see the remnants of my obsession, put my head in my hands, and closed my eyes. Unzipped, time now collected into fixed events that took on, in memory, a static quality, like the slightly awkward photographs of actors on a stage. The actors are straining toward the climax of their portentous melodrama. It is the last act of a didactic play, the crushing moment when iron lessons will be enunciated and the audience liberated at last into the cool night air.

On April 8, 2002, Eliot Spitzer had filed an affidavit in State Supreme Court detailing his investigations into Henry Blodget's group of Internet analysts at Merrill Lynch. Posted on the Attorney General's Web site, it made for depressing reading. Having seized the internal e-mails, Spitzer and his office were able to chronicle a pattern of outrageous cynicism. It seems the public ratings of "buy" were occasionally accompanied, inside the office, by outbursts of private distaste for the stocks in question. There were such comments as "fundamentals horrible" and "piece of junk" and "POS" (piece of shit) and "No hopeful news to relate," and so on. The mean flatness of the words, encountered now in cold print, was the final slap across the face of investor trust. Henry's Internet group had also, on several occasions, showed its analysis of certain companies to the companies themselves before releasing the material to Merrill's clients; the companies, not surprisingly, had requested adjustments in what was said about them. And the group had consistently pitched their ratings toward securing banking business and had then tabulated the results of their efforts for Merrill's higher-ups, with the consequence, as I knew, that Henry's compensation had jumped from $3 million in 1999 to $12 million in 2001.

On May 21, Merrill agreed to pay a fine of $100 million for failing to address conflict of interest within its own walls. The link between compensation for analysts and investment banking would be severed—a split that ended the possibility of any analyst at Merrill or anywhere else ever earning $12 million a year. So Henry's malfeasances (and not just Henry's, of course) wound up destroying the joyride for an entire profession.

I was all frozen up, my heart set against him, but I had to see him one last time, to hear what he would say. At the end of the summer, I met him again in the Village. He had changed cafés— this new one, Doma, at Seventh Avenue and Perry Street, was lighter, brighter, not so grotto-like, with little paintings and sculptures hanging on the walls. As before, Henry was sitting at a table with his laptop, working on his book. His appearance was the same, his face a mask of good humor, but he had locked himself into a defensive posture. What about the e-mails? Oh, he said, they were no more than the product of office exasperation.

"It's like football players gathering into a huddle and saying, 'Isn't the coach an asshole?'"

Sorry, but it wasn't much like that. At the same time that the "football players" were grousing to each other, outside the huddle they were touting the stocks and misleading a lot of people, who then lost millions of dollars. What he said to me sounded like a legal defense, as if he expected to be hit with a criminal charge from either Spitzer or New York City District Attorney Robert M. Morgenthau. I was pained by the spurious analogy and said nothing. The empty space in his long face was now filled in; he was publicly revealed as duplicitous, his charm a mechanism for fooling others and possibly himself. Set against him now, I still had to ask: What was the difference between us? After all, we both had got caught up in the boom. But I had hurt only myself, and he had hurt others. He would now have to meet his fate, whatever it was, on a lonely path. I had let him go—and I had let a part of myself go, too. I couldn't help him, and I wasn't sure that I wanted to. But I felt a pang at the same time, because it was his candor, which I had so much admired when I first met him and he had leaned across the table and spoken and listened with such atten-tion—the natural frankness of a young man who hasn't yet es-tablished an elaborate set of defenses and wants to appeal to colleagues—yes, his *candor* had got him into trouble. If he had not blurted the truth into friendly ears at the office, he wouldn't have been singled out by Eliot Spitzer. There were other ana-lysts, equally culpable, their ratings equally misleading or unreli-able, who had been shrewder about cloaking what they really thought. They may have lost credibility, but by remaining stony and silent, they had avoided Henry's kind of trouble—Henry Blodget, who had risen and fallen as fast as anyone in American financial history. He *was* the bubble.

The actors stood on the stage, straining for the end; and again, in the office, I thought, *What a period this has been!* In May, on the twenty-second, Sam Waksal had resigned from ImClone. "All the attention was falling on me," he said to me at his loft, with the usual broad smile, "and people were forgetting the drug." He said this as if his resignation from the company he had built for eighteen years was no big deal, just a temporary

301

arrangement until the storm blew over. Racing around at his party, he was madly chipper.

But on June 12, 2002, at 6:30 A.M., Sam was arrested at home. The feds arrived, and he let them in, still wearing his pajamas, and asked them to delay putting on the cuffs—he didn't want his daughter Aliza to see him in that condition. He was cuffed outside, on Thompson Street, and hustled into a waiting van, wearing slacks and an open shirt, with reporters shouting questions at him. Obviously the media had been tipped off. The word must have come down from the Justice Department to give him the full treatment. On the news, for the rest of the day, there were shots of him doing the "perp walk." In this society, the end for a fallen celeb is severe in its banality. The jeering media punishes anyone it has helped build up, and the perp walk becomes not just a nasty phase in your life but your public identity for years. Sam was charged with insider trading and perjury. They also took his passport away, as if he were some sort of roguish "flight risk" about to abscond with assets, like the fugitives Robert Vesco and Marc Rich.

In the office, months later, I was still stunned. Dear God, he had dragged his Holocaust-survivor father into this! I then remembered another detail of what Sam had told me about Jack Waksal's wartime experience: He had watched his three-year-old sister get shot in the head by the Germans at the beginning of the occupation. And yet, despite such catastrophes, he had survived. And played his double game with the Americans after the war. In the end, Sam's conscious emulation of his father's bravado and duplicity wound up pulling his father into fraud, an irony that could break anyone's heart.

For months I had been sick of irony, but another one, of course, quickly intruded itself: After Sam's arrest, his notoriety was brushed aside by his association with Martha Stewart. The law of celebrity took over, and the queen of good living was a juicier target for the media than a bony biotech executive with an incomprehensible drug and peculiar social habits involving intellectuals as well as rich people. Martha Stewart also sold ImClone on December 27, the day before the FDA refusal was made public, and her claim that she had earlier placed a stop-loss order with Merrill, selling the stock if it went below $60, was an apparent lie.

In my magazine-carpeted office, I was saying dumb things to myself like "I may have lost almost a million dollars, but at least I still have my job and my reputation and I'm not going to the slammer." I needed to reassure myself, because the illusions continued to fall. For one, I would have to rethink my belief that entrepreneurial skill manipulating the capital markets was the best way to develop exciting new drugs. Sam raised hundreds of millions, floated the company, retrofitted a factory in New Jersey, ramped up production, brought in investment big shots like Carl Icahn and Pete Peterson, made his deal with Bristol—and it was all based on his ability to tell a story. What earlier had seemed marvelous now seemed sinister. Since the laws allow managers, in advance of performance, to exercise options and enrich themselves, even when the product is just a theory, the system offers a structural temptation to dishonesty, false promises, and fantasy—even more enormous a temptation (in fact, unique) when the product in question is a therapy for cancer, and people are willing to throw money at mere possibilities. So I made a tentative answer to my heavy question dragged out of the subway a couple of years earlier, the question provoked by the South Sea Bubble of 1720: "Is there something inescapably criminal in the process of quickly raising money for a new enterprise?" The answer, of course, is that there's something *escapably* criminal, and that's why we need regulators, prosecutors, and an ethics that the ambitious and wealthy will live by. The lowest estimate of Sam's recklessness was that he betrayed cancer patients for a loft, a few paintings, a house in the Hamptons, and a whiff of celebrity. The highest estimate—mine—was that he was intellectually, morally, and emotionally incapable of facing the truth and by degrees slipped into fraud rather than admit he had screwed up. Either way, the system didn't do enough to discourage bad behavior.

With a groan I remembered my last time at Sam's loft. It was on June 5, 2002, exactly one week before he was arrested. A good crowd, maybe fifty people, had turned up to hear Ann Douglas, a professor of English at Columbia, talk about film noir in the forties, the culture of New York, and the culture of Los Angeles, and Sam, wearing jeans, loafers without socks, and a pink shirt, was even more relaxed than usual. In the middle of the evening, walking through the loft with a wineglass in my hand, I conferred with a friend, a literary intellectual of rather severe judgment. My friend said to me, "I don't want to give up my belief in him." Then he paused and uttered this astonishing sentence: "I would loan him money if he needed it." This from a man who probably had very little money. When my friend said that, I realized that more was on the verge of disappearing than a pleasant regular evening for a few privileged people. Sam had injected romantic faith into the world. He inspired loyalty, even sacrifice. People saw their aspirations enacted in him; they were grateful, despite everything.

At the end of the evening, I caught Sam and said, "You're so irrepressible, I can never tell what's going on with you."

"Yes, that's my secret."

"You mean I can never pluck out the heart of your mystery."

"No, you can't," he said, laughing, as he walked off, and I was hit by alternating waves of admiration and contempt so intense that I had to retreat to a corner of the room to sort out my feelings. This con man, this trifler, this buffoon—who was yet so appealing—had lied to everyone. He had wanted to avoid everyone's knowledge, even mine, though I could do him no harm. He was always playing the game, right to the end, hoping for one more day on top, one more person to charm.

That was in June. Surrounded by dead bubble magazines in September, I knew it was time to look at this greed thing again.

Dennis Kozlowski of Tyco tried to avoid taxes on his art purchases. Martha Stewart's take from her sale of ImClone stock was $228,000. Amazing, amazing, for each of these two had control of assets worth $1 billion or more. The money they got in trouble over was *peanuts*. So there it was. Behavior that seemed irrational to the rest of the world was perfectly rational to the greedy person: *You must never pass up any opportunity to make money or avoid loss.* These two, I guessed, had always acted this way; only this time they got caught. In my conjugation of greed's many forms back in the winter of 2000—when I saw so many positive sides to it as a human force—I managed not to emphasize the most obvious thing, the insatiability, the insistence on more and more, forever and ever. And why not? Because I had feared that most obvious part of greed.

There was one great American writer who understood greed very well. In her portrait of Undine Spragg in the bitterly funny 1913 novel *The Custom of the Country*, Edith Wharton created a gorgeous monster. Undine, a provincial beauty, arrives in New York and marries into a distinguished old family, then leaves her husband and child, marries a European aristocrat weighted down with tapestries and furniture, and leaves him as well. A stunning American woman, superbly dressed, she makes terrific entrances into Parisian salons but loses everyone's interest within minutes. Undine is essentially asexual; indeed, she is bored by all topics but money and power, and the book ends with her stranded in a state of wealthy dissatisfaction. "Even now, how-

305

ever, she was not always happy. She had everything she wanted, but she still felt, at times, that there were other things she might want if she knew about them." In other words, further knowledge would only make her more predatory. In Wharton's terms, there is no cure for this condition, no resting place, no promise of satiety and ease in the future, when Undine might attain peace. At its worst, then, greed is a fixed quality, like an unappeasable sexual perversion. There are laws to protect us from people so afflicted, though in America the legal structure is more an enabler than an active discourager of greed.

Yet I couldn't leave it there. The desire for money sharpens the appetite for life, particularly in middle age. I work harder at my writing now than I did when I was younger. To do decent work and to get well paid for it is one of the great blessings of a democratic capitalist society. And to get hold of a piece of a growing economy is also a blessing. I could not give up the positive valence of greed as a goad to performance and risk.

My thoughts on greed had become a tangle. So let us try to pull the mess apart and make some order. Let us to come to an end. Originality isn't the issue here; usefulness is the issue. Since September 11, I had been back in Great Books mode, and now I thought, "Every man his own Aristotle. Take a shot at it. Hold off the derision. Don't be afraid to be simple." Let us ask, as Aristotle would have asked, What are the ends of life? What do we live for? In other words, what are our ethics, what is our character—the things for which we strive, for which we make sacrifices? And where does greed, for good and ill, fit into the ends of life?

The ultimate ends of life are these:

First, existence itself—survival. After September 11, when it became clear that Americans *as Americans,* apart from their personal qualities, could be eliminated by religious totalitarians without any guilt whatsoever—after that event, survival, more than ever, becomes a daily preoccupation. And I add to survival all that makes for physical happiness and well-being, since survival itself is not enough for most of us. One would have to include shelter, security, health, all the body comforts that enhance sensual pleasure. Even a touch of luxury. The literal-minded will balk at luxury placed under this heading, since luxury, by definition, is splendor in excess of what is necessary to survive. But I am listing the ends not the necessities of life, and the desire for luxury as an extension of sensuous pleasure seems legitimate as a goal. The desire for a few extraordinary comforts is not corrupting, it's merely human. A few lusts, a few wants . . . I would buy that Audi with its Ming-blue metallic paint glowing in the sun, I would buy it someday.

Second: Love in all its forms, not just erotic and romantic love, and not just family love, but friendship, mentorship, teaching of every variety; cultivation of living things, animals, and land; even caring for machines if they are useful or beautiful enough.

Third: Achievement, and pride in achievement—what the Greeks called "spiritedness" and we call prowess or ability, and its rewards in money and prestige. The desire to do well and to be recognized for it. In a commercial civilization like ours, the danger of self-betrayal—"selling out"—may be a constant threat, but the shrewdest survivors know how to avoid it, they know how to sell without selling out.

Fourth: The desire to attain knowledge in all its forms; and the making and appreciation of craft, art, and entertainment.

Fifth and last: A coherent metaphysical or biological portrait of how existence works—God, the devil, the Big Bang, natural selection. I know many people live without any such idea. The notion of karma holds no interest for them, they are not pantheists, though they may lack the energy to be atheists—they don't regard spiritual clarity or the strenuousness of belief as

307

necessary, they merely accept the tribal or local belief as a social convenience. The rest of us seek some answer to the eternal questions, some insight into the two eternities that Nabokov wrote about.

So where does greed fit in? Money hunger is necessary for many as a motivation for hard work and its recognition. It tickles and then enables the desire for luxury. It answers to the ends of life, and therefore to ethical sense, in those two ways — that is, only in its minimal forms. The rest of greed is perversion, or at least a deformation of character, and not just in such recent instances as CEOs lifting money from shareholders. Greed in its extreme form is a deformation of one's general relation to money. Georg Simmel was good on this subject. Simmel, the great German sociologist, brought out his voluminous study, *The Philosophy of Money,* in 1900, only a few years after Veblen completed *The Theory of the Leisure Class.* Money, says Simmel over and over, has no character of it own, or rather, its character is neutral, devoid of qualities. There are those, of course, who disagree and have compared money to blood or semen or whatnot — shit, in Dickens's *Our Mutual Friend* and Freud's psychology. But these are unconscious associations and metaphorical mystifications, and I preferred Simmel's definitional literal-mindedness:

> Money is the institution through which the individual concentrates his activity and possessions in order to attain goals that he could not attain directly. . . . It is restricted to being a pure means and tool in relation to a given end, has no purpose of its own and functions impartially as an intermediary in a series of purposes.

At what point does your relation to this pure tool change? Obviously, when money becomes an end in itself rather than a means. And when does that happen? I wanted to be wealthy, and

I didn't make it, and the messiness and inconsequence of my life over the previous three years might be answer enough — at times, I acted as if money were an end in itself, and I came close to betraying my true calling, which was writing. To fill out my scheme for others, however, I needed to ask, How does one define wealth in this extravagant country? If one knew the answer, one might be able to set some practical limit on greed.

At this point, I'm afraid, I will incur the ridicule of moralists. Certainly anyone from a society less affluent than ours will be appalled by my answer, while the American families living at the median — $43,000 a year — will utter a few silent curses, and rightly so. What I'm doing here, however, is suggesting ethics for big shots. To be wealthy in America you need two nice places to live, one in the city and one in the country, and $5 million in liquid assets (some would add a private plane and another $15 million, but such people are nuts). It takes more than that to build a large company, of course; I'm speaking merely of personal wealth, and with two places to live and $5 million — a great deal of money, by any standard — you can pick up and go from street to meadow and then back, you can live amid beauty. How does one arrive at such an amount? How does one draw a line beyond which the pursuit of additional money begins to turn into the destructive extravagance of greed? By applying my little scheme of life's ends and also Simmel's formulations. For it is not necessary, I believe, to build liquid assets of more than $5 million in order to attain the great ends of life — survival, love, achievement, knowledge, or belief. You cannot amass greater amounts of money than that without beginning to see money as an end in itself and then taking on what Simmel calls the characterless quality of money. That is, you have few significant passions outside it. You become cynical, and assume an instrumental view of friendship and of everything else — how does it make me richer? You turn yourself, not money, into a tool.

The powerful cannot continue to blandly assert, "I did nothing illegal," that infuriating phrase which covered a host of barbarities. Is it too much to ask CEOs and Wall Street types to observe the simple requirement that they build corporations and shareholder value and accept the appropriate rewards and glory due them without robbing other people? Possession without dispossession? And that they submit all other desires for money to the simple tests — Does this desire benefit the company, benefit shareholders? And does it answer to the ends of life in any way that makes sense? Is that naive? Or is it the opposite of naive, a requirement without which investing will never again attain the widespread trust, the excitement, the sheer fun of the great boom years of the nineties? That's what it comes down to. On Wall Street, ethical behavior, and the trust that it inspires, is not some prissy system of safeguards for shrinking violets. On the contrary, it is precisely the force that makes the entire roaring, tumultuous, risk-loving, irrational, baffling, thrilling, many-faceted carnival benefit a larger and larger number of people in the first place. Ethical behavior helps keep the market alive; it keeps the market liquid and surging. It makes us all prosperous.

But enough. Take off the toga. Sitting in the office amid dusty copies of the *Journal* and dead Internet magazines, I could come no closer than that to an Aristotelean ethics of greed. It was time to tend my own garden, clean house — my own house, literally. I was sprucing up the apartment. I was going to sell it, at last.

28

Slowing Down

Quarterly Report, October 1, 2002
Cumulative Net Losses $900,000

OBSERVED from the rear, Sam Waksal stood up straight in court on the morning of October 15, 2002—not ramrod straight, in the military cliché, but with a slight bend that was actually rather graceful. Physically, he appeared at ease as he rested his right hand, knuckles down, on the surface of a table and listened to the judge. I stood behind him and off to the right, leaning against a paneled side wall in Federal Court, Southern District of New York, as Sam pleaded guilty to six federal charges and heard Judge William H. Pauley III say that he had the power to sentence him to sixty-five years in prison.

"Do you understand that the maximum penalty for bank fraud is thirty years imprisonment, followed by a fine of one million dollars or twice the pecuniary gain that you have realized from these transactions or twice the amount you have cost others?"

"I do, your honor."

Over and over, the judge asked, "Do you understand?" A possible ten years for securities fraud (i.e., insider trading), five for obstruction of justice, years more on the other counts. And all Sam could say — this man who could talk his way in and out of anything, who could sell snake oil to a snake — all he could say was "Yes, your honor" and "I do, your honor."

For months, I had been half-welcoming his comeuppance. But in the courtroom I was shocked. The law could do this. The law had the power to crush a wealthy and well-connected man. The moment was like something out of Dickens. The judge was polite but implacable. He made Sam recite his crimes, which he did, in outline, reading from notes: "Based on my information from the FDA, which I knew would depress the value of ImClone's stock, I caused my daughter to sell her shares. . . . On or about January 12, 2002, in order to hide certain personal financial records, I ordered my staff to limit the SEC's access to those records . . ." And so on. He had forged the signature of a company lawyer to a letter attesting that he still possessed assets that he had in fact disposed of; he had lied, swindled. The judge reminded him several times that a guilty plea, once entered, cannot be withdrawn. He understood that, too.

Sam Waksal had destroyed himself by making mistakes of almost unimaginable stupidity. By engaging in insider trading — which is sometimes easy to detect — he caused his earlier crimes to come to life. And by getting his own family in trouble, he sealed his fate. Once the feds could bring charges against his father and daughter, he lost his room to maneuver. Even if he were willing to give them the names of other people he had tipped off, they could always force him to plead guilty by threatening to put Aliza and Jack Waksal in jail. The old man had survived the Nazis, but at the age of eighty, he would not survive a prison sentence.

But now, Sam was doing something almost noble—he was trying to save his father and daughter by sacrificing himself. He crafted his guilty pleas so as to absolve the two of them, and after months of negotiation, he had arrived at an apparent understanding with federal prosecutors that they would leave his family alone. An understanding, but not a deal. He was pleading guilty but not entirely co-operating, at least not yet—not turning in names of other people he might have tipped off. Seven charges against him remained outstanding. In effect, he threw himself on the court's mercy, and the legal analysts in the media thought his strategy very risky. The prosecutors could bring additional evidence to bear on him in a pre-sentencing hearing that could lengthen his years in federal prison. He was counting on the leniency of the judge. He was still gambling.

I looked at the people sitting behind him in the rows of benches. They were all reporters—everyone was taking notes. Sam's brother, Harlan, now the CEO of ImClone, was there, and Sam's lawyers, but I didn't see a single person from the candlelit soirees and high-rolling Christmas parties. It was just like Gatsby's funeral: No one showed up. Did his friends stay away to avoid witnessing his shame and embarrassing him further? Or did they turn away from the disaster, cravenly, cynically, with a laugh or a wave of nauseated pity? In any case, they didn't show.

Would I have come down to the court out of friendship alone? I had been following his adventures for two and a half years and needed desperately to understand him. I would have come down out of puzzlement, perhaps. And maybe, at the last minute, out of loyalty, too. In the jury box, in front of Sam, and off to the left, two artists sat with pads, drawing the face that I couldn't see. But what did they find there? Shame? Or was it defiance, even a glimmer of pride in the totality of his self-immolation? I didn't catch a glimpse of his expression until, the confessions finally over, the courtroom broke up and Sam suddenly turned around. He was gray, unsmiling, his eyes were sunken. He looked terrible. This was not pride.

He might have seen me. I couldn't tell. I lingered for a few minutes as his lawyers gathered around, and then I walked out, following the reporters into an elevator and down to the ground floor of the federal courthouse, where I found a telephone and called my office. But I couldn't leave the building. I didn't want to leave. Did I hate this man or not? Did I want him in prison?

In the hallway, on the ground floor, I remembered something Sam had told me about his birth. When Sam was born in Paris in the late forties, his mother, Sabina, was astonished. She had never felt him moving. All through the pregnancy, she thought she was carrying a dead fetus. It was, of course, a mythical birth, perfectly congruent in style with Jack Waksal's escape into the river and his bravura double-dealings. But was it true? Sam thought it was true, which is what matters, for, of course, he had never stopped moving since springing to life, Lazarus-like, from an apparently stillborn state. The first time I met him, at his loft in 2000, he seemed the most restless man I had ever seen, and the longer I knew him, the more activities I heard about. For instance, he bought lofts in SoHo and Tribeca, refitted them, and sold them at a profit, and when the insider-trading scandal broke, one of his buyers decided to sue him for shoddy workmanship — the place, he claimed, was falling apart. Sam seemed to invent ways of getting into trouble. He was so *busy*. And now he was going to federal prison. What could be a greater agony for a restless man than to be confined for years?

Another datum from Sam's myth-haunted origins: Entering the United States at Ellis Island, in 1951, when he was three and a half, he had long hair with a bow and he looked like a girl. The immigration officials made him "drop trou" to prove his parents' claim of masculinity. He told me this story with some

314

delight. Whether true or not, the tale suggested that his ability to dissemble, and the unknowability of his identity, had begun a long time ago. As a grown-up, he had, it turned out, a fabulous record of faking. On September 27, 2002, just before his guilty plea, the *Wall Street Journal* published an article by Geeta Anand retracing Sam's research career prior to setting up ImClone in 1984. At each of his jobs in those years — at Stanford, the National Cancer Institute, Tufts, and Mount Sinai Hospital in New York — he began with a brilliant idea, a fascinating research project, followed by a claim of unusual results. And just when he was scheduled to show his proofs, something went wrong — the beaker spilled in the refrigerator; the lab mice, genetically transformed, developed infections and died or turned out never to have existed. Or the claims were not borne out by the actual lab books — the results were fake.

It was "the dog ate my homework" over and over, and of course, the dog struck again, eating the "homework," as Sam said to me when describing the absence of proof in the Erbitux trials. This long record of flimflam, which hammered the last nail in the coffin of his reputation, reinforced my theory that Sam was less a conscious scoundrel than a fantasist who couldn't produce the goods. After each research failure, he would talk his way into a better job, and the previous boss, fearing a defamation suit, or perhaps thinking it was none of his business, kept quiet. Sam drifted upward, reached the pinnacle, and then fell in an instant to the tabloids and the prison yard, an American fool for the ages. But I still couldn't hate him, and I remained in the long corridor of the courthouse, which led to the front of the building on Pearl Street. Plaques, there were plaques on the wall with grave words about the law printed on them, and I stared at them without seeing a thing. Finally, Sam arrived on the ground floor with his lawyers and made his way down the corridor. He was going to face the cameras waiting outside the building. As he came toward me, I stepped out from the wall and offered my hand and wished him luck.

The handshake was firm, the gaze saddened but direct. He thanked me, nodding slightly, without a smile, but there was an instant of recognition, an acknowledgment of some bond, perhaps, just as there had been when I had said something interesting at one of his parties and he had flashed me a look. And then he continued down the corridor, and went out to face the furies in front of the courthouse on Pearl Street. Outside, before the press, he read a statement saying how sorry he was, how good a company ImClone was, how much he believed in Erbitux. When he was done, an enormous person from his lawyer's office wrapped his arms around the disgraced entrepreneur and hustled him through the pushing and shoving crowd of photographers and deposited him into the back of a darkened van. Behind the shrouded windows, Sam's face was invisible. Very quickly, the photographers and reporters dispersed, and I walked away from the courthouse in tears.

A few weeks later, I stood in the living room of a small apartment, looking south, over the tops of old brownstones and town houses. Below, in the backs of the houses, there were patios with trellises and little gardens, a hibachi or two. On a wooden sundeck, a pair of white cats wrestled, and then nipped and chased each other. The apartment was only a few blocks from the big place on West End Avenue. I was going to sell the old apartment and live in something much smaller.

The sky was open above the brownstones, but off to the right stood a series of enormous and clumsy residential towers put up by Donald Trump along the Hudson River. It was the great builder's latest assault on good sense, and Trump, as if he didn't have enough real estate in New York, planned to put up many more buildings along the river, including another monstrosity right next to a distinguished old structure on 72nd and the river, the Chatsworth. The tower would block the river views that the elderly folks living in the Chatsworth had enjoyed for a half century. It wasn't enough for Trump to own; he had to dispossess—that was the spirit of big money in this age. In my new apartment, despite Trump's invasion, the light was still good and the rooms were cheerful, though they were in a sorry state. The previous tenant had lived in the apartment since 1938. The kitchen linoleum was stained and cracked, the old cabinets were yellow, and the drawers, refusing to budge, suddenly burst out when you tugged, nearly falling to the floor. But I would make it new.

Cathy was finishing a novel, her sixth, in which a woman leaves her husband for another woman. She was living in her rental a few blocks away and would buy her own place the following spring. The real estate market in Manhattan, after booming for years, was finally softening a bit. Yet the apartment on West End was still a gold mine, worth $1.5 million or a little more. I had hated to leave the place so much that I had rarely thought of it as an investment, but of course, it *was*. For us, as for many Americans, real estate in the end had been a better deal than stocks. Now I was ready to go, eager to get out. I was restless, even disgusted. My prize, my cave, my tomb. *Leave* it, and know that leaving it was not dying. *Staying* in the place was dying. Why had it taken me over three years to see that I was expiring there? No woman worth having would join me in a place in which another woman had reigned. Suddenly I was excited by the idea of renovating the 1938 wreck a few blocks away.

After retiring the primary mortgage and also a home-equity loan, and then paying taxes, Cathy and I would each clear a good bit of money. Maybe—dare I say it?—this was the right time, now, in November 2002, to put fresh cash into the market. My friends rolled their eyes in dismay: "Hasn't this guy learned *anything?*" But the market was way, way down, a good time to invest.

The Nasdaq composite index hit a low of 1114 on October 9, 2002, a drop of 3934 points, or 78 percent, since March 10, 2000. At the end of the third quarter of 2002, our liquid assets, soon to be split, were down almost a $1 million on paper since the peak. One million . . . gone. It was so much money that thinking of it made me numb. You couldn't mourn that kind of loss the way you mourned the loss of, say, $50,000. I was beginning to feel like one of those men in South Carolina grinning into a TV camera after his home has been demolished in a hurricane. He was alive.

When I added up our totals, I realized that we now had about the same amount of money that we had laboriously saved and put into the market over a period of many years. In absolute terms, then, we hadn't lost our money, but we had failed to reap profits by getting out of the market anywhere near the peak, and we had lost the many years in which the money could have been invested in bonds, steadily earning income. My friend James Stevens, having lost $700,000 on paper, was also back to where he started. Jim had got out altogether back in June and had given his remaining assets to his brother's brother-in-law, the conservative money manager working in the Midwest—the manager who had told him two years earlier, when Jim was invested in just a few tech stocks, that he was crazy. Tech was now over as an investment, Jim said. Certainly a lot of products had fizzled, and by October 2002, the 100 largest tech companies had lost money in the aggregate for five straight quarters. Yet tech still accounted for about 14.5 percent of the S&P 500 index, and Scott Thurm and Ken Brown of the *Journal* pointed out on October 18 that "three times in the past quarter-century, tech has faced downturns and an uncertain future. Each time, new ideas, along with relentless improvement of existing products, brought the industry back to life in unforeseen ways, though some innovations took years to bear fruit."

All right, then. With a loud sigh, and a determination not to let myself feel like a fool, I resolved to look into the new thing, "Wi-Fi," or wireless fidelity — radio waves that operated in a commonplace, unregulated area of the spectrum, along with microwave ovens and digital satellite radios. The waves didn't extend very far — three, four hundred feet, good enough for linking computers in an office but also good for delivering Internet access at airports and hotels and malls. Something like 27 million business travelers carried their laptops along with them and regularly drummed their fingers with irritation as they wasted one, two, even three hours in an airport lounge. What if you could tune your laptop into the radio waves? The tiny Palm Pilot could be brought back to life by Wi-Fi; even better, a laptop receiving a serious dose of Internet on a full screen was a newly empowered machine. Intel had announced it would put a Wi-Fi radio on its Pentium chipset; it was investing in companies developing Wi-Fi networking.

There was no obvious Wi-Fi stock to buy in November 2002, but the whole area could be hot someday, it could take off, and my heart flipped a few times and my head throbbed, because I did not want to lose more money with another set of stupid investments. Yet I knew, as did everyone else, that those who invested in a new technology at the early stages and then got out did very well indeed. One didn't want to learn the wrong lesson — stay out of the market altogether — from the Internet and telecom crashes. That would be a way of being stupid twice, and a simple defeat of imagination and will. The market always came back . . . eventually.

Whatever my quavers in the summer over see-through real estate, American capitalism was not about to expire. No, it was righting itself, slowly threshing out the excesses of the nineties, taking its time — another six months, another year, maybe another eighteen months, and then expansion would begin again.

Meanwhile, the Winter Garden with its soaring trees and views of the harbor had been rebuilt, and there were signs of life even in the New Economy. On the Internet, retail sales had picked up, and Amazon was turning a profit. As financial writer James Surowiecki pointed out in *The New Yorker*, Henry Blodget, whatever his malfeasances, was right about Amazon in the end. Grant him that. And Ravi Suria, the Lehman bond analyst who received kudos in 2000 for insisting that Amazon would not be able to service its debt, was wrong.

In the fall of 2002, I took a look now and then, peeking through my fingers, and the entire market started to climb in the second week in October and continued to climb into November, and I knew, chastened but not quite inert, that if I ever did put fresh money in, I would go slowly, moving as cautiously as a father entering the room of a sleeping child. Slowly, and gently, very gently. And despite my looking for some way of getting in on Wi-Fi, I would return to the old strategy of diversification, which, as Jonathan Clements never tired of pointing out in the *Journal*, was the best way to build wealth over the long haul. With a sigh, I accepted the unexciting conventional wisdom, for it provided some measure of calm. Now that I had lost so much money, I was finding it easier to sleep at night—easier than when the market was at the peak and I *might* lose it. Loss came as a kind of relief, and the truth was that my wife and I, divorced, would survive. We would have less money, we would cut back, we would work, we would earn, we would love our boys, we would survive. Indeed, we would do more than survive. The truth—it had taken me more than three years to see it—was that Cathy was right to leave. I was grateful to her now for having the guts to get up and go rather than let the marriage harden into a bitter stalemate.

Was I insane in 2000? I was demoralized, that's for sure, demoralized and panicked, not just by the ending of my marriage but by the idea of splitting the growing nest egg in two. I felt cheated in some way, and afraid of poverty in old age, and I abandoned realistic optimism in favor of desperate optimism. And there was more, as I now knew: My disappearance into what Nabokov called the second eternity was not imminent, but it was no longer an event impossible to imagine. My emotional life had died, hadn't it?—vanishing into pornography, adultery, isolation. And I was demoralized by something else, a victory, actually—the closing down of any serious opposition to free-market capitalism. Capitalism was so powerfully and obviously triumphant worldwide that in a celebratory panic I rushed to embrace it. Like a convert lost in a frenzy of devotion, I threw myself into the new religion, and I forgot all the ways it could fool you, betray you, undermine you.

Finally, I was thrown by what seemed an irreversible decline. Leaving aside a spiritually impoverished avant-garde, commerce ruled a good part of the arts, and the abashed retreat of the arts from the center of so many lives, and the shift of creativity to technology, to science, to medicine, and to business, had left me wondering if I had not devoted my life to a waning force. Looking for a popular movie that was also a work of popular art, I was often ragged and unsatisfied in 2001 and 2002, though I was suddenly back in business in the fall of 2002 with the release of 8 Mile, the first picture devoted to a nasty-faced genius-punk. Eminem's movie was certainly not great, but it was alive.

In the tradition of *Rocky* and *Saturday Night Fever*, the movie is a shrewdly engineered piece of proletarian pop—a story of triumph—but, like Eminem's enraged lyrics, *8 Mile* has its own kind of vile candor. The great Mexican cinematographer Rodrigo Prieto (*Amor Peros*) keeps the visual palette ugly and raw—gray skies, damp streets, dank factories, graffiti-covered buildings. *8 Mile* is about *Detroitismo* in all its misery of sunken hopes and defiance. The

321

movie says, "Out of this junk, out of the self-hatred and anger that grows from living amid junk, rappers will make their art."

Renewal forged out of economic failure and cultural despair—now, that was something to cling to in late 2002. *8 Mile* told the story of the white rapper's origins in a straightforward way, rather than selling it with two hours of flashing music-video images. I took the aesthetics of *8 Mile* (not Eminem's performance, but the style of the movie as directed by Curtis Hanson) as a blessing and a confirmation, because I also needed to slow down, I needed to stop jabbering at people and listen more. I knew this three years earlier, but I acted as if I didn't know it. I longed for duration, but had forgotten how to achieve it.

By the end of 2002, I was more convinced than ever that our modern relation to time was screwed up. What would be the result if George Gilder's all-optical network became a reality? I mean, what would be the philosophical and psychological benefits apart from the overwhelming value of the network as a way of delivering imperiled minority cultures like jazz and old movies to our homes? As a tech guru advising investors, Gilder might have been a mountebank, but his hopes were still worth listening to. Gilder, you remember, longed for the end of waiting, the onset of simultaneity. In *Telecosm*, he described a family of the future. Everyone rises in the morning, and immediately father, mother, daughter, and son are learning from the Web, doing business on it even as they brush their teeth. They will accomplish routine tasks in a few minutes. But then what will they do with the time they have saved?

Since human beings through history have thrived through work, most people will use their liberated time to perform more valuable economic activity. Using the web, they will be able to work far more

322

efficiently, collaborating with the top experts everywhere and serving the markets around the globe. . . . Under capitalism, where profit comes from serving others, this release of entrepreneurial energy will be more morally edifying than the "leisure" diversions that many imagine to be the end and meaning of life.

So there you have it. The final triumph. We will work so hard that we will banish leisure altogether. The time we save, then, is not something we can deposit in a bank and withdraw when we need it, it is time taken away from the apparently immoral waste of art, entertainment, friendship, and thought. Now, this extraordinary denouement has its comical as well as its tragical side, since Gilder is a libertarian and his book is ostensibly a celebration of freedom. Yet his model family, at the apex of its alleged control over life, simply disappears into the network; or rather, each man, woman, and child takes the network into his being, and becomes a series of gleaming nodes without a center, connected to everyone in the world but not to himself.

I reject this utopia utterly. Obviously, it's a nightmare. In the modern world, time was the point, all right—not saving it, but expending it opulently, with the maximum sensuous unfolding of pleasure. The experience of duration I had been looking for—it couldn't have been anything else—was falling in love. The slow dinner, the filled-to-the-brim silences, the articulated pauses and renewals. Love slows you down. But at first, at fifty-nine, love is hard, a kind of painful displacement. Living by yourself for a few years, you build up the defensive egotism of loneliness, the proud habits and responses that sustain the peculiar project of isolation. You tell yourself that you are self-sufficient; you can read, sleep, work when you want. Love knocks all those ego props down. The woman I suddenly fell in love with in October was fifty-six years old, a distinguished person; she had ideas and passions and spirit, and golden skin, too—she was a knockout, in fact—and she slowly pulled me out of isolation, the sour egotism of "self-sufficiency." I was not divorced, but emotionally I was free, and she was free, too—her children were grown up—and we devoted long hours to each other and did cornball, movieish things like walking across Central Park in the rain. Lying side by side, we were astonished by our good luck. Love is harsh and demanding but tender beyond measure, too, for when you are in love, you experience time as slowly as anyone can.

When Cathy left, I became irrationally exuberant so as not to be dead. Like a starting pitcher who is removed from the game and slams his glove against the dugout wall and kicks the water cooler and knocks over a trash can and then kicks the *can*, too, I had acted out my grief, throwing money furiously away rather than moldering in my cave. But now the market assumed its proper proportion in life, as a minor passion, something to visit now and then.

How could you give up on the market completely? Love of the stock market is built into an American's experience of time. I'm not joking. Remember, as Heidegger says, we are all of us "running ahead" to our past. That is, we have only the future, which approaches and then passes us by—it becomes the present, and instantly (indeed, continuously) the past, falling somewhere behind us. So how do we think of the future, the only time we've got? In a wealthy country with a $10 trillion economy, we think of it with hope. Wonderful things will happen to us, to our children, our friends. We will become rich, distinguished, loved. Of the wonderful things we dream about, perhaps only one of them becomes true, so contemplation of the future is, for most of us, more satisfying than the actual experience of the future. Which doesn't stop us in this country from constructing new hopes and being freshly disappointed as well as satisfied—on and on, in an endless cycle. Given this experience of time and hope in a wealthy country, it's very hard—indeed psychologically impossible—for us to think of the market going down or staying down forever, even if it does stay flat for periods, as the saturnine Robert Shiller pointed out. And this hopefulness is not some foolish illusion, it's central to the American temperament and to the longtime success of the stock market, which does, as we know, rise over time. For Americans, even if we are running ahead to our past, time is on our side. We can be suckered by apparent success, but the greater fault is to be suckered by loss.

The living-room walls, wrinkled, looked like a set of unmade beds that had hardened through the years. The kitchen needed to be gutted, and the bathroom was so old that the porcelain had worn away, revealing the steel body of the sink. Max was at college, but Tommy would still be staying with me part-time, and I took down and moved the wall between our bedrooms, giving him and his brother (when he came home) a bigger space—I would make it new. Like many Americans after the crash, I had decided to cut back, reduce expenses, live more modestly. Not forever, but certainly for now. From somewhere—high school, maybe—I remembered one of the few French phrases that were actually useful: *Reculer pour mieux sauter.* Step back in order to spring forward. The economy was resilient, and now that I had ceased chasing role models in my late fifties, I was beginning to think that I was resilient, too.

Looking south from the living room, I saw the brownstones below, a few trees in pots, wooden benches for assignations in the dark, the remnants of an older, slower, more gracious New York; and I saw the new Trump towers, which blocked out some of the light. I wanted the slower gracious life; and I was also drawn to the life made possible by technology and entrepreneurial hustle and greed, which both excited and frightened me

at the same time. I would always want both. There was no reso-
lution — there couldn't be, not for any of us, we Americans. But
at least I was ready to move on. I would die, and knowing that,
I would live more slowly and more happily, filling time as best
as I could, one moment after another, in a chain of pleasure that
would last as long as I could forge one link to the next.

Epilogue: Debts to Society

ON April 28, 2003, Henry Blodget was banned from working on Wall Street for life. He also agreed to pay a fine of $4 million, known legally as a "disgorgement" of profits. The two punishments emerged as part of a deal struck between regulatory bodies (including the SEC) and state prosecutors on one side and ten major investment firms on the other. The firms, including Merrill Lynch, neither admitted nor denied allegations that they routinely offered misleading stock research in order to secure investment-banking business. As part of the settlement, however, they agreed to pay fines of $1.4 billion, of which $367 million would be set aside as compensation for victims. The settlement also called for a number of reforms, including the clear separation of stock research from investment banking.

Some six weeks later, on June 10, 2003, Sam Waksal was sentenced to seven years and three months in federal prison by

Judge William H. Pauley III. He was also fined $3 million. "The harm that you wrought was truly incalculable," Pauley said, rejecting Sam's plea for leniency. Sam was the first CEO to be convicted in the scandals that became public in 2001 and 2002, and would be the first to go to jail. ImClone's stock, which had fallen to a low of $5.24 after the FDA refusal and the publicity about the insider-trading charge, closed at the end of the day at $36.30. The stock had been going up all spring on rumors that Erbitux had been successfully tested overseas by ImClone's German affiliate, Merck. The results of the tests were announced on June 1, only nine days before Sam Waksal's sentencing, at the annual conference of the American Society of Clinical Oncology. They were virtually the same as the successful results that Im-Clone had announced two years earlier from trials that the FDA had disallowed.

On the day of Sam Waksal's sentencing—June 10, 2003—the Nasdaq composite index closed at 1627. It was up 22 percent for the year and over 40 percent from its low on October 9, 2002. Experts on CNBC and in the financial press debated whether the run-up was just another bubble or the beginning of a new bull market.

Bibliography

This is a subjective work fueled by actual events. Much of the information that provoked and enabled my writing came from CNBC, the *New York Times*, and the *Wall Street Journal*. I have not seen the need to gum up the text by footnoting readily available information, but I would like to express my admiration and, from a readerly distance, my affection for such talented reporters and writers as Louis Uchitelle, Gretchen Morgenson, Floyd Norris, Jonathan Feurbringer, Alex Berenson, and Richard W. Stevenson of the *Times;* Greg Ip, E. S. Browning, Aaron Lucchetti, Randall Smith, and Jonathan Clements of the *Journal;* Gene Epstein and Alan Abelson of *Barron's;* and the entire gang at CNBC, who, despite my ragging them during the worst days of the bear market, have taught me a great deal. From time to time, I also dipped into *Business Week, Forbes, Fortune, The Industry Standard, Fast Company, Red Herring, Variety,* and The Street.com. James J. Cramer's impassioned outbursts in print and on television were a frequent stimulant. Articles and books that were of particular help I have noted below.

Amis, Martin. *Money.* New York: Penguin, 1986.

Anand, Geeta. "In Waksal's Past: Repeated Ousters," *Wall Street Journal,* September 27, 2002.

Aristotle. *The Nicomachean Ethics.* Oxford: Oxford University Press, 1980.

St. Augustine. *City of God.* London: Penguin, 1984.

Bellow, Saul. *Humboldt's Gift.* New York: Viking, 1975.

———. *Ravelstein.* New York: Viking, 2000.

Berman, Paul. "Terror and Liberalism," *The American Prospect,* October 22, 2001.

———. *Terror and Liberalism.* New York: Norton, 2003.

The Bible (King James translation). New York: New American Library, 1974.

"The Birth of a Cancer Drug," *Business Week,* July 9, 2001.

Brooks, David. *Bobos in Paradise: The New Upper Class and How They Got There.* New York: Simon & Schuster, 2000.

Cassidy, John. *Dot.Con.* New York: HarperCollins, 2002.

———. "The Greed Cycle," *The New Yorker,* September 23, 2002.

Chancellor, Edward. *Devil Take the Hindmost: A History of Financial Speculation.* New York: Farrar, Straus & Giroux, 1999.

Cox, Michael W., and Alm, Richard. *Myths of Rich & Poor.* New York: Basic, 1999.

Cramer, James J. *Confessions of a Wall Street Addict.* New York: Simon & Schuster, 2002.

Denby, David. *Great Books.* New York: Simon & Schuster, 1996.

———. "The Quarter of Living Dangerously," *The New Yorker,* April 24–May 1, 2000.

———. "The Speed of Light," *The New Yorker,* November 27, 2000.

Dreiser, Theodore. *The Financier.* New York: Penguin, 1995.

D'Souza, Dinesh. *The Virtues of Prosperity.* New York: The Free Press, 2000.

Epstein, Gene. "Extremism Is No Vice When Selling Books," *Barron's,* May 8, 2000.

Fairley, Peter. "The Microphotonics Revolution," *Technology Review,* July–August 2000.

Fitzgerald, F. Scott. *The Great Gatsby.* New York: Scribner, 1995.

———. *The Crack-Up.* New York: New Directions, 1945.

Frank, Robert H. *Luxury Fever.* New York: The Free Press, 1999.

——— and Philip J. Cook. *The Winner-Take-All Society.* New York: Penguin, 1996.

Frank, Thomas. *One Market Under God: Extreme Capitalism, Market Populism, and the End of Economic Democracy.* New York: Doubleday, 2000.

Friedman, Thomas L. *The Lexus and the Olive Tree.* New York: Anchor, 2000.

Galbraith, John Kenneth. *The Great Crash.* Boston: Houghton Mifflin, 1997.

Gilder, George. *Microcosm: The Quantum Revolution in Economics and Technology.* New York: Touchstone, 1990.

———. *Telecosm.* New York: The Free Press, 2000.

———. *Gilder Technology Report* (monthly, 2000–2002).

Gladwell, Malcolm. *The Tipping Point.* Boston: Little, Brown, 2000.

Glieck, James. *Faster.* New York: Pantheon, 1999.

Gopnik, Adam. "The Habit of Democracy," *The New Yorker,* October 15, 2001.

Gordon, John Steele. *The Great Game: The Emergence of Wall Street as a World Power 1653–2000.* New York: Scribner, 1999.

Grace, Eric S. *Biotechnology Unzipped: Promises and Realities.* Washington, D.C.: Joseph Henry, 1997.

Groopman, Jerome. "The Thirty Years' War," *The New Yorker,* June 4, 2001.

Gross, Daniel. *Bull Run.* New York: Public Affairs, 2000.

Hecht, Jeff. *Understanding Fiber Optics,* 3rd edition. Upper Saddle River, N. J.: Prentice-Hall, 1999.

Heidegger, Martin. *The Concept of Time.* Oxford: Blackwell, 1992.

Howells, William Dean. *A Hazard of New Fortunes.* New York: Modern Library, 2002.

———. *The Rise of Silas Lapham.* New York: Penguin, 1983.

James, Henry. *The Spoils of Poynton.* London: Penguin, 1989.

Karabell, Zachary. *A Visionary Nation: Four Centuries of American Dreams and What Lies Ahead.* New York: HarperCollins, 2001.

Kindleberger, Charles. *Manias, Panics, and Crashes: A History of Financial Crises,* 4th edition. New York: Wiley, 2000.

Kurzweil, Ray. *The Age of Spiritual Machines.* New York: Penguin Putnam, 1999.

———. *The Loss of Happiness in Market Democracies.* New Haven: Yale University Press, 2000.

Levitt, Arthur. "Renewing the Covenant with Investors" (speech), Securities and Exchange Commission, May 10, 2000.

Malkiel, Burton G. *A Random Walk Down Wall Street.* New York: Norton, 1999.

Nabokov, Vladimir. *Speak, Memory.* New York: Putnam's, 1967.

Negroponte, Nicholas. *Being Digital.* New York: Knopf, 1995.

Phillips, Kevin. *Wealth and Democracy.* New York: Broadway, 2002.

Prud'homme, Alex. "Investigating ImClone," *Vanity Fair,* June 2002.

Rand, Ayn. *The Fountainhead.* New York: Signet, 1996.

Rivlin, Gary. "The Madness of King George," *Wired,* July 2002.

Robbins-Roth, Cynthia. *From Alchemy to IPO: The Business of Biotechnology.* Cambridge, Mass.: Perseus, 2000.

Rose, Frank. "Telechasm: Can We Get to the Future from Here?" *Wired,* May 2001.

Schama, Simon. *An Embarrassment of Riches: An Interpretation of Dutch Culture in the Golden Age.* New York: Knopf, 1987.

Schor, Juliet B. *The Overspent American.* New York: Harper Perennial, 1999.

———. *Do Americans Shop Too Much?* Boston: Beacon Press, 2000.

Schor, Juliet B., and Holt, Douglas B., editors. *The Consumer Society Reader.* New York: The New Press, 2000.

Sennett, Richard. *The Corrosion of Character.* New York: Norton, 1998.

Shiller, Robert J. *Irrational Exuberance.* Princeton: Princeton University Press, 2000.

Siegel, Jeremy. *Stocks for the Long Run,* 2nd edition. New York: McGraw-Hill, 1998.

Simmel, Georg. *The Philosophy of Money* (edited by David Frisby), 2nd edition. London: Routledge, 1990.

Spitzer, Eliot, et al. Affidavit in Support of Application for an Order Pursuant to General Business Law Section 354, April 8, 2002.

Surowiecki, James. "Doom, Incorporated," *The New Yorker,* May 20, 2002.

————. "The New Economy Was a Myth, Right?" *Wired,* July 2002.

Trollope, Anthony. *The Way We Live Now.* London: Penguin, 1994.

U.S. House of Representatives. An Inquiry into the ImClone Cancer-Drug Story. The Committee on Energy and Commerce, Subcommittee on Oversight and Investigations, June 13, 2002.

Veblen, Thorstein. *The Theory of the Leisure Class.* New York: Penguin, 1994.

Wharton, Edith. *The Custom of the Country.* New York: Scribner, 1997.

Woodward, Bob. *Maestro.* New York: Simon & Schuster, 2000.

About the Author

David Denby is a staff writer and film critic for *The New Yorker* and was formerly film critic of *New York* magazine. His first book, *Great Books* (1996), was a finalist for the National Book Critics Circle Award. He lives in New York City.

Acknowledgments

I would like to thank Michael Pietsch for helping me gain control of my materials, Pat Strachan and Lynn Warshow for detailed editorial help, and Kathy Robbins for innumerable acts of professional guidance and personal friendship.

A number of friends and colleagues read parts or all of the manuscript and made vital and useful suggestions. I am indebted to Peter Blauner, Henry Finder, Adam Gopnik, Margot Hentoff, Peggy Kaye, Janet Meyers, David Remnick, Susan Rieger, Stephen Schiff, Cathleen Schine, Deborah Solomon, and Pearl Solomon. Robert Lupi was a useful sounding board for many of the book's ideas.

My *New Yorker* colleagues John Cassidy and James Surowiecki shared their knowledge with me and graciously answered my questions.

Apart from those mentioned in the text, a number of investment professionals and journalists talked over their trade and aired their beliefs. I particularly enjoyed my learning sessions with *New York Times* reporter and macro-economics analyst Louis Uchitelle and investment banker Mack Rossoff. Steve Frank of CNBC clarified a number of issues. Matt Geller, biotechnology analyst at CIBC-Oppenheimer, and Marc Bruneau, CEO of the consulting company Adventis, offered their friendship and knowledge on repeated occasions. Venture capitalist Burt Alimansky, redoubtable organizer of investment conferences, was very helpful at the beginning of the project. My indebtedness to all these people leads me to insist that any misconceptions in the text are entirely my own responsibility.